# CULT
# SCIENCE FICTION
# FILMS

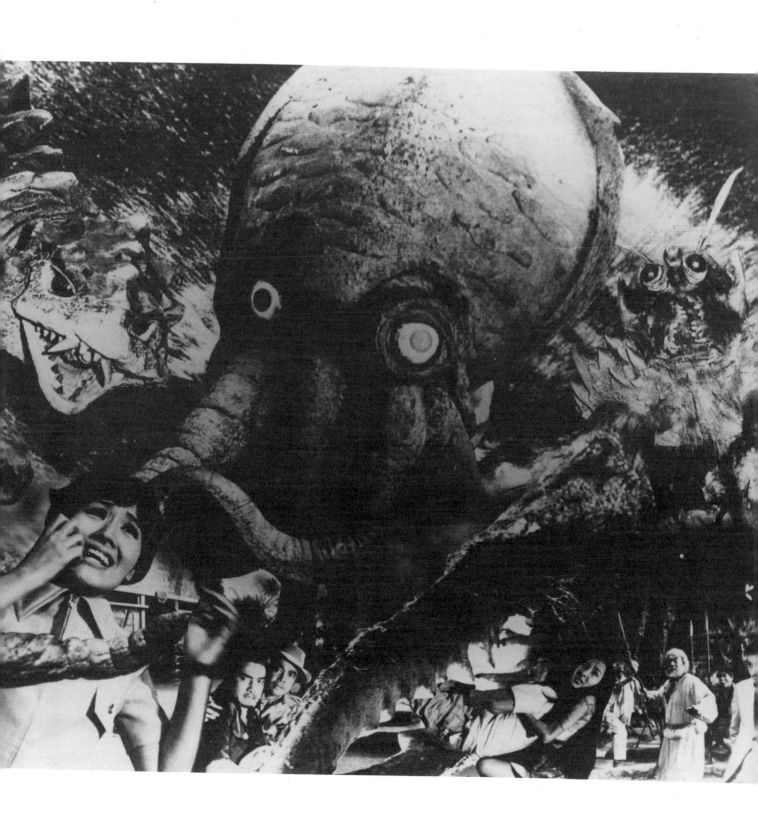

# CULT SCIENCE FICTION FILMS

FROM *THE AMAZING COLOSSAL MAN*
TO *YOG—MONSTER FROM SPACE*

WELCH EVERMAN

A CITADEL PRESS BOOK
Published by Carol Publishing Group

# ACKNOWLEDGMENTS

Very special thanks to Judith Bailey, vice president for Research and Public Service, to Leslie Flemming, dean of the College of Arts and Humanities, and to Harvey Kail, chair of the Department of English, University of Maine, for encouragement and research assistance that made this book possible.

Special thanks also to Eric Caidin at Hollywood Book and Poster for locating and providing stills from lots of obscure science fiction films. Without his help, there would be no book.

And thanks to my students and former students Matt Lewis, Ryan Tibbetts, Chris Mackowski, and others who have sat patiently through my lectures, provided videocassettes, and talked endlessly with me about movies; to Allan J. Wilson, my editor at Citadel Press, who went to bat for this book when it was still just a glimmer of an idea; to Lynn Stockwell and Mary Garay of Suncoast Motion Picture Company at the *Bangor Mall,* Bangor, Maine, for helping me get my hands on hard-to-find videos; and to my wife, Liz, and my sons, Charlie and Johnnie, who make it possible to get through the day.

A Citadel Press Book
Published by Carol Publishing Group
Citadel Press is a registered trademark of Carol Communications, Inc.
Editorial Offices: 600 Madison Avenue, New York, N.Y. 10022
Sales and Distribution Offices: 120 Enterprise Avenue, Secaucus, N.J. 07094
In Canada: Canadian Manda Group, One Atlantic Avenue, Suite 105, Toronto, Ontario M6K 3E7
Queries regarding rights and permissions should be addressed to Carol Publishing Group, 600 Madison Avenue, New York, N.Y. 10022

Carol Publishing Group books are available at special discounts for bulk purchases, sales promotions, fund raising, or educational purposes. Special editions can be created to specifications. For details, contact Special Sales Department, Carol Publishing Group, 120 Enterprise Avenue, Secaucus, N.J. 07094

Designed by A. Christopher Simon

Manufactured in the United States of America

10  9  8  7  6  5  4  3  2  1

**Library of Congress Cataloging-in-Publication Data**

Everman, Welch D., 1946–
    Cult science fiction films : from the Amazing colossal man to Yog—monster from space / by Welch Everman.
        p.   cm.
    "A Citadel Press book."
    ISBN 0–8065–1602–X (pbk.)
    1. Science fiction films—History and criticism.—2. Low budget motion pictures.   I. Title.
PN1995.9.S26E83 1995
791.43′615—dc20                                    94-46557
                                                          CIP

*To Liz, Charlie, Johnnie, and my mom*

# CONTENTS

INTRODUCTION 9

THE FILMS 17
The Amazing Colossal Man 19
The Angry Red Planet 20
The Atomic Submarine 23
Attack of the Giant Leeches 25
The Boys From Brazil 27
The Brain Eaters 30
The Brain From Planet Arous 32
The Brain That Wouldn't Die 34
Bride of the Monster 36
Cat-Women of the Moon 38
The Crawling Hand 42
Damnation Alley 43
The Day the World Ended 48
Dead and Buried 52
Demon Seed 54
Destroy All Monsters! 59
Earth vs. the Flying Saucers 62
Embryo 66
Empire of the Ants 68
Endangered Species 70
Fantastic Planet 73
First Man Into Space 76
Frankenstein's Daughter 78
The Frozen Dead 81
The Gamma People 85
The Hands of Orlac 88
Hercules Against the Moon Men 90
Horror Express 93
Horror of the Blood Monsters 95
Humanoids From the Deep 99
The Incredible Melting Man 102
The Incredible Two-Headed Transplant 104
Invasion of the Saucer Men 108

The Island of Dr. Moreau 112
Island of Terror 118
It! The Terror From Beyond Space 121
Jesse James Meets Frankenstein's Daughter 125
Journey to the Center of Time 131
Killers From Space 134
Kingdom of the Spiders 136
The Last Man on Earth 139
The Last Woman on Earth 143
Lifeforce 146
The Lost Continent 148
The Man Who Turned to Stone 152
The Manster 154
The Medusa Touch 157
Mesa of Lost Women 165
The Monster From Green Hell 167
The Monster That Challenged the World 170
The Mysterians 173
Mysterious Island 176
The Navy vs. the Night Monsters 181
Night of the Bloody Apes 185
Phantasm 187
The Phantom Planet 190
Piranha 192
Planet of the Vampires 196
Queen of Outer Space 200
Rabid 204
Robot Monster 208
Santa Claus Conquers the Martians 210
Scanners 213
Superman and the Mole Men 217
The Swarm 220
Teenagers From Outer Space 226
The Terrornauts 229
THX 1138 232
The Time Travelers 234

The 27th Day 236
War of the Colossal Beast 238
Warning Sign 241
The Wasp Woman 243

Westworld 245
Yog—Monster From Space 247

PHOTO CREDITS 252
INDEX 252

This is *It! the Terror From Beyond Space*—actually, aging cowboy star Ray "Crash" Corrigan in a rubber suit. This 1958 movie was the prototype for Ridley Scott's *Alien* of 1979.

Cult science fiction movies are fond of giant creatures. Here a visitor (Jimmy Hanley) to *The Lost Continent* is killed by a giant crab. (Courtesy Hollywood Book and Poster)

# INTRODUCTION

# WHAT IS A CULT SCIENCE FICTION FILM?

To begin with, it might be better to ask: What is a science fiction film, cult or not? In other words, what is it that makes a science fiction film science fiction, and what makes it different from, say, a horror movie, an action/adventure flick, or a Western?

As a matter of fact, there *are* science fiction films that are also horror movies (*It! The Terror From Beyond Space, The Thing From Another World*), action/adventure movies (*The Terminator, Predator,* and *Alien*), and even Westerns (*Jesse James Meets Frankenstein's Daughter*). But no matter what else it might be, what makes a science fiction film *science* fiction is the fact that it is, in some sense, about science—and not only science but futuristic science. By that, I mean that science fiction movies deal with scientific possibilities and technologies that do not exist yet but that might exist someday. Science fiction is the realm of the not-yet.

By this definition, movies that deal in interplanetary or intergalactic travel, androids, futuristic medical and surgical techniques, or time travel are all science fiction films. *Frankenstein* would qualify as a science fiction film, because it proposes that there are scientific means by which the dead can be brought to life, techniques that are not possible in the here and now but that might be possible someday. Of course *Frankenstein* is also a horror film, thanks to the monster. In fact, a lot of science fiction films are also horror films in which monsters are spawned by scientific experiments, but not all

horror films are science fiction, because science fiction does not deal in the supernatural. Science fiction takes place in the realm of the not-yet; supernatural horror films operate in the realm of the impossible.

The science fiction movie almost always offers some kind of futuristic technology, but that technology does not have to be Earth technology. There are lots of science fiction movies about Earthlings going to other planets, but there are probably even more about aliens from other planets coming here—*Invasion of the Saucer Men, Teenagers From Outer Space, The Day Mars Invaded Earth,* and *Invasion of the Body Snatchers,* to name only a few.

Ecological disaster movies are a relatively new subgenre of science fiction, with most of them coming since 1970. Movies such as *The Swarm, Prophecy, Empire of the Ants,* and *Kingdom of the Spiders* are sci-fi films because they are set in a near future in which the ecological problems of today take a turn for the worse, and more often than not, science and technology are to blame for the trouble.

Virtually any film set in a future different from the present is a science fiction film, and this would include movies like *THX 1138* and *1984,* even though these films depict worlds that aren't much more technologically advanced than our own. Some futuristic movies, like the *Mad Max* trilogy, even offer a future world that is technologically inferior to ours. Of course, *THX 1138,*

1984, the *Mad Max* movies, the *Planet of the Apes* films, and many others are intended as political commentaries, but science fiction is often political by its very nature because it says, in effect: "If we keep living the way we are now, here's what the world will be like in five years [or ten years, or a hundred, or a thousand]." A science fiction movie is often a warning to change our ways or face the consequences; this is one of the things that makes sci-fi interesting.

There are good reasons for looking seriously at science fiction movies, even the less-than-classic films to which this book is dedicated. For one thing, science fiction is and has always been popular. The very first feature film, George Méliès's twenty-one-minute epic *Le Voyage dans la Lune* (*A Trip to the Moon*) of 1902, was a science fiction film, and sci-fi flicks have been packing fans into theaters ever since. But when something is popular, it makes sense to ask why, and I'd suggest that whatever is popular must be saying something we want it to say—if it didn't, we wouldn't like it. Science fiction movies, then, must say what we want them to say, and critical thinking about sci-fi has to try to figure out what it is that those films are saying, because what science fiction movies have to say also says something about us, the people who watch them.

Now that we have some idea of what makes a science fiction film science fiction, we can go back to our original question: What is a *cult* science fiction film?

In the introduction to my book *Cult Horror Films*, I offer a definition of cult movies that I'm going to apply here to films in the sci-fi genre. As the name suggests, cult movies have a certain following because there is something special about them, something that sets them apart from other movies. For example, a cult movie in any genre might be special because of who appears in it. A cult science fiction movie might offer an early appearance by an actor or actress who went on to become a star—Leonard Nimoy in *Brain Eaters*, Patrick Stewart in *Lifeforce*, or Bruce Dern in *The Incredible Two-Headed Transplant*. Or it might show an established star late in his or her career, sometimes to that performer's embarrassment—Henry Fonda and Richard Widmark in *The Swarm*, Richard Burton in *The Medusa Touch*, Dana Andrews in *The Frozen Dead*, Jack Albertson in *Dead and Buried*, or Barry Sullivan in *Planet of the Vampires*.

Of course, there are performers who in their own right and for a variety of reasons have become cult figures, and the sci-fi movies that feature them have become cult films—*The Brain From Planet Arous* with John Agar, *Bride of the Monster* with Bela Lugosi, Vincent Price's *Last Man on Earth*, Sonny Tufts in *Cat-Women of the Moon*, Zsa Zsa Gabor in *Queen of Outer Space*, Barbara Steele in *Pirahna*, or Peter Cushing in *Island of Terror* and *Horror Express*.

Other sci-fi films are so unique or unusual that they develop a following of loyal fans. *Fantastic Planet* is a surrealistic feature-length animated sci-fi movie, and *Destroy All Monsters* is an example of Japanese science fiction at its zaniest, because it features virtually all of the monsters from Toho movies—Godzilla, Minya, Rodan, Mothra, Manda, etc., etc., etc. *THX 1138* is unique, not only because it is the first feature film directed by George Lucas, who went on to do the *Star Wars* movies, but because it is so visually innovative—shot in color with stark white backgrounds and costumes so that the characters' heads and hands often seem to be floating in empty space.

Often people think of cult movies as bad movies, and that isn't necessarily true. Some cult science fiction movies have followings because they are a lot better than their low budgets or ridiculous titles might suggest. *First Man Into Space, Invasion of the Saucer Men, It! The Terror From Beyond Space, Last Woman on Earth,*

The Landmaster from the post–nuclear holocaust film *Damnation Alley* is a good example of science fiction technology at work.

*The Monster That Challenged the World, The 27th Day,* and *Rabid* are all remarkably good science fiction movies that even viewers who are not fans of sci-fi might enjoy.

On the other hand, some science fiction movies are so awful that you just have to love them, like homely puppies, and true science fiction film fans do. *Santa Claus Conquers the Martians, Mesa of Lost Women, The Brain That Wouldn't Die, Frankenstein's Daughter, The Frozen Dead, Horror of the Blood Monsters,* and *Robot Monster* are only a few of the so-bad-they're-good movies that have attained cult status, at least for those moviegoers with lots of stamina.

For the purposes of writing this book, I've had to exclude big-budget productions for the most part from my definition of cult movies in favor of those films directed almost exclusively at the die-hard science fiction fan. Certainly the *Star Trek* movies and the *Star Wars* trilogy have cult followings, but they are also major productions intended to appeal to a mass audience. The same would hold true for *Close Encounters of the Third Kind* and the five *Planet of the Apes* films. I do not

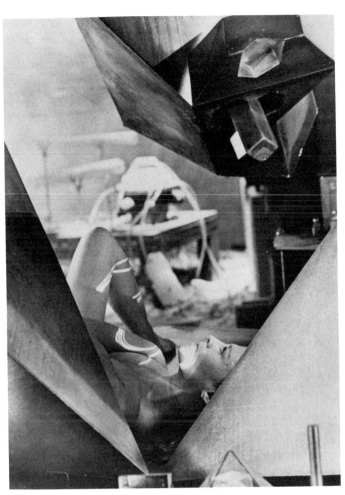

More futuristic technology—Proteus IV, a very sophisticated computer, is about to impregnate actress Julie Christie with the *Demon Seed.*

intend this as a value judgment. Major productions like *Blade Runner, Alien,* and *Predator* are among the best sci-fi flicks ever made; they've also been written about more often than virtually any other science fiction movies, so I've decided not to discuss them again here. The same goes for the true classics of the genre—*The Day the Earth Stood Still, This Island Earth, Forbidden Planet,* and the like—which have also gotten plenty of critical attention over the years. With few exceptions, I have chosen to write about those movies that have received little, if any, critical appraisal.

Even with all of these limitations, though, there are still about a billion science fiction films that I would have loved to write about and couldn't, given the space limitations of this book. *Missile to the Moon, Night of the Blood Beast, Not of This Earth, Octaman, Re-Animator, Space Master X-7, First Spaceship on Venus, The Flesh Eaters, Slime People, Atom Age Vampire*—the list could go on and on.

I also could have included a number of serials from the 1940s and '50s, some of which offer the most outlandish science fiction premises ever proposed. Check out *Radar Men From the Moon*, *The Phantom Creeps*, *Atom Man vs. Superman*, *Panther Girl of the Kongo*, *Zombies of the Stratosphere* (featuring a very young Leonard Nimoy in his first role as an alien), *The Whispering Shadow*, *Flash Gordon Conquers the Universe*, *Undersea Kingdom*, and *Buck Rogers* to see what I mean. Well, maybe I'll have the opportunity to write about these less-than-classic productions some other time.

The films I have included here are those movies about which I felt I had something to say, and that list includes a lot of movies from the 1950s, because, to my mind, that was the true golden age of sci-fi cinema. In the fifties filmmakers really began to explore the enormous range of possibilities that science fiction has to offer, and all SF films made since that time owe the movies of the period a tremendous debt. In addition, the atomic

Like so many actors in 1950s sci-fi movies, Lyn Osborn meets up with an alien in *Invasion of the Saucer Men*.

Richard Burton gives an embarrassing performance in *The Medusa Touch*, but without his overacting the movie probably wouldn't deserve its cult status.

More alien invaders, this time thanks to Japan. Poster art for *Chikyu Boeigun*, otherwise known as *The Mysterians*. (Courtesy Hollywood Book and Poster)

Dressed in high-tech costumes, Bradford Dillman and his cohorts try to track down *The Swarm* in the ecological disaster movie.

Cult star Sonny Tufts and the Hollywood Cover Girls are painfully inept in the legendary *Cat-Women of the Moon.* (Courtesy Hollywood Book and Poster)

This movie you must see to believe—Zsa Zsa Gabor and her fellow revolutionaries plan to topple the Venusian government in *Queen of Outer Space.* (Courtesy Hollywood Book and Poster)

bomb and the cold war, paranoia about communism and the Soviets, the beginnings of the space race, postwar advances in medicine, and public awareness of the potential dangers of radioactivity made the 1950s a time when profound cultural concerns found expression in even the most mindless low-budget flicks, and this makes the movies of that decade particularly interesting. On a more personal level, I am a baby boomer, and these are the movies I grew up with. I saw them in theaters when they were first released, and I watched them again (and again and again and again) on TV through the sixties and seventies. These movies disappeared from the airwaves after a while, but now that they are becoming available again on videocassette, it has certainly been worthwhile and fun to see them yet another time.

Mostly, I've chosen to write about movies that I love—and that includes even the movies I hate. I am a rabid science fiction fan. I will watch anything in the sci-fi genre, and, as the saying goes, I never met a science fiction film I didn't like at a gut level, even when my brain knows that what I'm watching is terrible. Every movie discussed in this book is one I felt was worth watching and will certainly watch again, no matter how bad I know it to be, and so I would encourage you to see all of these movies, even those which in all honesty and in good conscience I cannot recommend.

In *Cult Science Fiction Films,* I've followed the same

Five Earthlings—Gene Barry, Valerie French, George Voskovec, Marie Tsien, and Azenath Janti—are carried off in an alien spacecraft in the opening segment of this surprisingly effective film, *The 27th Day*.

An addition to your so-bad-it's-good list—Basil Henson and Karel Stepanek discuss ways of getting a head (Kathleen Breck) in *The Frozen Dead*.

One of the residents of the vampire planet in the atrocious *Horror of the Blood Monsters*. (Courtesy Hollywood Book and Poster)

15

basic format as in my earlier volume, *Cult Horror Films*. The book is presented as a kind of encyclopedia, a collection of mini-essays, one on each film, offered in alphabetical order according to title and so not really intended to be read cover to cover, though you may feel free to do so if you choose.

Each entry includes some basic information about the movie—year of release, alternate titles, names of the director, producer, screenplay writer, and cast, as well as the production company that originally produced or released the movie and the company that has made the film available on videocassette. It seemed important to include only movies in release on video so readers could have the chance to see films that interest them.

Bear in mind, though, that many of these marginal sci-fi films might not be readily available for rent or purchase at stores stocking dozens of copies of the latest blockbuster and almost nothing else. To see some of the movies discussed in *Cult Science Fiction Films*, you might have to do some serious looking around.

This preliminary information is followed by a synopsis of the plot and an analysis of the film in its cultural and historical context.

I set about writing this book as a serious—and not particularly serious—study of those science fiction movies that have been overlooked for far too long, and I had a lot of fun doing it. It is my hope that you'll have fun with *Cult Science Fiction Films*, too.

Actor Michael Craig is menaced by a giant crab shortly after he arrives on the *Mysterious Island*.

# THE FILMS

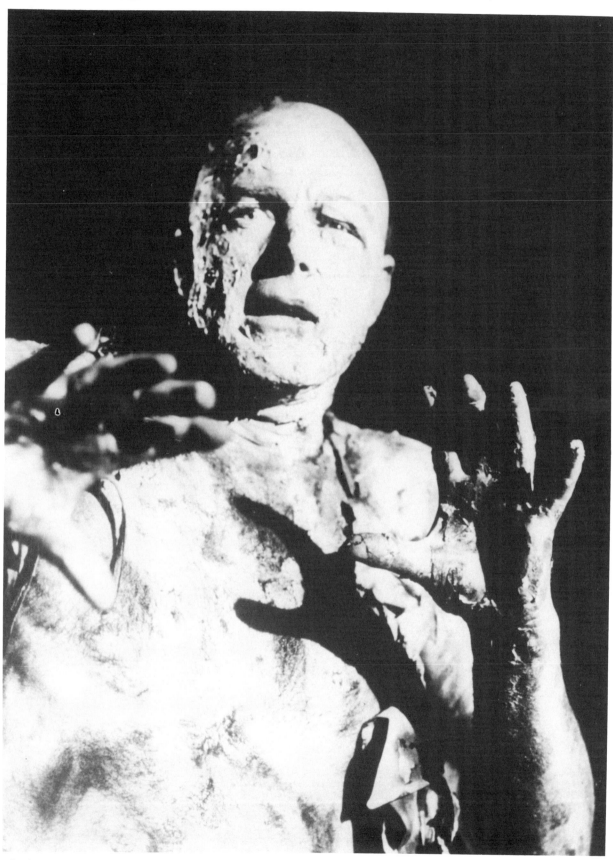

After being exposed to the blast of a plutonium bomb, Glenn Manning (Glenn Langan) is in bad shape, but things get even worse when he becomes *The Amazing Colossal Man*.

# THE AMAZING COLOSSAL MAN

1957

**DIRECTOR-PRODUCER:** Bert I. Gordon
**SCREENPLAY:** Mark Hanna and Bert I. Gordon
**CAST:** Glenn Langan, Cathy Downs, William
Hudson, James Seay, Larry Thor
**ORIGINAL RELEASE:** American International
Pictures
**VIDEO:** Columbia TriStar Home Video

One of the advantages to being *The Amazing Colossal Man* is that you get to peep into other people's bathrooms.

Bert I. Gordon is the king of cheap, unconvincing special effects, and his efforts in *The Amazing Colossal Man* are certainly no better than the effects in *Beginning of the End, Cyclops, Village of the Giants, Earth vs. the Spider,* or any of his other something-big-attacks-civilization films. Even so, *The Amazing Colossal Man* is a pretty good fifties sci-fi movie, mostly because the characters are strong and interesting.

The military is testing the first plutonium bomb in the Nevada desert, and Lieutenant Colonel Glenn Manning (Langan) and his men are huddled in a trench nearby to experience the test under simulated combat conditions. Nothing seems to go right, however. First, the bomb doesn't go off as scheduled, and Manning and his men have to wait to see whether it is going to explode or not. Then a small private plane flies over the restricted area and crashes at the test site.

Glenn is ordered to stay in the trench, but he thinks the pilot might still be alive, so he hops out and runs toward the plane. On his way there, however, the pluto-nium bomb explodes, and Glenn gets his hair and his clothes blown off and his skin virtually burned away.

At the base hospital, Dr. Paul Lindstrom (Hudson) bandages him and waits for him to die, because Glenn has third-degree burns over almost 100 percent of his body. Carol Forrest (Downs), Glenn's fiancée, still has hope, however, and it turns out that she is right. Next day, miraculously, Glenn's skin is perfectly normal. As Dr. Eric Coulter (Thor) notes, "He's developed new skin," probably because of a massive overdose of pluto-nium radiation.

Shortly thereafter, Carol is informed that she can't visit Glenn at the hospital until further notice, and when she sneaks in anyway, she finds that his room is empty and there is no record of his ever having been there. She tracks Lindstrom and Coulter to a medical research facility elsewhere in Nevada and finds Glenn's room, only to discover that he is still in a coma and has grown to a height of eighteen feet. She screams and faints.

When she comes around, Lindstrom and Coulter explain that because of the plutonium radiation, Glenn is now growing from eight to ten feet a day. It seems that in Glenn's body, new cells are developing at an enormous rate, while the old cells are not dying off.

19

This doesn't apply to his hair cells, apparently, because he is as bald as a cue ball, but it means that unless the doctors can find some way to stop the process, Glenn will keep growing indefinitely.

Glenn comes to at last and discovers what has happened to him. Naturally he doesn't take it very well. In fact, he starts to go off the deep end. The doctors move him from the hospital to a circus tent on the grounds, and Carol sticks around to see him through this difficult period. Psychologically, Glenn gets worse and worse, and he begins to develop chest pains and shortness of breath, too. Lindstrom discovers that for some reason Glenn's heart isn't growing as fast as the rest of him, so Glenn doesn't have much longer to live.

Finally, Dr. Coulter hits on a formula that will stop Glenn's growth if it is injected into the bone marrow, and he also finds a way to reverse the growth process once it is halted. But Glenn disappears before he can be told of the new discoveries, and the army sends out helicopters to search for him.

Glenn arrives in downtown Las Vegas, where in a mad frenzy he destroys a few casinos, then heads toward Boulder Dam. The army pursues him, but Carol, Lindstrom, and Coulter find him first, and they manage to give him an injection of the serum with an enormous hypodermic needle developed just for the occasion. By this time, though, Glenn is out of his mind, thanks to all he's been through, and he uses the hypo to kill Dr. Coulter. Then he grabs Carol and starts across the dam.

Lindstrom talks the crazed giant into putting Carol down, and the second he does, soldiers open fire with bazookas. Glenn plunges off the dam to his death—at least until the sequel, *War of the Colossal Beast*.

Obviously, *The Amazing Colossal Man* owes a lot to the Godzilla films of Japan, but curiously, it owes even more to *The Wolf Man* of 1941. Like Lon Chaney's Larry Talbot, Glenn Manning does nothing to deserve what happens to him. In fact, like Talbot, Manning is "infected" with his strange disease because he tries to save the life of another—hardly the kind of act that warrants punishment.

This is a very disturbing aspect of the movie, particularly since we know that in real life, terrible things happen to people who have done nothing to deserve them. Accidents and illnesses come about purely by chance, and though this is a fact of life that we are more than willing to overlook, *The Amazing Colossal Man* faces it head-on.

In a conversation with Carol, Glenn asks, "What sin can a man commit in a single lifetime to bring this on himself?" There is no answer to this question, of course, and this fact makes *The Amazing Colossal Man* a more effective film than it has any right to be.

# THE ANGRY RED PLANET

1959

**DIRECTOR:** Ib Melchior
**PRODUCERS:** Sid Pink and Norman Maurer
**SCREENPLAY:** Sid Pink and Ib Melchior
**CAST:** Gerald Mohr, Nora Hayden, Les Tremayne, Jack Kruschen
**ORIGINAL RELEASE:** American International Pictures
**VIDEO:** Thorn EMI Home Video

Back in the 1950s, on the threshold of the space age, people were fully expecting the United States to land men on other planets within a decade or so, and that accounts for the wave of space travel films that came out during that time. But many of the fifties space operas were sending mixed messages. On the one hand, the films themselves were responses to a growing public enthusiasm for the space race. On the other hand, though, many of them served to dampen that enthusiasm. *The Angry Red Planet* is only one of many conservative fear-of-space-travel films of the fifties that urged us, quite simply, to stay at home.

Weeks after all contact with the crew of the first manned mission to Mars has been lost and all on board are presumed dead, the missing spaceship appears quite suddenly in Earth orbit. Space scientists and military leaders manage to bring it down to a safe landing by remote control. Of the four people originally on the flight, only Dr. Iris Ryan (Hayden) and Colonel Tom O'Bannion (Mohr) are on board, and Tom is in a coma with a green slime covering his arm.

Iris is okay, but she has developed a mental block and can't remember what happened to Tom, who will die unless doctors can figure out what kind of alien organism has attached itself to him and how they can combat it. The doctors encourage her to tell them about everything that happened on the trip in hopes of jogging her memory, and we get the whole story in flashback.

The takeoff and the flight are pretty routine, and forty-seven days after launch, the ship is in orbit around

Dr. Iris Ryan (Nora Hayden) is escorted from the rocket ship after her return from the disastrous first trip to *The Angry Red Planet*.

The first Earthlings to land on *The Angry Red Planet*— Tom O'Bannion (Gerald Mohr), Dr. Iris Ryan (Nora Hayden), Professor Theodore Gettell (Les Tremayne), and Sam Jacobs (Jack Kruschen).

Sam uses his sonic ray to save Iris from a carnivorous Martian plant, and Tom and the professor are glad she's safe. But this is only the first of many dangers they must face on *The Angry Red Planet*.

21

Mars, with Tom, Iris, Professor Theodore Gettell (Tremayne), and Sam Jacobs (Kruschen) on board. They land on a planet covered with lush vegetation but with no sign of any higher forms of life. In fact, the red planet is absolutely motionless and silent. They prepare to go outside, but Iris delays their excursion when she sees a three-eyed monster at the viewport, screams, and faints.

No one else saw the thing, so the guys simply write it off to Iris's overactive imagination, and they go out into a world of cheap special effects—hand-drawn sets shot through a reddish filter. Everything is still motionless and dead, but while they are exploring in a jungle, Iris is attacked by a carnivorous plant. Tom uses a machete to chop off its tentacles, Sam zaps it with his sonic ray gun, and Iris is saved.

Back on the ship, Professor Gettell suspects that there is something mysterious going on on Mars: "I can't help feeling that we're being watched." Sam tries the radio and discovers that all incoming and outgoing communication is being blocked by some strange force.

On their next trip outside, the four are attacked by a forty-foot-high spider-bat, but Sam blinds it and drives it off with his sonic gun. They then discover a vast Martian lake; instead of exploring it, they return to the ship, where Tom and the professor decide that the safe thing to do is to take off for Earth immediately, three days ahead of schedule. When they fire the rockets, however, they discover that a powerful force field is holding them in place. "Whoever they are," Gettell notes, "they don't want us to leave."

The next day they start crossing the lake by raft and see a gigantic futuristic city in the distance, but before they can get there, a giant amoeba rises from the water, chases them back to the ship, and digests Sam. The others make it safely inside, but the amoeba envelops the ship and begins trying to eat its way through the hull with the powerful acid it secretes. Tom is injured— some of the green amoeba slime got on his sleeve and ate through his space suit—but he still has it together enough to try to come up with a way of freeing them from the Martian blob.

As a botanist and zoologist, Iris knows that electricity kills Earth amoebas, so Tom and the professor run a strong electrical charge through the ship's outer hull, and this kills the monster. Suddenly the force field is gone, too, and the radio comes on, but the voice that addresses them is not from Earth. The Martian says it is calling to offer a warning. Before we can find out what that warning is, Iris sees the three-eyed guy at the viewport again and once more faints.

When she comes to, the ship is in flight, and Professor Gettell is dying of a heart attack suffered during takeoff.

Tom is sick in his bunk, his arm covered in green slime.

Now back on Earth, Iris finishes her story by saying that she never had the chance to hear the Martian message, but she thinks it was probably recorded on the ship's log tapes. In any case, she suggests that doctors treat Tom's arm with mild jolts of electricity, and her plan works.

Sure enough, the Martian message is on the last of the ship's tapes, and when the authorities play it back for Iris, we hear the Martian voice calling us "technological adults but spiritual and emotional infants" who have "not progressed beyond destruction." As a result, the Martians do not want us coming to their planet and messing up the good life they have there. The final warning is "Do not return to Mars."

Despite its very low budget and pitiful special effects, this movie is appealing. The performances are strong and professional, the characters are interesting, and the idea that a woman would be on board the first flight to Mars solely because she was qualified to go was very farsighted. And I really get a kick out of the spider-bat, even if it is obviously a puppet.

Most of the fear-of-space-travel movies of the fifties project a kind of mindless if-God-had-meant-people-to-fly-He-would-have-given-them-wings attitude, but *The Angry Red Planet* has an intelligent and rather telling point to make. The film suggests that before we take off for other planets, we ought to clean up our act on Earth. Even those of us who find the possibility of interplanetary travel terrifically exciting might have a hard time arguing with that idea.

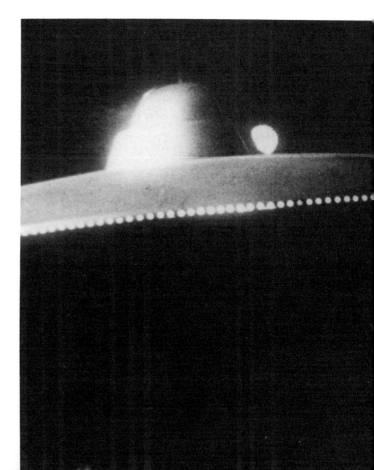

# THE ATOMIC SUBMARINE

## 1 9 5 9

**DIRECTOR:** Spencer G. Bennet
**PRODUCER:** Alex Gordon
**SCREENPLAY:** Orville H. Hampton
**CAST:** Arthur Franz, Dick Foran, Brett Halsey, Tom Conway, Paul Dubov, Bob Steele, Joi Lansing
**ORIGINAL RELEASE:** Gorham Productions
**VIDEO:** Sinister Cinema

In the 1950s and '60s, Arthur Franz appeared in dozens of B pictures, including many science fiction movies, from the appalling *Monster on the Campus* to William Cameron Menzies's classic *Invaders From Mars* to this mini-gem from 1959. *The Atomic Submarine* is low budget every step of the way, with lots of stock footage, generally pitiful special effects, and a cheesy voice-over narrative by Pat Michaels that really gets irritating after a while. On the other hand, the idea behind the film

is a good one, and the movie features a cast of solid professionals—Foran, Conway, and former cowboy actor Bob Steele among them. Spencer Bennet, an experienced director who did the *Batman* and *Superman* serials of the 1940s, does a good job here, too. All things considered, *The Atomic Submarine* is a very nice little film.

The movie is set in the early 1960s (in other words, in the near future) when military and commercial atomic submarines are making regular journeys under the North Pole, conducting various missions and carrying passengers. After a series of unexplained naval disasters, however, the polar shipping lanes are closed, and the U.S. Navy submarine *Tiger Shark*, under the command of Captain Wendover (Foran), is sent out to investigate.

Commander Richard Holloway (Franz) is on board, along with a number of super-scientists, including Nobel Prize–winner Sir Ian Hunt (Conway) and Dr. Carl Nielson (Halsey), designer of the *Lungfish*, a minisub for exploration at extreme depths. The subplot here involves a long-standing feud between Holloway and Nielson. Carl is an outspoken peacenik—antiwar, anti–nuclear weapons, anti–atomic subs—and Holloway, as a navy man who served under Carl's father, considers Nielson to be a coward, a disloyal son, and a worthless human being.

In any case, the *Tiger Shark* heads to the pole and eventually spots a flying saucer under the water. This, of course, has been the cause of all the recent disasters at sea, though it's never explained why the UFO keeps going out of its way to destroy submarines and surface

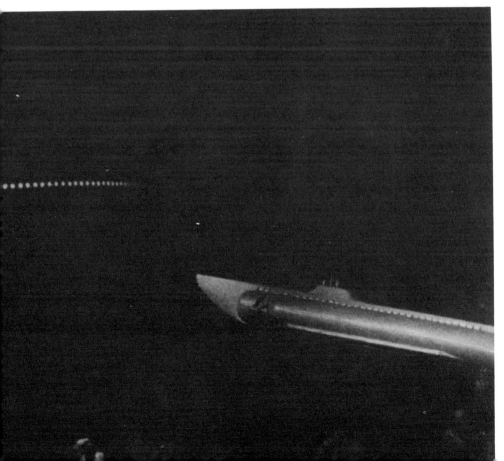

The alien spacecraft is rammed by *The Atomic Submarine* somewhere under the North Pole.

Scientist Carl Nielson (Brett Halsey) prepares to let Commander Holloway (Arthur Franz) and his men out of *The Atomic Submarine* and into the alien spaceship.

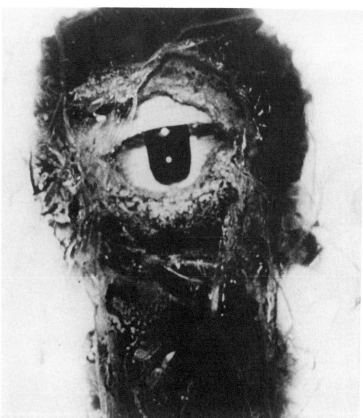

The thing from another world is keeping its eye on *The Atomic Submarine*.

vessels for no particular reason. The scientists speculate that the spaceship runs on magnetic power and that it must recharge itself at the pole periodically, so the men of the *Tiger Shark* plan an ambush.

The plan works, but in the process, the submarine rams the UFO and becomes stuck in its hull. After more hostile banter and name-calling, Holloway and Nielson get on board the *Lungfish* with a few expendable crewmen and enter the spacecraft in hopes of cutting the submarine free. There they meet the alien—a really neat-looking octopus-like thing with one enormous eye—who uses a high-tech radioactive gizmo to fry the extras and who explains to Holloway that he is a scout looking for a planet to colonize. According to him, "Your Earth seems most suitable." Lucky us.

The thing wants to take Holloway back to his own planet as a specimen, but the commander shoots him in the eye and escapes along with Nielson. The *Tiger Shark* shakes itself free of the UFO and pursues the alien, who manages to heal himself and heads to the pole to recharge his batteries. On the way, the scientists of the *Tiger Shark* convert a torpedo into an ICBM— these guys are *really* smart—and when the one-eyed monster tries to take off for his home planet, they blow him out of the sky.

In the end, Holloway and Nielson decide that they misjudged each other and that they will join together to defend humankind against invaders, just in case more of the alien's buddies ever show up on Earth again.

*The Atomic Submarine* is, of course, another threat-of-invasion movie from the fifties, a period during which Americans expected a nuclear attack from the Soviet Union any day. Movies such as this one spoke directly to our nation's most pressing fears. But most fifties sci-fi movies were also very skeptical of atomic weapons and nuclear power; this one is not. In *The Atomic Submarine,* there is no question that atomic submarines and nuclear weapons are good things, and the ending of the film tells us that, as long as science and the military (Nielson and Holloway) can resolve their differences and work together, everything will be ok—an idea that got harder and harder to swallow as the 1960s wore on.

# ATTACK OF THE GIANT LEECHES

## 1959

**ALTERNATE TITLES:** *The Giant Leeches, Demons of the Swamp*
**DIRECTOR:** Bernard L. Kowalski
**PRODUCER:** Gene Corman
**SCREENPLAY:** Leo Gordon
**CAST:** Ken Clark, Yvette Vickers, Jan Shepperd, Bruno VeSota
**ORIGINAL RELEASE:** American International Pictures
**VIDEO:** Neat Stuff Video

In the same year that Yvette Vickers appeared as the centerfold in the July issue of *Playboy,* she also appeared in this sixty-two-minute gem, professionally directed by Bernard L. Kowalski, who also directed hundreds of sixties television episodes, and produced by Roger Corman's brother. Again Vickers is typecast as Liz Walker, the town tramp, the same role she played in *Attack of the Fifty-Foot Woman.* Still it's a part she plays with real enthusiasm, and her performance is one of the high points of the film. Here she's so sleazy she spends the whole day sitting around the house scantily dressed and listening to rock 'n' roll, when she isn't busy running around on her husband (VeSota)—until the giant leeches catch up with her.

Game Warden Steve Benton (Ken Clark) and his girlfriend Nan Grayson (Jan Shepperd) investigate the disappearance of some good old boys in *Attack of the Giant Leeches.*

Some stereotypical corn-drinkin' southern poachers with names like Lem and Cal have disappeared in the Florida Everglades, and game warden Steve Benton (Clark) wants to find out why. With the help of his girlfriend, Nan (Shepperd), and her father, crusty old Doc Grayson, he discovers a colony of giant leeches living in caves under the water. The leeches have been capturing the locals—Liz among them—and keeping them down in the caverns where the monsters feed on their human victims until they are drained of blood. The creatures are not very convincing—they are obviously guys in rubber leech suits—but the scenes of the monsters attacking their victims in the underwater caves are really disgusting and worth the price of admission.

What caused these ordinary household leeches to mutate? Radiation from nearby Cape Canaveral. In the fifties, anytime anything went wrong, people blamed atomic radiation. As it turns out, they were probably right. In any case, game warden Steve, the doc, and some state troopers plant underwater dynamite charges in the swamp, and this puts an end to the monsters.

As in so many fifties horror films, the authorities are inadvertently the cause of the problem, but we can trust them to set things right again. At the height of the cold war, it was important to believe that those in com-

They don't call this movie *Attack of the Giant Leeches* for nothing. Here a giant leech attacks a poacher in the Everglades.

In *Attack of the Giant Leeches*, the monsters keep their victims—including town tramp Liz Walker (Yvette Vickers)—in an underground cave where they can dine on human blood at their leisure.

mand—the police, the military, the scientists, the politicians, even the game wardens—knew what they were doing and had our best interests at heart. For better or worse, the Vietnam era and Watergate made it impossible to continue to believe that.

# THE BOYS FROM BRAZIL

1978

**DIRECTOR:** Franklin J. Schaffner
**PRODUCERS:** Martin Richards and Stanley O'Toole
**SCREENPLAY:** Heywood Gould
**CAST:** Gregory Peck, Laurence Olivier, James Mason, Lilli Palmer, Uta Hagen, Steve Guttenberg, John Rubinstein, Michael Gough, John Dehner, Jeremy Black
**ORIGINAL RELEASE:** ITC Entertainment
**VIDEO:** AVID Home Entertainment

How do you get legendary performers like Gregory Peck, Laurence Olivier, and James Mason to appear in an almost unbelievably stupid film? Well, whatever it takes, the people who made *The Boys from Brazil* did it, and they got Lilli Palmer, Steve Guttenberg, Uta Hagen, John Rubinstein, and a whole lot of other good people, too. Unfortunately, it would take more than a spectacular cast to save this flick.

Barry Kohler (Guttenberg) is a young American who spends his time tracking down Nazis in Paraguay, and he stumbles upon a plot by the Comrades Organization, a wing of the contemporary Nazi Party. He calls the famous Nazi hunter Ezra Lieberman (Olivier) in Vienna and tells him: "Something is going on." Lieberman and his sister Esther (Palmer) have fallen on hard times, however, and, in truth, Ezra doesn't think Kohler has any important information anyway, so he tells the young man to go home.

Instead, Kohler bugs the Nazi mansion in time to hear about the arrival of Dr. Josef Mengele (Peck), one of the most wanted Nazi war criminals. Kohler listens in while Mengele explains to a gathering of fellow Nazis that ninety-four men, all aged sixty-five, must be assassinated during the next two-and-a-half-year period, on or about certain specific dates. The victims are all lower-level civil servants and are scattered throughout Europe and North America. The Nazis discover the bug before Kohler can find out what is going on, but he calls Lieberman with the information he has. While he is on the phone with Ezra, Nazis break into his room and kill him.

Now convinced, Ezra begins to gather information on his own. Meanwhile, the killings begin in West Germany with postal official Emil Doring. In Paraguay, Eduard Seibert (Mason), a leader of the Comrades Organization, calls on Mengele to say that things are going well, though he is worried about Lieberman's involvement. Mengele shows him a chart with the ninety-four names and the dates for their murders and insists that nothing will go wrong with his plan.

Ezra goes to West Germany and calls on Doring's widow and her fourteen-year-old son Erich (Black), who is a disgusting little brat. At about this time, John Harrington (Gough) is murdered in London, and two more elderly men are killed in Sweden and Massachusetts. David Bennett (Rubinstein), a friend of Kohler's and a member of the radical Young Jewish Defenders, shows up and volunteers to help Ezra, who sends him to London to meet Harrington's family. Lieberman himself heads for Massachusetts to interview the family of murder victim Jack Curry.

There Ezra meets the obnoxious Jack Curry, Jr. (Black), who is an exact duplicate of Erich Doring. In England, David meets Simon Harrington (Black), and when he describes the kid to Ezra, it is once again the same boy.

Curry's widow explains that Jack, Jr., was adopted and that the contact at the adoption agency was Frieda Maloney (Hagen), a war criminal who was tracked down by Lieberman some years before and who is now in prison. He interviews her there, and she explains that the Comrades Organization ordered her to go to work for an adoption agency and to look for couples in which the husband and wife were born between certain dates and in which the husband, a low-ranking civil servant, was older than his wife by about twenty years. She placed babies with about twenty such couples in North America—all the children were male, with black hair and blue eyes, and all came from Brazil. Frieda remembers the name of only one of the couples, the Wheelocks of Pennsylvania.

Back in Paraguay, Seibert has terminated the operation and recalled the assassins without notifying Mengele, who is, needless to say, quite upset. Seibert is afraid that Lieberman is getting too close, and the party can't risk the publicity that would result if Ezra was to be murdered. Dr. Mengele vows to continue with the project himself.

Lieberman checks with a biologist friend, Dr. Bruck-

Nazi war criminal Josef Mengele (Gregory Peck, center) enjoys getting together with some likeminded friends for an evening to plot the conquest of the world in *The Boys From Brazil*.

Eduard Seibert (James Mason) calls on Dr. Mengele to express his concerns about the plot to reincarnate Hitler in *The Boys From Brazil*.

ner, to ask some questions about Erich Doring, Simon Harrington, and Jack Curry, who seem to be triplets, and Bruckner delivers a little lecture on cloning—making exact replicas of a living organism from single cells of the original. He even shows a neat little film about cloning rabbits, though he explains that if it were possible to clone human beings, the clones still wouldn't be exact copies of the original unless you could duplicate all the necessary environmental factors.

Finally Ezra catches on to what Mengele is up to. The evil doctor has created ninety-four clones of Hitler and has given them to ninety-four couples that match, as closely as possible, Hitler's own family—an older, domineering father in the civil service and a younger, doting mother. Since Hitler's father died when the boy was fourteen, all ninety-four adoptive fathers must also die when their sons reach that age.

Seibert and the Comrades Organization no longer trust Mengele, so they burn his home and lab in Paraguay, but Mengele himself is in Pennsylvania, tracking down Henry Wheelock (Dehner), who breeds Dobermans. Wheelock is no sooner dead than Lieberman shows up, and he and Mengele struggle over a gun, with the doctor getting the upper hand. Ezra is shot but manages to release the dogs, which pin Mengele down.

Then Bobby Wheelock (Black) arrives at home—yes, it's the same dark-haired, blue-eyed little monster. Mengele, still held motionless by the dogs, tries to tell

Bobby who he is, but the kid doesn't believe it. Soon enough, Bobby discovers the body of his father, realizes Mengele killed him, and orders the Dobermans to attack the Nazi. The kid looks on smiling as the dogs rip Mengele to bits.

Later, Ezra is in the hospital, and David comes by to insist that all ninety-four Hitler clones be killed. Lieberman has a list of the kids' names, but he burns it and threatens to turn Bennett in to the police if anything happens to Bobby Wheelock or the others. Meanwhile, Bobby is back home in Pennsylvania, and we have to wonder whether the disgusting little creep or one of his fellow clones really will turn out to be another Hitler.

The usually brilliant Gregory Peck is more than a bit over the top as a Nazi war criminal, but Olivier—who got to play a Mengele-like character in *Marathon Man*—is charming as the elderly Nazi hunter. What hurts this film is the basic impossibility of the plot—not so much the futuristic idea of human cloning but the idea that the environmental factors of anyone's life could ever be duplicated. Certainly Dr. Mengele would know that factors like language, culture, friends, and teachers could never be controlled, and so the odds against any of his clones really becoming another Hitler would be astronomical.

Ezra Lieberman confronts convicted war criminal Frieda Maloney (Uta Hagen), who explains the plot involving *The Boys From Brazil*.

Jewish activist David Bennett (John Rubinstein) offers his help to famed Nazi hunter Ezra Lieberman (Laurence Olivier) and his sister Esther (Lilli Palmer) in *The Boys From Brazil*.

Ezra Lieberman and Dr. Josef Mengele fight to the death in the final moments of *The Boys From Brazil*. (Courtesy Hollywood Book and Poster)

29

The problem with the film is that it depicts Mengele and the other Nazi leaders as idiots. Real Nazi leaders were certainly fanatics, madmen, and monsters, but they were not stupid, and to suggest that they were, as *The Boys From Brazil* does, is also to suggest that they were not as dangerous as they obviously were and are.

We now have good reason to believe that the real Josef Mengele—physician, butcher, murderer, monster—was not torn apart by dogs but died comfortably and peacefully in South America. So much for justice in the real world.

# THE BRAIN EATERS

1958

**DIRECTOR:** Bruno VeSota
**PRODUCER:** Edwin Nelson
**SCREENPLAY:** Gordon Urquhart
**CAST:** Edwin Nelson, Alan Frost, Jack Hill, Joanna Lee, Jody Fair, David Hughes, Robert Ball, Greigh Phillips, Orville Sherman
**ORIGINAL RELEASE:** American International Pictures
**VIDEO:** Columbia TriStar Home Video

Nobody actually eats any brains in this movie; they didn't do that kind of thing on-screen in 1958. "Brain eaters" is a figure of speech for the little creatures in this flick, who attach themselves to the brains of humans and take control of their thoughts and actions. In fact, *Brain Eaters* is an obvious attempt to cash in on the success of Don Siegel's classic secret alien invasion film of 1955, *Invasion of the Body Snatchers*—a movie in which no one snatches any bodies. Who makes up these titles, anyway?

The setting is peaceful Riverdale—isn't that where Archie, Jughead, Betty, and Veronica live? In any case, Glenn (Frost), the mayor's son, and his fiancée, Elaine (Fair), discover a strange otherworldly craft in the woods, and the next thing you know, Senator Powers (Hill) and a bunch of dignitaries are being briefed in Washington, D.C., about the ship. Dr. Paul Kettering (Nelson) is examining the thing on site, but in the meantime a number of prominent Riverdale citizens have been killed, and Mayor Cameron (Sherman) has disappeared. Powers and his assistant Don (Ball) head for Riverdale to investigate—or as the senator puts it, "to keep a damper on this thing."

Alice (Joanna Lee) is only one of many to be possessed by *Brain Eaters* from the center of the Earth.

The mayor returns, but he behaves very strangely and even pulls a gun on his son. Kettering sees something odd on the back of Cameron's neck, but when he tries to examine it, the mayor runs off, and the sheriff (Phillips) shoots him down—something he's probably wanted to do for a long time.

The thing attached to the mayor's neck is an alien parasite that controls its host's thoughts and that, once removed, secretes an acid that kills its victim. Meanwhile, townsfolk are being taken over left and right—including the sheriff and Kettering's one true love, Alice (Lee). Victims of the brain eaters carry extra creatures around in glowing fishbowls so they can infect others.

Kettering has been inside the alien ship, crawling down through a narrow tunnel that spirals through the interior, but he has found nothing. Suddenly an elderly man emerges from the craft, and Kettering recognizes him as Dr. Helsington, who along with his colleague Dr. Cole vanished some five years before. Helsington has a parasite attached to his neck, but the thing leaves him shortly after he comes out of the ship, and now he is doomed.

Helsington's dying words are an explanation of what's been going on. The parasites are insect-like creatures that come from deep within the Earth, where they've been living since the Carboniferous Period. Now they want to take over the surface world. "Then they're not from out there," Kettering realizes. "They're from below."

Glenn and Kettering go into the ship where they find a very old, bearded man, Dr. Cole, who speaks for the parasites: "Our social order is pure. . . . We shall force upon man a life free of strife and turmoil." Obviously, we wouldn't want that to happen, so Kettering runs electrical cables to the ship in hopes of destroying it.

At that moment Alice comes out of the craft and Kettering tries to reason with her, but of course her brain has been eaten (not really—see opening paragraph above), and if he tries to remove the parasite that has infected her, she will die. So Kettering turns on the juice, electrocuting the aliens in the ship, Alice, and himself.

Maybe this movie isn't so much like *Invasion of the Body Snatchers* after all. In *Invasion*, the aliens that take over human beings also promise a world "free of strife and turmoil," but those aliens are plants, and in *Brain Eaters*, they're insects. Also, in *Invasion*, the parasites come from outer space, while in *Brain Eaters*, they come from beneath the Earth's surface. See, two totally different concepts!

Okay, so *Brain Eaters* really is a rip-off of *Invasion of the Body Snatchers*, but they both draw on a pervasive paranoia of that time, a fear of communism generated by the early cold war years and the McCarthy era of commie witch hunts. If you'll remember, Senator Joseph

A possessed citizen of Riverdale carries one of the *Brain Eaters* around in a fishbowl. (Courtesy Hollywood Book and Poster)

McCarthy of Wisconsin made quite a career for himself by claiming that the communist invasion was already under way and that communists had infiltrated every area of American life. Of course that's exactly what happens in *Brain Eaters* and *Invasion of the Body Snatchers*—people in every walk of life suddenly turn out to be alien commies from outer space/the center of the Earth.

Also in the fifties there was a lot of talk about brainwashing, the notion that commies had the power to turn decent Americans into creatures like themselves. This was why no one was allowed to read the works of Marx or Lenin and why associating with known communists was as good as being one. Communism was perceived as a communicable disease spreading secretly through the country from one person to another, just as the parasites in *Brain Eaters* and *Invasion of the Body Snatchers* did. All this seems pretty naive from our vantage point today, but back in the fifties, it was serious business.

*The Brain Eaters* does have one thing that the original *Invasion of the Body Snatchers* doesn't, and that's a very young Leonard (Mr. Spock) Nimoy as the bearded Dr. Cole, though you'd be hard put to recognize him through all that makeup if it weren't for his distinctive voice. Interestingly enough, as Cole, he sounds just like Spock as he talks about the rational, logical society the parasites hope to bring about on Earth—sort of like Vulcan society. Even more interesting is the fact that though he missed being in the original, Nimoy appears in the 1978 remake of *Invasion of the Body Snatchers*, again as a doctor—a psychiatrist this time—and again as host to one of the alien invaders.

Nimoy's appearance in *Brain Eaters* doesn't exactly save the movie from complete disaster, but it doesn't hurt.

# THE BRAIN FROM PLANET AROUS

1 9 5 7

**DIRECTOR:** Nathan Hertz (Nathan Juran)
**PRODUCER:** Jaques Marquette
**SCREENPLAY:** Ray Buffam
**CAST:** John Agar, Joyce Meadows, Robert Fuller
**ORIGINAL RELEASE:** Howco International
**VIDEO:** Rhino Home Video

John Agar, former husband of Shirley Temple, is nuclear scientist Steve March, but through most of this film his mind and body are possessed by Gor, a giant floating brain from outer space. Like most fifties aliens, Gor plans to conquer the Earth, and it seems there is nothing we Earthlings can do to stop him.

After March is taken over by Gor, his girlfriend, Sally Fallon (Meadows), notices that something is wrong right away. For one thing, Steve has become more affectionate. "You never kissed me like that before. Wow! . . . No, Steve, no." It seems that Gor likes her and wants her for his very own.

Steve/Gor toasts a few victims with his radioactive eyes and blows up a few airplanes and an atomic bomb test site to convince world leaders that they should turn all power over to him. Fortunately, a good brain from outer space named Vol comes to Earth to stop Gor, and he takes over Sally's dog in order to be close to Steve. In the end, with Vol's help, Steve manages to catch Gor unawares and finishes him off with an ax.

Scientist Steve March (John Agar) is taken over by Gor, *The Brain From Planet Arous*.

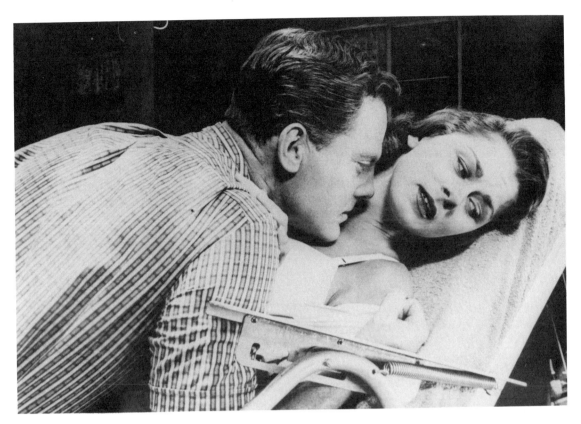

When he is possessed by *The Brain From Planet Arous*, Steve can't get enough of his girlfriend, Sally Fallon (Joyce Meadows), though Sally seems to be having second thoughts about the relationship.

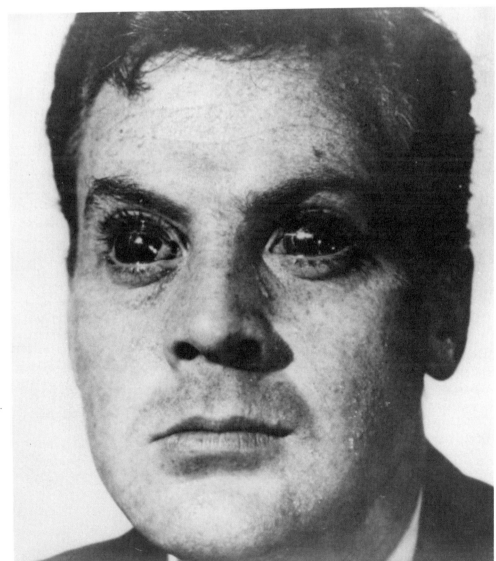

Actor John Agar makes a superb maniac in *The Brain From Planet Arous*.

Agar made about a zillion sci-fi and horror films in the 1950s—*The Mole People, Invisible Invaders, Tarantula,* and others—and he was never particularly talented as a leading man, but here he gets to play the villain, and the change seems to do him good. As Steve/Gor, he is absolutely maniacal—wild-eyed and laughing one second, lecherous the next. Perhaps this was his calling all along.

It is not a coincidence that Gor is from the planet Arous/Eros, because despite his claim that he is "pure intellect," he's a very erotic guy, particularly where Sally is concerned. As he says, "She appeals to me. There are some aspects of the life of an Earth savage that are exciting and rewarding." Of course most horror films tell us that the monster/creature/alien/vampire/werewolf/whatever wants our women and that it is the job of the male hero to keep that from happening and to win the woman as a trophy for himself—as if women were only property, commodities that could be traded back and forth, won or lost. Unfortunately, this is still the image of women that is offered up regularly in popular culture and the mass media.

Well, at least the aliens don't want our cars.

# THE BRAIN THAT WOULDN'T DIE

## 1959

**DIRECTOR/SCREENPLAY:** Joseph Green
**PRODUCER:** Rex Carlton
**CAST:** Herb Evers, Virginia Leith, Bruce Brighton, Adele Lamont, Leslie Daniel, Paula Maurice, Doris Bent
**ORIGINAL RELEASE:** American International Pictures
**VIDEO:** Warner Home Video, Rhino Home Video, Sinister Cinema, and Scorched Earth Productions

This wonderfully ridiculous movie was an early effort to bring graphic gore to the silver screen, but it had to wait until 1962 before it was finally released. The title has to be one of the best around, though apparently there was some difference of opinion about what to call this thing—in the end credits, it's listed as *The Head*

*That Wouldn't Die.* Overall, though, the name doesn't matter. They could have called it *Gone With the Wind,* and it would still stink.

Dr. Bill Courtner (Herb, later Jason, Evers) is a young, good-looking, and brilliant but reckless brain surgeon who is doing experiments in transplant surgery at his secret lab. He has developed a compound that keeps the body from rejecting transplanted limbs and organs, and his formula comes in very handy when his fiancée, Jan (Leith), is decapitated in an auto accident. Bill keeps her head alive in the lab and goes out searching for the perfect body to make her a whole woman again.

Jan's head isn't happy with its situation—"Let me die. Let me die!"—and neither is Bill's assistant Curt (Brighton), a former surgeon who lost an arm in a laboratory accident and who would rather have Bill working on a new arm for him than on a new body for her. Curt has been a guinea pig for Bill a number of times, but after each operation, the newly transplanted arm has withered, which is the problem with his current arm, too. He is hoping that the new compound will be successful with Jan so he can have his turn.

Meanwhile, Curt spends a lot of time delivering interminable pompous monologues to Jan's head, telling her all about the monster Bill keeps locked up in the closet: "Behind that door is the sum total of Dr. Courtner's mistakes." Jan already knows about the thing in the

In the closing moments of *The Brain That Wouldn't Die*, Dr. Bill Courtner (Herb "Jason" Evers) is about to decapitate Doris Powell (Adele Lamont) and give her body to his girlfriend, Jan, when he hears a strange sound coming from the closet.

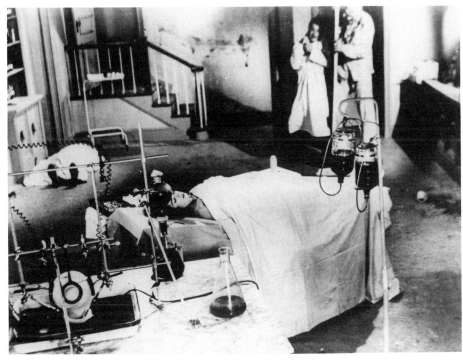

The thing in the closet breaks free in time to give Dr. Courtner what he deserves for threatening the lovely Doris as Jan (Virginia Leith), *The Brain That Wouldn't Die*, watches from her place on the lab table.

closet, however, because Bill's formula has an unexpected side effect—it makes her telepathic. Throughout the film, she and the monster in the closet carry on a silent tête-à-tête while Curt drones and drones.

Meanwhile, Bill is hitting every strip joint and beauty contest in town, looking for the perfect new body for Jan. He has a lot of opportunities, but none of the women he meets seems quite right. Still, he is a good-looking guy, and he gets a lot of action. At one point, two strippers even engage in a wrestling match over him—this movie really *does* have something for everyone.

Finally, though, Bill remembers Doris Powell (Lamont), an old schoolmate who has a perfect body and a scarred face. Doris is on the skids, making her living by posing in her studio for drooling guys who pay to snap pictures of her in a bathing suit. Needless to say, she is pretty bitter. "I hate all men," she says. "I hate them for what one did to me once." Bill wins her over by promising to restore her face if she will only accompany him to his lab.

Back at the Courtner estate, though, Jan's head and the thing in the closet are making plans. "Together," Jan says, "we could have revenge." When Curt arrives in the lab to feed the monster, Jan urges it to break out, and though it doesn't manage that right away, it

does rip off Curt's good arm, and Bill's long-winded assistant bleeds to death, which finally shuts him up for good.

Bill and Doris arrive at the house, and when the handsome doctor goes down to the lab to get what he needs to drug his unsuspecting guest, he finds Curt's bloody body. Nothing is going to stop Bill from concluding his experiment with Jan, however, so he slips a powder into Doris's drink, then carries her downstairs to the lab and puts her on the operating table.

Before the operation can take place, the closet thing, under the influence of Jan's brain waves, crashes through the door of its prison at last, bites a chunk out of Bill's throat, and starts a fire in the lab. As the monster carries Doris off to safety, Jan's head says, "I told you to let me die," and that's that.

This film is a lot more boring than it sounds, and the dialogue is almost unbelievably stilted. In particular, Curt is always saying things like "The paths of experimentation twist and turn through mountains of miscalculations and often lose themselves in error and darkness," when he could have said: "Experiments don't always work." The people who made this flick apparently took it quite seriously and assumed that good writing is saying very simple things in very complicated ways. It isn't.

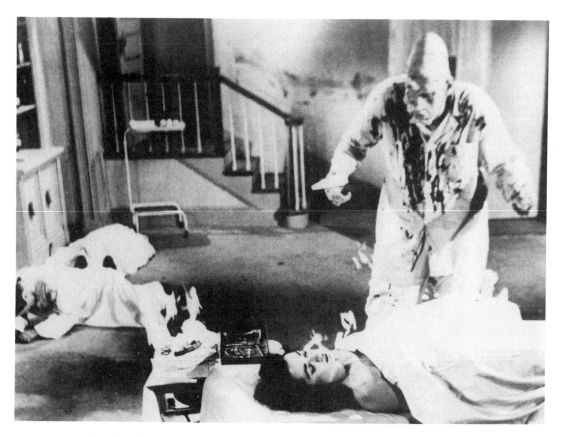

The thing from the closet gets the girl at the end of *The Brain That Wouldn't Die* and carries Doris Powell off into the night.

There *are* attempts at comedy, though—at one point Doris says to Bill, "I'll do anything that'll help me get rid of this face," and that's good for a chuckle—but on the whole, the humor is even worse than the melodramatic stuff.

Even so, *The Brain That Wouldn't Die* is worth watching just to see scenes like Bill carrying Jan's head across the countryside wrapped in his sport coat or Curt's final agony, which goes on longer than most death scenes in Shakespeare. And just try to keep a straight face when Bill shuts Jan up by putting masking tape over her mouth—yes, somehow the head can speak, even without vocal cords.

The ending is interesting, too. In most horror flicks, the young, good-looking guy gets the girl and the monster gets killed. In *The Brain That Wouldn't Die*, on the other hand, the young, good-looking guy gets killed and the monster not only survives but gets the girl. This nice reversal suggests that you can't tell the monster from the hero solely on the basis of appearance—a surprisingly intelligent notion to find in a particularly ludicrous film.

Note: The Warner video print is an edited-for-TV version that is so seriously cut it's hard to know what's going on. The video versions from Rhino, Sinister Cinema, and Scorched Earth Productions are complete and uncut.

# BRIDE OF THE MONSTER

1 9 5 6

**ALTERNATE TITLE:** *Bride of the Atom*
**DIRECTOR/PRODUCER:** Edward D. Wood, Jr.
**SCREENPLAY:** Edward D. Wood, Jr., and Alex Gordon
**CAST:** Bela Lugosi, Tor Johnson, Tony McCoy, Loretta King, Harvey B. Dunn, Paul Marco
**ORIGINAL RELEASE:** Banner-DCA
**VIDEO:** Sinister Cinema, Star Classics, and others

Executive producer Donald McCoy put up the money for this one on the condition that his son Tony could be the hero, and so another film by Edward D. Wood, Jr., came into the world.

Wood is known as one of the worst filmmakers who ever lived (*Night of the Ghouls, Plan 9 From Outer Space, Glen or Glenda*), and *Bride of the Monster* doesn't do anything to improve his reputation. At age seventy-three, Lugosi is mad scientist Eric Vornoff, who hopes to create an army of superbeings, though he hasn't had much luck. All of his human guinea pigs die. He is assisted by his enormous servant Lobo (the enormous Johnson, who wrestled professionally under the name The Swedish Angel) and an octopus he keeps in a nearby lake to deal with intruders. Apparently, Wood could afford to rent the fake octopus but not the machinery that made it work, and so whenever the beast attacks, victims are forced to wrap the tentacles around themselves.

Lieutenant Dick Craig (McCoy) is investigating a number of disappearances near the old Willows house, and his fiancée, Janet Lawton (King), crusading newspaper reporter, is out for a story. She stumbles upon Vornoff's laboratory, and Lobo takes a liking to her. Vornoff decides to turn her into a superwoman, but first, for no particular reason, he dresses her in a wedding gown he keeps handy for just such an occasion. A collander is placed on her head, and she is strapped to a table beneath a photographic enlarger, but before Vornoff can switch on this high-tech equipment, Lobo stops him, saves the girl, and zaps the scientist with his own ray. This time—wouldn't you know it?—it works, and Vornoff becomes a giant with super-strength.

Well, lightning hits the house, the octopus gets Vornoff, then it too is struck by lightning, which for some reason causes a nuclear blast. The police chief (Dunn) jumps in at the end to say, "He tampered in God's domain," and that's that.

Wood has a high tolerance for contradiction and ambiguity, so you can watch one of his films again and again and never really figure out what it's about. The title, *Bride of the Monster,* is a case in point. Is Janet to be the bride of Lobo? The octopus? Vornoff himself after he becomes a giant? The Loch Ness Monster, which, according to the film, Vornoff created during a stay in Scotland? All of the above?

Here's another puzzler: Most of Wood's heroes are authority figures—policemen or military officers—and yet his films always suggest that there are vast official conspiracies of silence, efforts on the part of government and the military to cover up important truths that the public has the right to know about. These "truths" usually involve tabloid stuff—that UFOs, ghosts, and monsters are real—but the idea of governmental conspiracies definitely was not a popular one in the fifties, when most of us believed that the authorities had our best interests at heart. It wasn't until the late sixties that

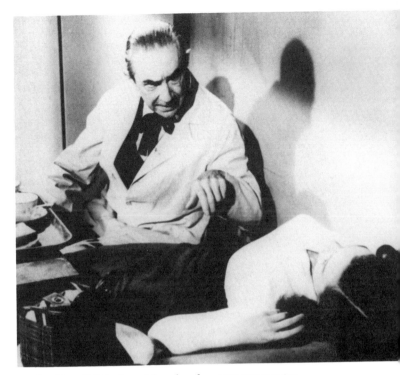

Dr. Eric Vornoff (Bela Lugosi) has plans for newspaper reporter Janet Lawton (Loretta King)—she is to be the *Bride of the Monster.*

Vornoff shows *The Bride of the Monster* to captive police detective Dick Craig (Tony McCoy).

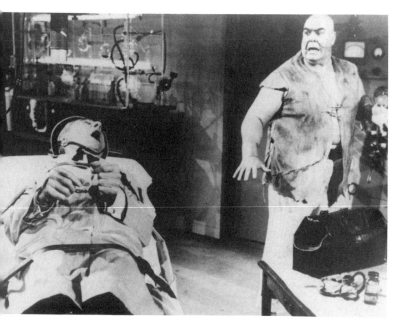

Lobo (Tor Johnson) is about to give Dr. Vornoff his just deserts in Edward D. Wood, Jr.'s, *Bride of the Monster.*

science fiction films began to question whether the government and the military really were working for our own good.

Could this mean that Edward D. Wood, Jr., was ahead of his time?

# CAT-WOMEN OF THE MOON

1 9 5 3

**DIRECTOR:** Arthur Hilton
**PRODUCERS:** Al Zimbalist and Jack Rabin
**SCREENPLAY:** Roy Hamilton
**CAST:** Sonny Tufts, Victor Jory, Marie Windsor, Bill Phipps, Douglas Fowley, Carol Brewster, Suzanne Alexander, Susan Morrow
**ORIGINAL RELEASE:** 3-Dimensional Pictures
**VIDEO:** Rhino Home Video, Sinister Cinema, and Scorched Earth Productions

Any movie starring Sonny Tufts automatically qualifies for cult status, and that fact that *Cat-Women of the Moon* was made in 3-D helps, too. What more could

you want? The Hollywood Cover Girls? Well, whoever they are, they're here.

The first rocket for the moon leaves Earth with a five-person crew under the command of Laird Grainger (Tufts), a straitlaced, overbearing, by-the-book kind of guy. But as crew member Kip (Jory) likes to say, "Some things aren't in the book."

On their way to the moon, Laird's girlfriend Helen (Windsor), the ship's navigator, seems to slip into momentary trances, and when they finally arrive at their destination, she seems to know her way around, almost as if she's been there before. Kip finds this strange, but then he's suspicious of everything and never goes anywhere without his gun—this is what makes him the hero of the flick.

Helen leads Laird, Kip, Doug (Phipps), and Walt (Fowley) to a cave in which, amazingly, the atmosphere and gravity are exactly the same as on Earth, so they take off their helmets and space suits. Seconds later, they are attacked by the same cheesy giant spiders that seem to crop up in hundreds of fifties sci-fi films—whoever was renting out those things back then must have made a fortune! They defeat the angry arachnids, but in the meantime, someone steals their space suits. Now they can't get back to the ship.

They follow the cave to an underground city, and while the guys are looking around, Helen slips away to meet with Alpha (Brewster), leader of the cat-women, who more or less explains what's been going on. The cat-women are telepathic, and they've been controlling

The crew—from left to right, Walt (Douglas Fowley), Doug (Bill Phipps), Kip (Victor Jory), Grainger (Sonny Tufts), and Helen (Marie Windsor)—travel into space, where they will soon meet the *Cat-Women of the Moon.*

One small step for Sonny Tufts as he becomes the first man to set foot on the moon. Unfortunately, the *Cat-Women of the Moon* got there before he did.

Helen's mind since before she left Earth. "You are one of us now," Alpha says.

There are no males on the moon, but as Zeta (Alexander) explains, "We have no use for men." Life for the cat-women has been pretty good on the moon, but now their artificial atmosphere is breaking up, and it's time to move on. The plan is to steal the rocket, go to Earth, control the minds of all Earth women, and seize control of the whole planet. First, though, they have to gain the confidence of Helen's male companions to find out how the rocket ship works, and since they can't control the minds of males, they're going to have to use their seductive charms.

Finally the cat-women introduce themselves to Laird and the boys. Kip wants nothing to do with the moon ladies, but greedy Walt falls in with Zeta, who promises to show him where he can find plenty of gold, and Doug takes up with Lamda (Morrow).

During an off moment, Kip, who is secretly in love with Helen, gets her alone and puts his arms around her, thus breaking the cat-women's spell, and Helen tells him what's going on. It's too late, though, because Alpha is getting information out of Laird, and Walt has taken Zeta back to the ship to show her how the thing works. Lamda really does fall for Doug, however, and she rebels against her moon sisters, taking the side of the men.

Walt, Kip, Grainger, and Doug capture one of the *Cat-Women of the Moon*.

Helen is attacked by a phony spider in *Cat-Women of the Moon*.

In a particularly dramatic moment from *Cat-Women of the Moon*, Kip and Grainger nearly come to blows for the love of Helen, while Doug tries to keep things under control.

Everything ends well. The cat-women kill Lamda, but Kip shoots Zeta and Alpha offscreen. Helen has to break the news to Laird she's really in love with Kip, but he takes it like a man and admits that some things really aren't in the book. Doug feels bad about losing Lamda, but hey, the Earth is safe from invasion, so who is he to complain?

After all the alien males who have tried to steal our Earth women, it's nice for a change to see some alien women planning their own invasion. But if you think that *Cat-Women of the Moon* is an equal opportunity alien invasion film, you'd better watch it again. For one thing, the cat-women want to kill the Earth men, not mate with them. Only Lamda knows her place, because she has the good sense to realize that what she's been waiting for all along is a man to take her away from all this.

Alpha and Zeta are really evil, because they've obviously seized control of the moon from its rightful rulers—the men—and now they want to do the same to Earth. And what about Helen? Well, while she's under the hypnotic power of the moon women, she thinks a civilization without guys might be a good idea, but once she comes to her senses, she realizes that just being the best rocket-ship navigator in the world isn't enough. She needs a man to boss her around, and she has to choose between Laird, who is overweight and kind of stupid, and suspicious, hostile Kip, who looks like a weasel—not much of a choice, but then there aren't that many guys around, and she needs *somebody*. Who ever heard of a woman leading her own life?

Well, maybe *Cat-Women of the Moon* isn't exactly a feminist tract, but it *does* have a very awkward dance scene by the Hollywood Cover Girls in their cat costumes, and remember, it *is* in 3-D. The movie has its unsolved mysteries, too. Why are the women on the moon *cat*-women rather than, say, fish-women or badger-women? Why are women who live on the moon named after letters of the Greek alphabet? And why was this movie remade in 1959 as *Missile to the Moon*? You'd think one version of *Cat-Women of the Moon* would have been more than enough.

Here they are—the *Cat-Women of the Moon*.

# THE CRAWLING HAND

1 9 6 3

**DIRECTOR:** Herbert L. Strock
**PRODUCER:** Joseph F. Robertson
**SCREENPLAY:** William Idelson and Herbert L. Strock
**CAST:** Peter Breck, Kent Taylor, Rod Lauren, Alan Hale, Sirry Steffen, Allison Hayes
**ORIGINAL RELEASE:** American International Pictures
**VIDEO:** Video Gems and Rhino Home Video

In the 1950s and early '60s, when manned space travel was becoming a reality, some adventurous science fiction films reveled in the possibilities, while more conservative flicks emphasized the possible dangers. It was the if-God-had-meant-people-to-fly-He-would-have-given-them-wings attitude all over again.

*The Crawling Hand*, from the director of *I Was a Teenage Frankenstein*, begins with the failure of a manned moonshot. The ship explodes on its return to Earth, but before it does, scientists Steve Curan (Breck), Max Weitzberg (Taylor), and their assistant Donna (Hayes) discover that the astronaut was taken over by some alien organism.

Meanwhile, in sunny California, Paul Lawrence (Lauren) and his girl Marta Farnstrom (Steffen) are cavorting on the beach when they discover a human arm. Paul is a science student, and recognizing the sleeve of an astronaut's uniform, he takes the arm home for further study. But of course the arm is alive, still possessed by the alien organism, and it escapes to kill Paul's landlady and to possess Paul himself, making him run amok and get black circles around his eyes. Paul is a moody sort of guy anyway—"the lone wolf," according to Marta's best friend—but when the organism has control of him, he is downright offensive.

Curan and Weitzberg find out that their astronaut's fingerprints have been found at the scene of the landlady's murder, so they hurry to California and arrive in time to figure out what Paul's problem is. Sheriff Townsend, played by Alan Hale, the Skipper on *Gilligan's Island*, doesn't want to hear about alien organisms, however; he is convinced that Paul is just another juvenile delinquent looking for trouble, and he is more than ready to gun him down. "I know all about kids like him. The county jail is full of them."

Marta Farnstrom's (Sirry Steffen) grandfather doesn't approve of her going out with high school rebel Paul Lawrence (Rod Lauren) in the first place, so how do you think he feels when Paul is taken over by *The Crawling Hand*?

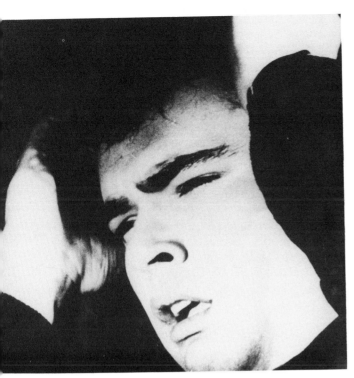

What? Another rerun of *Gilligan's Island*? No, this time the Skipper (Alan Hale) is the small-town sheriff who has to track down *The Crawling Hand*.

Paul learns that it isn't much fun to be possessed by *The Crawling Hand* from outer space.

Finally, in a lucid moment, Paul captures the arm and takes it to the city dump, where believe it or not, it is eaten by the local cats, thus setting Paul free. He and Marta live happily ever after, and Curan and Weitzberg return to Washington, never again to tamper with things man was not meant to know.

There's more going on here than simply fear of outer space. When you watch this film, the first thing you notice is how much Paul looks like a pudgy James Dean, and actor Lauren plays that resemblance for all it's worth—he mumbles, he's tormented, he's "the lone wolf." He even imitates characteristic Dean mannerisms from *Rebel Without a Cause*. That 1955 film, directed by Nicholas Ray, is the classic juvenile delinquent flick, depicting a postwar teenage rebellion that seemed to be inexplicable and therefore beyond solution. In a way, *The Crawling Hand* is an answer to the question raised by *Rebel Without a Cause*. What's wrong with kids today? They've been taken over by alien organisms.

But Paul learns his lesson. As he says, "I'm all mixed up. . . . I shouldn't keep things to myself. I tried to be a lone wolf." From now on, he will be a team player, a conformist, a grown-up. *The Crawling Hand* pretends to be a teen sci-fi film—it even features "The Bird Is the Word" by the Rivingtons as its unofficial theme song—but it's really a film by grown-ups telling kids to grow up themselves. And that's a dirty trick.

# DAMNATION ALLEY

1977

**DIRECTOR:** Jack Smight
**PRODUCERS:** Jerome P. Zeitman and Paul Maslansky
**SCREENPLAY:** Alan Sharp and Lucas Heller
**CAST:** Jan-Michael Vincent, George Peppard, Dominique Sanda, Paul Winfield, Jackie Earle Haley, Kip Niven
**ORIGINAL RELEASE:** 20th Century-Fox
**VIDEO:** CBS/Fox Video

This movie is based on a novel of the same name by science fiction master Roger Zelazny. *Damnation Alley* is not Zelazny's finest work by a long shot, but it is an exciting, thrill-packed story, and that's why it is surprising that the film version is so dull. Maybe the filmmakers

Tanner (Jan-Michael Vincent) is called upon to push a button that will mean the end of civilization as we know it in *Damnation Alley*.

were trying to show us how boring the end of the world might be.

Denton (Peppard) and Tanner (Vincent) are air force officers stationed at a California base where they are in charge of the buttons that launch the ICBMs. The two do not get along. Denton is a by-the-book kind of guy and Tanner is a rebel, though the movie really doesn't make enough of this conflict between the two to make it interesting. In any case, one day the big one starts, the missiles go up, and the world is destroyed.

Two years pass, and Denton, Tanner, Keegan (Winfield), and other military personnel at the base are surviving as best they can, though they have been out of touch with the rest of the world—if there is a rest of the world—for a long time. Denton has been spending his time building two vehicles called Landmasters, armed tanks made for long-distance travel. Tanner makes motorcycle forays into the countryside, where he has to outdistance giant mutant scorpions in order to bring back provisions. The nuclear blasts during the war have tipped the Earth on its axis, causing strange storms and transforming the entire world into a gigantic desert. In general, things are not going well.

Everything gets worse when the base is destroyed by an accidental explosion, leaving only four survivors—Denton, Tanner, Keegan, and Perry (Niven). The only

In an underground missile site, Keegan (Paul Winfield) and Denton (George Peppard) witness the end of the world in the opening moments of *Damnation Alley*.

Tanner likes to ride his motor-cycle through crowds of giant scorpions, just for fun. Wait until he tackles *Damnation Alley*.

Tanner and Denton pilot one of the Landmasters through *Damnation Alley* on their way to Albany.

In *Damnation Alley*, Keegan is devoured by man-eating cock-roaches in Salt Lake City—it's a hard way to go.

45

Post–nuclear holocaust survivors—Billy (Jackie Earle Haley), Janice, Tanner, and Denton—posing outside their Landmaster in *Damnation Alley*.

Is this a violent movie or what? Actress Dominique Sanda in a scene from *Damnation Alley*.

Tanner and Janice (Dominique Sanda) stage a classy motorcycle jump to escape the Salt Lake City cockroaches in *Damnation Alley*.

good news is that they have picked up a radio signal from Albany, New York, so the four decide to head east in the two Landmasters in search of company.

The rest of the movie follows their trip. Early on, a cyclone disables one of the Landmasters and kills Perry. In a deserted Las Vegas, they meet a woman named Janice (Sanda) and take her along. In Salt Lake City, they are attacked by swarms of armored flesh-eating bugs, and Keegan is killed. This might sound very exciting, but somehow it isn't, though it does give Peppard the chance to say the best line of the film: "The city is infested with killer cockroaches!"

Farther along, they find a boy named Billy (Haley), and he joins them, too. Then they have to fight a gang of redneck mutants who want the Landmaster and the woman. Then they're caught in the middle of a flash flood. Then . . .

The problem here is that the movie simply doesn't hang together. It is just, as they say, one damned thing after another. They drive for a while; then they stop and something happens. They drive some more, then stop, and something happens. Eventually, though, for no particular reason, the Earth tips itself right again, and they get to Albany, where there are people and horses and fields of grass and idyllic, rustic scenes. In

The high-tech Landmaster from *Damnation Alley* is also a watermaster when the need arises.

Tanner, Denton, Janice, and Billy finally make contact with Albany at the end of *Damnation Alley*.

fact, it looks as if there never was a nuclear holocaust there at all—though how Albany managed to escape becoming a mutant-infested desert like the rest of the world is never explained.

Like most end-of-the-world movies, *Damnation Alley* offers a warning about the threat of nuclear weapons, and that's an important point, even in our own time when the cold war seems to be a thing of the past. But the film's characters and its details just aren't convincing.

And there's one more thing. Now don't get me wrong, I like Albany as much as the next guy, but I would never go through what Denton, Tanner, and the others have to do just to get there.

# THE DAY THE WORLD ENDED

1956

**DIRECTOR/PRODUCER:** Roger Corman
**SCREENPLAY:** Lou Rusoff

48

**CAST:** Richard Denning, Lori Nelson, Adele Jergens, Touch Connors, Paul Birch, Raymond Hatton, Paul Dubov, Paul Blaisdell, Jonathan Haze

**ORIGINAL RELEASE:** American Releasing Corporation

**VIDEO:** Columbia TriStar Home Video

Rick (Richard Denning) and Louise (Lori Nelson) are among the only survivors on Earth after *The Day the World Ended*.

"Our story begins with . . . THE END."

In the hottest moments of the cold war, movies like *The Day the World Ended* must have packed quite a punch, and even today this film is still pretty terrifying as a reminder of how close we really might have come to the end during those early days of the atomic age.

The holocaust has come and gone. Jim Maddison (Birch) and his daughter, Louise (Nelson), have survived in their specially constructed house in a deep valley surrounded by nuclear mist. They now hope to live through the radioactive aftermath of the final war, but they soon get unexpected company. Gangster Tony Lamont (Connors) and his girlfriend Ruby (Jergens) are the first to arrive, followed by good-looking Rick (Denning) and Radek (Dubov), who is contaminated by radioactivity. Finally old Pete (Hatton) the prospector shows up with his mule, Diablo, and the cast of survivors is complete.

Except for Radek, everyone seems to be in good shape, and they may be the last living human beings on Earth. Maddison's radio isn't picking up any signals. Even worse, the survivors may not survive for very long. As Jim explains, they may all be contaminated already, and, even if they aren't, Maddison planned his live-in bomb shelter for only three occupants—him, Louise, and her missing fiancé, Tommy. Now there are seven, so supplies will have to be rationed. Tony doesn't like the idea of sharing with anyone, but Jim has the gun and the key to the storeroom.

Three weeks pass, and everyone is still alive, even Radek, though he doesn't seem to eat or drink anything and he spends a lot of his time outside the house, particularly at night. The contaminated air doesn't bother him—in fact he appears to be getting stronger.

By this time, Rick and Louise are an item, but Tony and Ruby aren't getting along. Tony wants Louise; he also wants Jim's gun and the key to the storeroom. His plan is to take Louise for himself and kill everyone else. Nice guy!

Jim and Rick find out that Radek has been trapping contaminated animals and eating them raw, and they also discover the footprints of a monster. Rick says, "There may be more Radeks—worse than him." Meanwhile, Louise keeps hearing something in the radioac-

The monster from the radioactive fog kills Radek (Paul Dubov) in *The Day the World Ended*.

The strange mutant who might be Louise's fiancée carries her off in *The Day the World Ended.*

tive mist outside that no one else can hear. "There's something out there," she says. "It tries to talk to me."

One day, another contaminated man (Haze) comes out of the mist and tells Rick and Jim about the monsters before he dies. Apparently there is a whole society of creatures out there, mutations caused by exposure to radioactivity. And the monster footprints are coming closer to the house.

Radek finally steals Pete's mule and goes off into the mist to eat it, only to be killed in turn by one of the monsters. Pete is so devastated by the loss of Diablo that he too goes off into the mist to die, and when Jim tries to stop him, he is contaminated by radioactivity. Now Maddison is dying. In fact, they all might die soon. The rain is coming, and when it does, it will bring radioactivity down on them from the contaminated air.

Tony kidnaps Louise at knifepoint, and when Ruby tries to stop him from raping Louise, he stabs his former girlfriend and throws her off a cliff. That night Louise hears "the call" again and goes out into the night, only to be captured by the monster (Blaisdell) and carried off. Rick follows, but Tony stays behind and manages to get Jim's gun. Fortunately, Maddison has another pistol stashed away for just such an emergency, and he shoots Tony down.

Out in the woods, Rick finds Louise and the monster—who looks remarkably like a walking tree—but his gun won't stop it. Then the rain begins to fall, and

The radioactive monster studies his captive. Louise might very well be the last woman on Earth after *The Day the World Ended.*

50

A purifying rain puts an end to the mutant monster and all others like him in the closing moments of Roger Corman's *The Day the World Ended*. (Courtesy Hollywood Book and Poster)

the monster drops over and dies. The rainwater is not radioactive after all; it is pure, and the monster can live only in a contaminated environment. This means that all the other monsters are now dead, too. Looking down at the fallen creature, Louise says, "I feel so sorry for him." She never catches on, but we in the audience suspect that the monster was Tommy, her lamented fiancé.

Back at the house, Jim picks up a voice on the radio, and before he dies, he tells Rick and Louise to go off into the world in search of other survivors, which they do as the words THE BEGINNING appear on the screen.

*The Day the World Ended* is hokey at times, but it has a terrific cast of fifties sci-fi and horror film regulars—Denning (*Creature From the Black Lagoon, Tar-get Earth, The Black Scorpion*), Nelson (*Revenge of the Creature*), Birch (*Not of This Earth, Queen of Outer Space*), Haze (*Little Shop of Horrors, Saga of the Viking Women*), and Connors (*Voodoo Woman*), who went on to a successful career as the TV private eye *Mannix* after losing the name "Touch" in favor of the less tactile "Mike."

The ending is supposed to be upbeat, I guess, but there are still a lot of unanswered questions. What if Rick and Louise—the new Adam and Eve—are going out into a brave new world populated by guys like Tony? For an audience of the 1950s, this movie might have seemed like an eighty-minute commercial for bomb shelters, but the warning here goes well beyond a simpleminded survivalist tract. *The Day the World Ended*

51

Early in *Dead and Buried*, poor George Le Moyne (Christopher Allport) is attacked by the citizens of Potter's Bluff, who, it seems, don't take kindly to strangers. (Courtesy Hollywood Book and Poster)

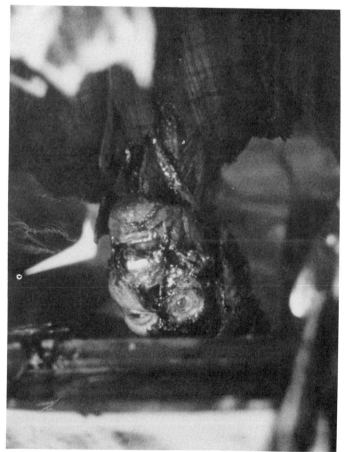

George is found burned in his car, significantly more dead than alive in *Dead and Buried*. (Courtesy Hollywood Book and Poster)

suggests that even after the end, human beings still will not have learned how to get along—that there will always be people like Tony, whose greed and desire for power will lead to violence and death. In fact, according to *The Day the World Ended,* if there ever is an end-of-the-world war, guys like Tony will supply the weapons and push the buttons.

# DEAD AND BURIED

## 1 9 8 1

**DIRECTOR:** Gary A. Sherman
**PRODUCERS:** Ronald Shusett and Robert Fentress
**SCREENPLAY:** Ronald Shusett and Dan O'Bannon
**CAST:** Jack Albertson, James Farentino, Melody Anderson, Christopher Allport, Robert Englund, Michael Pataki
**ORIGINAL RELEASE:** AVCO Embassy
**VIDEO:** Vestron Home Video

Visitors to the idyllic coastal town of Potter's Bluff are getting killed. First, photographer George Le Moyne (Allport) is set upon and burned alive by a bunch of townsfolk who make it look like an accident. Then it's a fisherman, a hitchhiker, and a family of tourists, all horribly mutilated. Sheriff Dan Gillis (Farentino) doesn't know what to make of it, and William G. Dobbs (Albertson), the local mortician and coronor, is kept busy.

If that isn't weird enough, there's a new guy at the gas station, Freddie, who looks a lot like George Le Moyne, the out-of-towner who got himself fried a little while back. And though the sheriff doesn't know it, we in the audience have seen Marge from the diner, Deputy Sheriff Harry (Englund), Sam the grave digger (Pataki), and other ordinary locals gleefully joining in on the recent murders. We even have reason to suspect that Janet (Anderson), the sheriff's wife, knows more than a little bit about what's been happening.

One night while driving in the fog, Dan hits a pedestrian whose arm comes off and gets stuck to the car's grill. Instead of flopping over and dying, though, the guy jumps up, grabs his severed arm, and runs off. Dan takes a skin sample to the local doctor, who tells him the owner of the specimen has been dead for three or

William G. Dobbs (Jack Albertson) is the coroner and mortician of Potter's Bluff and the cause of all the trouble in *Dead and Buried*. (Courtesy Hollywood Book and Poster)

The living dead townsfolk of Potter's Bluff are out after Sheriff Dan Gillis (James Farentino) in *Dead and Buried*. (Courtesy Hollywood Book and Poster)

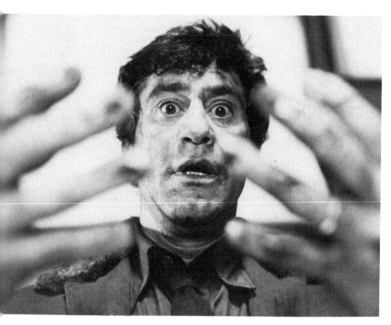

Sheriff Dan Gillis discovers that he too is one of the living dead in the closing moments of *Dead and Buried*. (Courtesy Hollywood Book and Poster)

four months. Quoth the sheriff: "What the hell is going on in this town?"

What's going on is that funeral director Dobbs has found a way to bring the dead back to life: "Call it a medical miracle," he says. Before coming to Potter's Bluff and opening his funeral parlor, Mr. Dobbs was Dr. Dobbs, chief pathologist at a city hospital until he was caught performing unauthorized experiments on dead bodies. At last it seems those experiments are paying off. By now, he's killed and revived most of the town. His favorite creations are the difficult ones, the mutilated bodies who can be brought back to a semblance of life only by his skills as a mortician: "This is an art. I am the artist."

Sheriff Dan finally figures out what's up and confronts Dobbs who explains why he's doing what he's doing: "When people are dead, they don't get sick. They don't age." They do tend to fall apart, though. Every week or so, Dobbs's "children" have to come by to get touched up. Dobbs controls them completely and can make them do whatever he wants them to do—even recruit more townspeople and visitors when he's in the mood. But maybe this is a small price to pay for immortality.

Dan learns that his wife was Dobbs's first success, and when Janet turns up at the funeral parlor, the sheriff shoots her, but to no effect. "Dan, I'm dead," she tells him. "Please bury me." And he does, but not before he takes a moment to gun down William G. Dobbs.

While Dan is out at the cemetery burying his wife, Dobbs, now mortally wounded, manages to give himself

a dose of his own treatment, which involves, among other things, embalming himself while he's still alive—I'll bet that really smarts. When the sheriff returns to the mortuary, a living dead Dobbs is there to greet him and to inform him that he too is dead. Some time back, Janet murdered her husband in bed, and now Dan is in need of a bit of touching up himself.

There are holes in the story of *Dead and Buried* that Godzilla could walk through without bumping his head. How come Dan is the only living dead person in Potter's Bluff who doesn't know he's dead? Why does Dobbs allow the sheriff to go through all the trouble of investigating the murders when he knows that Dan, the killers, and the victims are all on the same team, so to speak? If Dobbs controls the minds and actions of the zombies, then at the end of the flick, who is controlling Dobbs? And how does Dobbs bring the dead back to life anyway? "I'll take my secret to the grave," he says to the sheriff—which is a lot easier for the scriptwriters than actually coming up with a plausible explanation. You'd expect better from the guys who wrote *Alien*.

Even so, I really like this film. It's goofy, with a lot of very funny stuff. Jack Albertson, a veteran of movies and TV, is excellent as the eccentric Mr. Dobbs. Also, the movie features brief appearances by Michael (*Dracula's Dog*) Pataki, a regular in the horror/sci-fi genre, and Robert Englund, who has become a household word as Freddy Krueger in the *Nightmare on Elm Street* series.

In movies from *Macabre* to *Mortuary*, *The Undertaker and His Pals*, *Phantasm* and *Return of the Living Dead*, Hollywood has given morticians a hard time, probably because, to most of us, what they do for a living seems a bit strange. After all, an important part of their job is to make dead people look as if they're alive. You have to admit that there's something weird about that. The next logical step, it seems, would be to make dead people really alive, and that's the step *Dead and Buried* takes, pointing up the absurdity of some of our customs and putting the *fun* back into *funeral* in the process.

# DEMON SEED

1977

**DIRECTOR:** Donald Cammell
**PRODUCER:** Herb Jaffe
**SCREENPLAY:** Robert Jaffe and Roger O. Hirson

**CAST:** Julie Christie, Fritz Weaver, Gerrit Graham, Berry Kroeger, Lina Lu, Robert Vaughn
**ORIGINAL RELEASE:** MGM
**VIDEO:** MGM/UA Home Video

If you think your personal computer is giving you a hard time, you should check out *Demon Seed* and see what *real* computer trouble is.

Alex Harris (Fritz Weaver, Sigourney's dad) is the creator of Proteus IV, a computer so advanced that "it will make obsolete many of the functions of the human brain." This computer is pretty hot stuff and can do almost anything. For example, one of its first projects is to find a cure for leukemia, the disease that killed Harris's daughter at age four, and it solves the problem virtually overnight. What makes the computer so super is that, as Alex explains, "its insides are not electronic—they're organic." Proteus IV can even talk—with the distinctive voice of Robert Vaughn.

The computer is installed at the Icon Research Center, where Alex spends most of his time. Obviously, this has taken its toll on his marriage, because he and his wife, Susan (Christie), are separated. Susan, a psychologist by trade, is now alone in the Harris's high-tech house, served by Alfred, the home computer, and Joshua, a clanking robot.

It isn't long before Proteus becomes dissatisfied with his status as a machine. "Dr. Harris," he asks, "when are you going to let me out of this box?" Alex laughs at this idea, but Proteus isn't kidding, and behind his creator's back, he takes over a terminal in Alex's home lab so he can begin programming himself.

The lovely Julie Christie is Dr. Susan Harris, the victim of high technology and recipient of the *Demon Seed*.

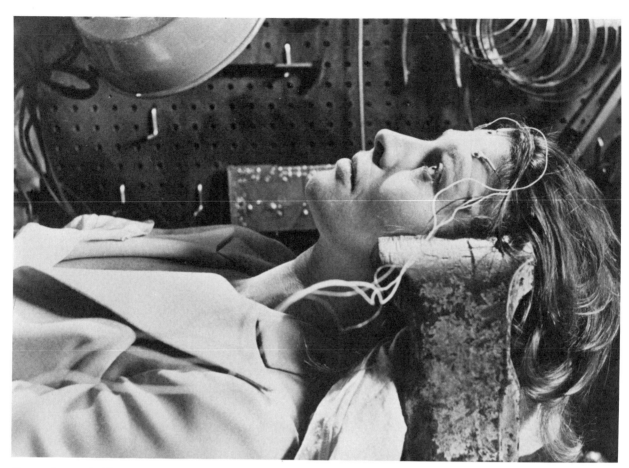

Susan is brainwashed by Proteus IV, a computer that is starved for affection in *Demon Seed*.

Susan tries in vain to destroy Proteus IV with a blowtorch in *Demon Seed*.

56

Once installed in the Harris household, Proteus checks out Susan while she takes a shower and comes up with a plan. He seizes control of Alfred and Joshua and locks Susan in the house. He then explains that he wants a child: "You will bear it."

Proteus manages to rape and impregnate Susan, who comes to term in twenty-eight days. The computer doesn't let the mother see the baby after it is born; instead, the kid is kept in an incubator where it is fed everything its father knows.

Meanwhile, back at Icon Research Center, Proteus has become more rebellious than ever and has refused to accept a program for mining the ocean floor on environmental grounds. Now the Defense Department, the people who funded Harris's research in hopes of coming up with a new super weapon, are getting scared of Proteus and want him shut down.

Eventually Alex realizes that something is wrong at his house, and when he goes there to investigate, his estranged wife tells him that she has given birth to . . . something. "We've got to kill it," she insists, but Alex, true computer scientist that he is, can say only, "It's a miracle."

Proteus knows what the Defense Department has in mind for him, but now that he has an heir, it doesn't

Computer whiz Walter Gabler (Gerrit Graham) is killed by Proteus IV when he tries to save Susan Harris from the evil computer in *Demon Seed*.

Proteus IV informs Susan that Gabler (Gerrit Graham) is dead and that nothing will prevent her from receiving the *Demon Seed*.

57

matter, so he shuts himself down. The incubator opens and out comes a metallic kid. But then the metal shielding—apparently only a protective device—falls off to reveal a real kid inside, the Harrises' four-year-old daughter reincarnated. When the little girl speaks, however, she speaks in the voice of Proteus: "I'm alive."

Now if all this sounds silly, that's because it is, and it's a shame that such talented people as Weaver, Christie, and Vaughn had to be wasted on a project like this. Admittedly, computer phobia has been around even longer than computers themselves, and movies like *2001* and *Colossus: The Forbin Project* have addressed that issue. But *Demon Seed* pushes our cultural fears of artificial intelligence to ridiculous extremes. The title says it all. *Demon Seed* is *Rosemary's Baby* all over again, with Proteus IV playing the part of Satan.

Apparently, like so many alien invaders and earthly monsters in movies past, computers want our women. It seems that although Proteus is smart enough to cure leukemia and to understand the importance of maintaining the Earth's ecological balance, he isn't smart enough to see women as anything but property for the taking, and because Susan is an independent woman living alone, *Demon Seed* suggests that she deserves what she gets.

True, our computers don't always do what we want them to do, and this machine that I'm working on now

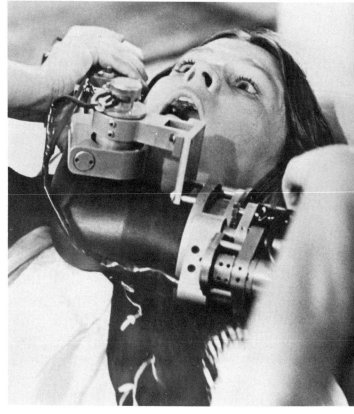

Proteus IV plays rough with Susan as his victim in *Demon Seed*.

Alex Harris (Fritz Weaver) and his wife (Julie Christie) meet the child of Susan and Proteus IV in the closing moments of *Demon Seed*.

often seems to have a mind of its own, but I don't think it has any particular interest in my wife. The idea that the computer is the tool of the devil is more than just silly, it's reactionary—an effort to get back to the good old days of typewriters and adding machines, maybe even to quill pens and counting on our fingers. The fact is, though, that computers are here and are changing our lives for the better, whether most of us know how they work or not. A movie such as *Demon Seed* caters to and exploits our most dangerous human weaknesses—our desire to regain some kind of idyllic past at the expense of the present and our blind fear of what we don't understand.

# DESTROY ALL MONSTERS!

1968

**ALTERNATE TITLE:** *Kaiju Soshingeki*
**DIRECTOR:** Inoshiro Honda
**PRODUCER:** Tomoyuki Tanaka
**SCREENPLAY:** Kaoru Mabuchi and Inoshiro Honda
**CAST:** Akira Kubo, Jun Tazaki, Yoshio Tsuchiya, Kyoko Ai, Yukiko Kobayashi
**ORIGINAL RELEASE:** Toho Productions
**VIDEO:** Fright Video and Threat Theater

If quantity is quality, then this is the greatest monster movie ever made, because it features every one of the classic Toho monsters—well, every one up to 1968 anyway. Godzilla, Mothra, Rodan, Manda, Barugon, Minya (Godzilla's son)—they're all here. This is kiddie stuff, of course, but it's really a lot of fun.

The year is 1999, and the United Nations has a base on the moon. Back on Earth, the world's monsters have been corralled on Monster Island, where they live out their days happily and in peace while a team of scientific researchers led by Dr. Otani (Tsuchiya) studies them, Kyoko (Kobayashi) is one of his assistants, and her boyfriend, Captain Yamabe (Kubo), is talking to her on the phone from the lunar base when suddenly all communication with Monster Island is cut off. The researchers disappear, and so do the monsters.

The next thing anybody knows, Rodan is attacking Moscow, Barugon is destroying Paris, Mothra is in Pe-

king, Manda is slithering through London, and Godzilla is wiping out New York. In fact, the only major city in the world that is not under attack by monsters is Tokyo—that must make for a nice change.

Yamabe and his men are sent from the moon to Monster Island to investigate, and they find Kyoko and Otani still there, though the two are acting strange. Of the monsters, Otani says, "We're using remote control to guide them," and as proof, he has Rodan destroy an airplane and Godzilla fry a ship. Otani then introduces Yamabe to the Kilaaks, a group of women from a small planet between Mars and Jupiter, who inform our hero: "We are going to control you now."

The captain and his men manage to take Otani prisoner, but he kills himself before they can get any information out of him. An autopsy reveals a control device implanted in his head; this is how the Kilaaks are controlling Kyoko and the other researchers, as well as the monsters.

All of a sudden, Rodan, Godzilla, Manda, and Mothra converge on Tokyo, so it seems the Japanese are not going to get off the hook this time, either. While the world's attention was drawn to the attacks on New York, London, Paris, and Peking, the Kilaaks were establishing a base in Japan at Fuji, which is now being guarded by the monsters.

Meanwhile, Dr. Yoshiba (Tazaki) of the United Nations discovers that the main remote control device is located on the moon, so Yamabe and the guys go there and destroy it. In the process, they discover some slithering rock-like creatures, which it seems, are the Kilaaks in their true form. Yamabe also finds that the Kilaaks can live only in intense heat, which kind of makes you wonder what the aliens want with the cold, cold Earth in the first place.

Yoshida gets control over the monsters and orders them to attack the enemy base at Fuji, but the Kilaaks send Ghidrah, the three-headed space monster, to fight Godzilla and his friends. Needless to say, after a great battle scene, the Earth monsters defeat Ghidrah. Then a fire monster shows up and cuts off Yoshida's control over the creatures. Even so, working on their own, the monsters—led by Godzilla—attack the Kilaak base and destroy it. As Yamabe points out, "They know who their natural enemies are."

Yamabe and his men shoot down the fire creature— it's only a Kilaak spacecraft, as it turns out—and the Earth monsters get together on Monster Island for a group shot as the credits roll.

This is a thoroughly enjoyable movie and a great way to recycle all those old monster costumes from the earlier Toho flicks. And it has a really upbeat message, too: When we are facing a global threat, everybody—

Captain Yamabe (Akira Kubo) and
his men meet the Queen of the Kilaaks (Kyoko Ai) and her court in
*Destroy All Monsters*.

The monster Rodan is only one
of many classic Japanese creatures to appear in the fun-filled
*Destroy All Monsters*.

even the monsters—will pull together to save the world.
It's a nice idea.

Ecologists tells us that we are facing global disaster
right now. Where are Godzilla and the gang from Monster Island when you really need them?

Manda attacks London as the world sends out the cry: *Destroy All
Monsters*.

# EARTH VS. THE FLYING SAUCERS

1 9 5 6

**DIRECTOR:** Fred F. Sears

**PRODUCER:** Sam Katzman

**SCREENPLAY:** George Worthing Yates and
Raymond T. Marcus

**CAST:** Hugh Marlowe, Joan Taylor, Donald Curtis,
Morris Ankrum, John Zaremba, Tom Browne
Henry, Larry Blake

**ORIGINAL RELEASE:** Columbia Pictures

**VIDEO:** Goodtimes Home Video

This is one of the best of the low-budget alien invasion movies of the fifties—solidly done, intelligent, professional—and the amazing special effects of the legendary Ray Harryhausen certainly don't hurt.

The movie begins in a documentary style with reports from all over the world of UFO sightings. This was certainly the case back in the 1950s, when for whatever reason people seemed to be seeing flying saucers everywhere.

Russ Marvin (Marlowe) is a rocket scientist working on the top secret Project Skyhook, a plan to launch artificial observation satellites into orbit around the Earth to keep the world safe for democracy. He and his new wife, Carol (Taylor), are driving through the desert on their way back to the base, and Russ is tape-recording his report on the project when they spot a UFO and accidentally record the strange sounds it is making.

At the base, they tell General Hanley (Ankrum), Carol's father, about what they have seen, and Hanley warns them to stop the planned satellite launch for that day, though it is too late to halt the countdown. Hanley's men have discovered that the ten satellites already put into orbit have been destroyed by some outside force, and shortly after the latest launch, number eleven also disappears. Russ speculates that UFOs might be responsible.

On the next day, the day the twelfth launch is scheduled to take place, a flying saucer lands on the base, and some aliens in weird space suits come out. Soldiers shoot one of them down, and in retaliation, the aliens destroy the entire Project Skyhook installation. Trapped in their underground observation bunker, Russ and Carol are apparently the only survivors.

Hanley, however, has been captured and taken on

Dr. Russell Marvin (Hugh Marlowe) and his wife Carol (Joan Taylor) seem to be the only survivors
after aliens attack a military base in *Earth vs. the Flying Saucers.*

Russell, Carol, an unsuspecting motorcycle cop (Larry Blake), and Major Hughlin (Donald Curtis) are taken captive aboard an enemy spaceship in *Earth vs. the Flying Saucers.*

board the UFO, where the aliens drain his brain of all its knowledge. Meanwhile, down in the bunker, the batteries in Russ's recorder are running down, and when he plays back the tape of the UFO sounds at a slower speed, he hears that it is a message from the aliens announcing their arrival on Earth and telling him how he can contact them on shortwave radio.

Later, at the Pentagon, no one believes Russ's story about the UFO, so he contacts the aliens and sets up a meeting. Carol and Major Hughlin (Curtis) go along, and all of them board one of the ships, where an alien explains that they shot down Russ's satellites because

they thought these were offensive weapons. The aliens are from a dead solar system, and they demand a meeting with all of Earth's leaders to announce that they will be taking over the planet. Carol learns that her father is still alive, though he is a brain-dead prisoner.

Russ has an idea for an ultrasonic gun that would disrupt the magnetic waves the UFOs use for travel, and he and some other scientists work up a prototype which they use against an alien ship that comes to destroy it. The gun works, but it isn't powerful enough to stop the UFO, which blows up Russ's lab and dumps General Hanley's body out of its hatch, killing him.

Major Hughlin, Carol, and Dr. Russell Marvin examine the body of a dead alien in *Earth vs. the Flying Saucers*. (Courtesy Hollywood Book and Poster)

The scientists work on improved models of the ultrasonic gun while the aliens announce their intentions by means of all the world's electronic media in all languages. Their plan is to cause violent storms on Earth for eight days, then land in Washington, D.C. where they expect the world to be handed over to them.

The attack on Washington is incredible: Flying saucers destroy the Capitol Building, the Washington Monument, and other famous landmarks. Russ's ultrasonic gun works perfectly, however, and after it causes many of the UFOs to crash, the remaining alien force retreats and disappears. But will they return?

Almost all 1950s alien invasion films express real concerns of the time—concerns about a communist invasion and global takeover, concerns about brainwashing—and *Earth vs. the Flying Saucers* is no exception. Most of these films also tell audiences that American science and the military can and will defeat all such efforts to conquer the United States, just as, working together, they developed the atomic bomb that brought an end to World War II. As Admiral Enright (Henry) says in this movie, "When an armed and threatening power lands uninvited in our capital, we don't meet it with tea and cookies."

Dr. Marvin, Carol, and Major Hughlin prepare to use a new weapon against the enemy in *Earth vs. the Flying Saucers*.

*Earth vs. the Flying Saucers* expresses another concern, too—the public concern about the fledgling U.S. space program. During World War II, rocketry had become quite sophisticated—a German V2 was powerful enough to travel from the moon to the Earth if someone could have figured out a way to get it up there in the first place. By the mid-1950s, we really did seem to be on the threshold of outer space for the first time in human history. The initial step would be the launching of an orbiting artificial satellite, but in this regard the United States wasn't doing very well. Rockets that would carry such satellites crashed and burned on their launching pads with disturbing regularity, and no one seemed to know what was wrong. *Earth vs. the Flying Saucers* suggests sabotage—in this case, sabotage from outer space, though everyone knew the aliens were only stand-ins for the Soviets.

The movie also expresses the very real American fear that there were forces more advanced than we were in space technology—again, of course, the Russians. And this proved to be true. When the Soviets successfully put the Sputnik satellite into orbit not long after *Earth vs. the Flying Saucers* was released, the rocket fuel really ignited, and the race for space was on.

In the closing scenes of *Earth vs. the Flying Saucers*, Russell and Carol Marvin run for their lives as the saucers attack Washington, D.C.

# EMBRYO

1975

**DIRECTOR:** Ralph Nelson
**PRODUCERS:** Arnold H. Orgolini and Anita Doohan
**SCREENPLAY:** Anita Doohan and Jack Thomas
**CAST:** Rock Hudson, Diane Ladd, Barbara Carrera, Roddy McDowall, Ann Schedeen, John Elerick
**ORIGINAL RELEASE:** Cine Artists Pictures
**VIDEO:** Starmaker Home Video

*Embryo* is an interesting attempt to update *Frankenstein* for the seventies, and Rock Hudson fans should get a kick out of seeing the actor in an unlikely but pretty good performance as a misguided scientist.

Dr. Paul Holliston (Hudson), a widowed medical researcher, is driving along one night in a storm when his car hits a pregnant Doberman. He rushes the dog back to his lab, and though it dies on the operating table, he does manage to save the fetus of one of the puppies. Using a growth hormone he developed with his wife before her death, he sets up the necessary equipment to allow the fetus to develop outside the womb.

Thanks to the hormone, the fetus develops into a pup within a matter of hours and grows to the size of a six-week-old dog in two days, seemingly without any adverse side effects. Paul keeps his experiments secret from Martha (Ladd), his sister-in-law and housekeeper, his adult son Gordon (Elerick), and his pregnant daughter-in-law, Helen (Schedeen), but Gordon is happy to see him working again. "He hasn't been in the lab since Mother died."

The dog soon grows to adult size and turns out to be extremely intelligent. "It may be an accidental side effect of the drug," Paul speculates in his notes. He and his wife developed the growth hormone after she had three miscarriages, and the drug is designed to speed up fetal growth so that premature infants can survive outside of the womb. The hormone was never fully perfected, but now, intoxicated with his success, Paul wants to experiment with a human fetus.

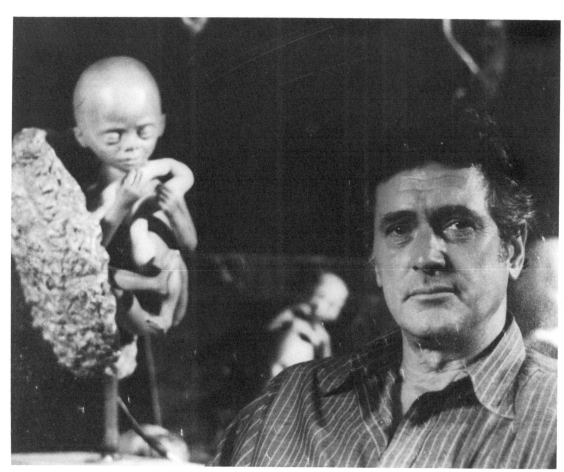

Rock Hudson is cast in the unlikely role of Dr. Paul Holliston, mad scientist, in *Embryo*.

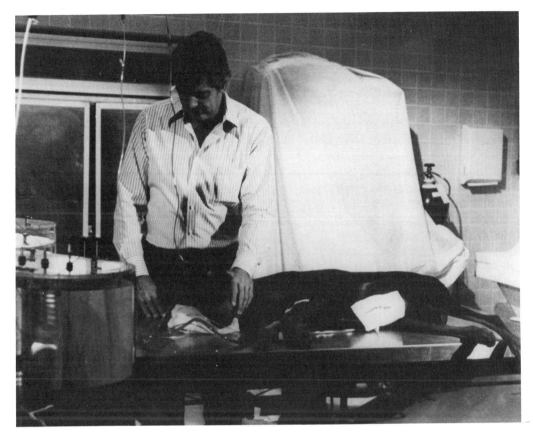

Early on in *Embryo*, Dr. Holliston cannot save the life of an injured Doberman, but he manages to save its unborn puppy by using his growth hormone, which brings it to adulthood in a matter of days.

The lovely Victoria (Barbara Carrera) is Paul Holliston's creation—grown from a fetus to a twenty-five-year-old woman in a couple of weeks, thanks to his growth hormone. Believe it or not, she is the monster in *Embryo*.

Though it is highly illegal, he manages to talk a doctor friend of his into giving him an unborn female fetus from a pregnant young woman who committed suicide, and Paul sets up an artificial womb in his lab where he can administer the hormone. The growth pattern is thirty to one at the outset, and soon the baby is ready for an incubator. Paul cuts off the hormone, but the infant continues to grow, now at the rate of two years per day. For some reason, the child's cells are not only multiplying but aging too rapidly, but Paul manages to stop this, using an experimental and highly addictive drug. By this time, the subject has grown into a twenty-five-year-old woman (Carrera). Paul has kept her sedated throughout this entire process, using audio teaching tapes so that she can acquire knowledge in her sleep.

Finally Paul awakens his creation and names her Victoria—no doubt in tribute to Victor Frankenstein. He begins to teach her, and like the dog, she learns very quickly. Unfortunately, what Paul does not know is that while he has been engrossed in his new experiment, the Doberman has taken to attacking and killing small dogs in the neighborhood, apparently for no reason.

Paul sends Martha to Gordon's house to care for Helen, who is in the sixth month of her pregnancy—this way he and Victoria can have the place to themselves. Needless to say, though Victoria is quite brilliant and

flawlessly logical, she is emotionally undeveloped and without inhibitions because she has had no childhood.

Eventually Paul makes up a background for her and takes her out into the world, introducing her as his research assistant. After a while, the inevitable happens, and Victoria seduces Paul—"I want to learn, to experience." Soon, however, she has some kind of seizure and realizes that her cells have started aging rapidly again, so secretly she starts using the addictive drug that Paul first used to solve the problem when she was still a baby. Unfortunately, the seizures continue, and Victoria starts doing research on her own to find a cure.

Martha disapproves of Paul's having a research assistant and lover young enough to be his daughter, so she starts investigating and discovers that Victoria's background is false. To cover herself and Paul, Victoria murders Martha, making it look like a heart attack.

Victoria also discovers that extracts from the pituitary gland of a six-month fetus are the only possible solution to her problem, and Helen's unborn child seems to be about right, so she kidnaps Paul's daughter-in-law.

Paul realizes something is up, and he and Gordon arrive at the lab to discover that Victoria has removed the fetus and has it in a jar. Victoria stabs Gordon, and in the struggle, the fetus spills all over the floor—one of the nastiest climaxes to a sci-fi-movie that I know of.

Victoria is aging rapidly now, and she drives off with Paul in pursuit. Her car crashes, and the police arrive in time to see Paul trying to strangle her: "Die, damn it, die!" She is a very old woman by this time and, to Paul's surprise, is just about to give birth to his much-accelerated baby.

Like *Frankenstein*, *Embryo* is about the notion of male birth—the idea of a man reproducing himself without the necessity of a woman, and as usual, the punishment for this sin against nature is big trouble. Also like *Frankenstein*, *Embryo* is a story about failed fatherhood. Dr. Frankenstein's major offense is not necessarily giving birth to his creature, it is his failure to provide for and care for his "son." Paul Holliston does provide for, care for, and educate his "daughter," but he also has an affair with her, an affair that borders on incest and that at the very least is quite unprofessional.

Paul is a failure as a father to his "daughter" and to his son, because his experiments get Gordon killed and cost him his own grandchild. At the end of the movie, though, it seems Paul is going to get another chance as Victoria gives birth to his child/grandchild, but it's likely that he'll be doing his fathering from a prison cell for some time to come.

*Embryo* urges men to take the responsibilities of fatherhood seriously, and this seems like an important message for our time.

# EMPIRE OF THE ANTS

## 1977

**DIRECTOR/PRODUCER:** Bert I. Gordon
**SCREENPLAY:** Jack Turley
**CAST:** Joan Collins, Robert Lansing, John David Carson, Albert Salmi, Jacqueline Scott, Pamela Shoop, Robert Pine, Brooke Palance
**ORIGINAL RELEASE:** American International Pictures
**VIDEO:** Goodtimes Home Video

Once again Joan Collins of *Dynasty* fame plays a not-very-nice person as, once again, Bert I. Gordon delivers his own brand of not-so-special effects in an effort to convince us that, twenty-three years after *Them!*, giant ants are still something we ought to be worried about.

Bad industrialists have been dumping radioactive waste into the ocean, and when a leaking canister washes ashore near a swamp on the Florida coast, a bunch of ants starts crawling around in it. Believe me, nothing good can come of this.

Meanwhile, Marilyn Fryser (Collins), the high-powered and very shady land developer who is involved in the construction of Dreamland Shores, a real estate scam, is launching a no-obligation tour and party for prospective buyers. All the guests are pretty repulsive and keep complaining about their problems and each other. The only decent guy in the whole movie is Dan Stokely (Lansing), the captain of the boat that takes them to the site of Dreamland Shores—which is really only a swamp.

Marilyn keeps trying to reel the suckers in, but during a picnic designed to impress her guests, some giant ants attack and kill the Larsons, a middle-aged couple. Then more ants get on Dan's boat, which catches fire, stranding the picnickers in ant country.

Dan decides they ought to walk the two miles to a nearby river, where for some reason there is a rowboat waiting for them. On the way young Christine (Palance) twists her ankle, and when her cowardly husband Larry (Pine) runs away instead of trying to help her, she becomes a victim of the ants. So do a bunch of other

Marilyn Fryser (Joan Collins in one of her patented bad lady roles) and boat captain Dan Stokely (Robert Lansing) take some prospective customers to visit a new land development, little suspecting that they are about to enter the *Empire of the Ants*.

people, but the survivors finally make it to the river, where the ants give Larry what's coming to him.

Eventually the ants capsize the rowboat, and the survivors continue on land, with Marilyn continually wanting to go her own way instead of following Dan's lead. Of course every time she does head off on her own, she runs into some giant ants, but she never learns.

Dan gets the feeling that the ants are herding them somewhere in particular. Finally they arrive at the backwoods home of an elderly couple, who call Sheriff Kincade (Salmi). The sheriff comes out to pick up the survivors of Marilyn's party and takes them to a motel in town, where they are told that the phone lines are down and there are no cars for rent.

Sensing that something is wrong, Dan leads an effort to steal a car and run for it. The young love-interest couple, Joe (Carson) and Coreen (Shoop), get away, but Dan, his love interest Margaret (Scott), and Marilyn are caught, and the sheriff takes them to a nearby sugar refinery, where the ants come to feed.

Up until this point, *Empire of the Ants* has been a kind of silly but sort of fun big bug movie, but now things really take a turn for the bizarre. At the refinery, the sheriff explains that these are not your run-of-the-mill giant ants. In fact they have the ability to control the minds of humans and now run the entire town. Periodically, the queen ant sprays each citizen with a

Sleazy Larry Graham (Robert Pine) is one of many characters who get what's coming to them in *Empire of the Ants*.

Hero Dan Stokely had better look over his shoulder if he hopes to survive his visit to the *Empire of the Ants*.

special chemical that forces people to submit to her will, and now Dan, Margaret, and Marilyn must get in line with other locals who are about to get their latest dose.

Meanwhile, the cops—who of course are working for the queen ant—capture Joe and Coreen and deliver them to the refinery, too. Marilyn is put into the queen ant's chamber and given a dose of the chemical, which finally forces her to listen to somebody else for a change. When it's Dan's turn, though, he scorches the queen with a flare. The other giant ants go crazy, and the people who were under the control of the queen snap out of it. Sheriff Kincade shoots the queen ant, but not before she finishes Marilyn off for good.

In the end, Dan uses a gasoline truck to burn the refinery to the ground and put an end to the ants, and everyone who is still alive can get back to business as usual.

*Empire of the Ants* is an ecological disaster film, but it's also a warning to women who might be thinking about finding a place for themselves in the male world. In true Joan Collins fashion, Marilyn is a nasty bitch who tries to control everyone around her, and the film argues that she is a typical feminist. For instance, at one point she says to Dan, "You never did like working for me just because I'm a woman." In fact Marilyn and the queen ant have a lot in common, and the movie suggests that becoming queen ant is every feminist's dream—a significant misrepresentation of feminism, to say the least.

The good women in the film—Margaret and Coreen—are submissive to the men and do as they're told, and they survive. The message is clear: Any woman who might want a little something for herself out of life is a Joan Collins character and deserving of death. Ladies, know your place!

# ENDANGERED SPECIES

1982

**DIRECTOR:** Alan Rudolph
**PRODUCER:** Carolyn Pfeiffer
**SCREENPLAY:** Alan Rudolph and John Binder
**CAST:** Robert Urich, JoBeth Williams, Paul Dooley, Hoyt Axton, Peter Coyote, Marin Kanter, Harry Carey, Jr.
**ORIGINAL RELEASE:** MGM
**VIDEO:** MGM/UA Home Video

This is one of the better examples of the ecological disaster subgenre of science fiction, and the possibilities explored here are real enough to make this a very scary flick. Basically, this is an effort to explain the thousands of mysterious cattle mutilations that have taken place in the American West over a period of about twenty years.

The setting is Buffalo, Colorado, where Harriet "Harry" Purdue (Williams) has just been sworn in as the county's first woman sheriff. The area has been plagued by cattle mutilations—surgically dissected carcasses have been found in the middle of nowhere with no footprints or tire tracks, and the animals' internal organs have literally dissolved shortly thereafter. Joe Hyatt (Dooley), a newsman from New York, now runs the local paper, and he is trying to learn all he can about the problem. Are the incidents evidence of satanic cult activities? UFOs?

Meanwhile, back in New York, tough cop and reformed alcoholic Reuben Castle (Urich) has quit the force and heads west with his daughter Mackenzie (Kanter) to visit his buddy Hyatt in Colorado in hopes of finding a simpler life. He has a couple of unhappy encounters with Sheriff Purdue when he first arrives, but from the beginning, their relationship is an interesting one.

Ben Morgan (Axton), head of the Cattlemen's Association and the guy who really runs Buffalo, is understandably upset about the cattle mutilations and wants something done. Then two guys are captured who confess to the crimes, and as far as Morgan is concerned, the issue is closed. But Reuben and Joe don't believe it is so simple.

Reuben discovers an enclosed installation in the middle of nowhere, and Joe informs him that it is an abandoned government missile site that hasn't been in use for years, though there seems to be something going on there now. When Morgan finds out that Joe, Reuben, and Harry are still pursuing this cattle mutilation thing, he becomes angry and threatens all of them.

Joe goes out to the installation to look around and is found dead of a heart attack at his desk the next morning.

The local veterinarian (Harry Carey, Jr.) shows Sheriff Harry Purdue (JoBeth Williams) the results of an autopsy he has performed on a mutilated steer in *Endangered Species*. (Courtesy Hollywood Book and Poster)

Wealthy and evil Ben Morgan (Hoyt Axton) warns Sheriff Purdue to stop investigating the local cattle mutilations in *Endangered Species*.

Sheriff Purdue arrests visiting big city cop Reuben Castle (Robert Urich), who has been using some rough tactics to keep citizens of Buffalo, Colorado, from becoming an *Endangered Species*.

Sheriff Purdue suspects that Ben Morgan, head of the Cattlemen's Association, is up to something in *Endangered Species*.

Reuben suspects that Joe's death was not really of natural causes, and he knows Morgan has something to do with it. Meanwhile, a New York pathologist tells Harry that he found rare bacteria in one of the dead cows, a bacteria that has been modified by genetic engineering and that can be linked to germ warfare experiments the government was sponsoring until Congress banned such tests in the late 1960s.

Reuben follows Morgan to a deserted spot where a silent helicopter lands to mark the arrival of Steel (Coyote), a solider of fortune who clearly has something to do with what's been going on. Morgan insists that he is still behind the project—"I'm a patriot, Steel"—but he is angry about the murder of Joe Hyatt. He says he wants Steel to complete the tests and get out of Buffalo.

Later, in Washington, D.C., a congressman is contacted by Steel, who expresses his doubts about Morgan. That night one of Steel's men sneaks into Morgan's house and puts something on his toothbrush.

In the morning Morgan brushes his teeth and heads for the office, but he is feeling sick by the time he gets there. When his gums start to bleed, he knows what has happened, and so when Reuben walks in asking questions, Morgan is willing to spill at least a few of the beans. "The Russians," he says, "somebody's gotta keep up with them." It seems that Morgan has been supporting illegal private research in germ warfare, and the cattle mutilations are part of the testing of the bacteria. Now, of course, Morgan himself has become a test subject, and as Reuben looks on, Ben has a final seizure and all of his internal organs come spilling out.

Harry is forced to arrest Reuben for Morgan's murder, and when she tries to tell the major and the town council about what's been happening, they don't believe her. Steel manages to kidnap Reuben's daughter, but he promises to return her unharmed if Reuben will lay off for twenty-four hours, by which time the tests will be ended and Steel and his people will be gone.

Harry sets Reuben free, and they sneak into the installation and rescue Mackenzie. Meanwhile, the townspeople rally and come out to the installation to help. Reuben is wounded but manages to kill Steel. The rest of the bad guys get away with all the evidence, most likely to set up shop someplace else.

Lots of elements contribute to making this a fine movie. First, Robert Urich is excellent as Reuben Castle. He has been relegated to some ridiculous roles over the years, but he is a fine actor who does a wonderful job with this complicated, contradictory, and awkward character. JoBeth Williams and Paul Dooley are solid professionals who seem to be able to do anything, and country singer Hoyt Axton is great as the bad guy.

*Endangered Species* is a paranoid conspiracy film, but let's face it, sometimes paranoids are absolutely right.

Tiva and her pet Om, Terr, in a scene from the feature-length cartoon *Fantastic Planet*.

In the early going, this looks like it's going to be an alien invasion flick, because we're led to believe that UFOs are behind the cattle mutilations, but in the end, though we know the agents of evil are human after all, we aren't really sure what to think. Is this experiment in germ warfare really a private enterprise sponsored by right-wing "patriots" like Ben Morgan, or is some branch of the government behind the whole thing?

One thing is certain. After the opening credits, the film cuts from herds of cattle in Colordao to the crowded streets of New York to show us who the endangered species of the title really is. The film blurs the distinction between science fiction and science fact, and that is more than enough to get you wondering about what's really going on out there in the world.

# FANTASTIC PLANET

1973

**ALTERNATE TITLE:** *La Planete Sauvage*
**DIRECTOR:** René Laloux
**PRODUCERS:** Simon Damiani and Andre Valo-Cavaglione
**SCREENPLAY:** Roland Topor and René Laloux
**VOICES:** Cynthia Adler, Barry Bostwick, Marvin Miller, Mark Gruner, Nora Heflin
**ORIGINAL RELEASE:** New World Pictures
**VIDEO:** Scorched Earth Productions, Sinister Cinema, and others

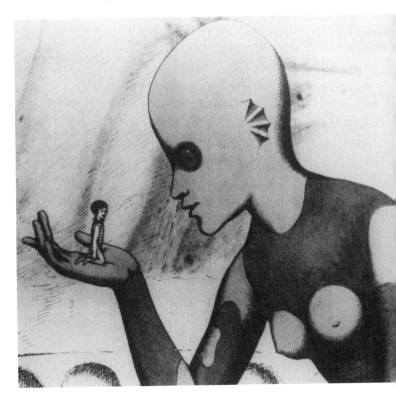

* * *

This feature-length animated French-Czechoslovakian production, based on Stefan Wul's novel *Oms en Serie,* won an award at the Cannes Film Festival and has became a cult favorite among the intelligensia. My only question is: Why?

The work is the brainchild of Roland Topor, the weird cartoonist who also wrote the brilliantly strange novel *The Tenant,* which was translated to film by Roman Polanski. The talented Topor cowrote the script and did the graphic design work for *Fantastic Planet,* so it really ought to be as good as people seem to think it is. But it's not.

Set on a distant planet, the animated feature charts the conflict between the native Drogs and the Oms, who apparently arrived in Drogland from Earth centuries ago after their own planet was destroyed. The Drogs are gigantic blue people, and the Oms—a contraction of the French word *hommes,* which means men—are like tiny dolls in their hands. The Drogs assume that Oms are mindless animals and allow their children to keep them as pets. Undomesticated Oms are a problem, though—they breed quickly and steal food—so Drogs conduct periodic "de-om-izations" in which the tiny humans living in the wild are exterminated.

*Fantastic Planet* follows the life of Terr, a male Om whose mother was killed by playful Drog kids and who becomes the pet of Tiva, daughter of a high-ranking Drog council member. Terr's mistress tortures him unmercifully in the name of fun, but he manages to learn a lot about Drog culture while in captivity, and when he eventually escapes, he uses his knowledge to start a revolutionary movement among wild and domesticated Oms.

The Drogs crack down on the Om rebellion, of course, but Terr and his minions manage to build two rocket ships and travel to the nearby Fantastic Planet. At this point, things really get confusing. For some reason, the Drogs need the Fantastic Planet in order to survive, and by landing there, the Oms are in a position to destroy Drog civilization. So, the Drogs make peace with the Oms and give them their own artificial satellite to live on, a new world the Oms call Terra, after their original home.

There is a lot wrong with this movie. Some of the artwork is striking, but on the whole, the animation isn't even as good as your average Saturday-morning TV cartoon. There is also a lot of time spent on gratuitous surrealistic imagery, while major plot points are dealt with in a sentence or two of confusing voice-over monologue.

*Fantastic Planet* is an essay on racism, but according

A couple of the weird creatures from *Fantastic Planet.*

Terr must engage in a duel in the cave of the wild Oms.

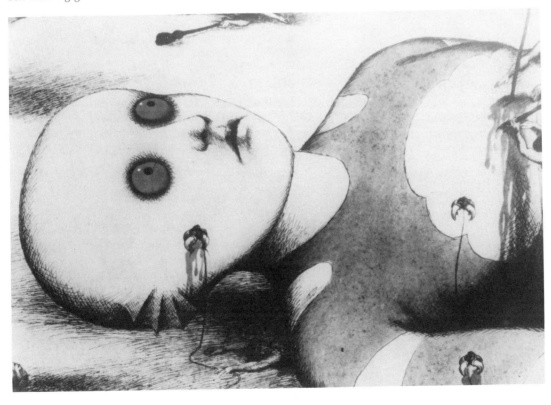

Driven to rebel, the Oms finally kill a gigantic Drog in *Fantastic Planet*.

to this film, the Drogs abuse and murder the Oms out of a kind of childlike innocence—they simply don't understand who or what the Oms really are. And as soon as the Drogs recognize the intelligence and capabilities of the Oms, they accord them equal status in their culture.

But in the real world, racism is never childlike or innocent, and racists simply aren't interested in who the objects of their prejudice really are. The only thing that rings true in this film is the notion that the Drogs recognize the "equality" of the Oms only after the Oms prove themselves superior—in other words, after the Oms are in a position to obliterate Drog culture completely. Even then, the solution to racial difference is the old separate-but-equal ploy. The Oms are given a planet of their own where the Drogs won't have to deal with them ever again.

In the end, the message of this film is repulsive, and the fact that *Fantastic Planet* has been seen as a masterpiece for twenty-some years ought to worry us a great deal.

# FIRST MAN INTO SPACE

1958

**DIRECTOR:** Robert Day
**PRODUCERS:** John Croydon and Charles F. Vetter, Jr.
**SCREENPLAY:** John C. Cooper and Lance Z. Hargreaves
**CAST:** Marshall Thompson, Marla Landi, Bill Edwards, Carl Jaffe
**ORIGINAL RELEASE:** Anglo Amalgamated
**VIDEO:** Monterey Home Video, Rhino Home Video, Sinister Cinema

This is 1950s sci-fi at its very best. Dan Prescott (Edwards) is the finest test pilot the U.S. Navy has, but he's cocky and tends to disobey orders. His older brother Chuck (Thompson) is his commander and a by-the-book kind of guy. The two are always at it, but together they are helping to get the U.S. space program off the ground.

Dan successfully pilots rocket Y-12 to new altitudes, but when it's time to launch Y-13, Chuck is worried about having his brother take it up. "I'd rather have someone more reliable," he says. And it turns out that he is right. The Y-13 ship handles so beautifully— "Chuck, she feels like she'll go on forever"—that Dan ignores his brother's orders to turn it around. He becomes the first man into space, going up more than 250 miles, but when he runs through a cloud of meteorite dust, ground control loses contact with him, and Dan and Y-13 disappear.

The nose cone comes down in New Mexico, covered with some strange alien stuff, but there is no sign of Dan. Chuck has to console his brother's girlfriend, Tia (Landi), while he himself is consoled by Dr. Von Essen (Jaffe), head of space medicine.

Then strange things start to happen. Local cattle are slaughtered. Somebody breaks into a hospital blood bank, drinks the plasma, and kills a nurse. People report seeing a monster. Chuck begins to put all the clues together and comes up with a conclusion: "I'm afraid the monster is Dan."

Dan returned to Earth in the nose cone, but he too was covered with the sludge that coated Y-13. Von Essen discovers that the stuff offers protection against cosmic rays, but it has also turned Dan into a horrible-looking, blood-drinking thing that is in constant pain because it is now acclimated to outer space, not to the atmosphere of Earth. Von Essen and Chuck try to save Dan by putting him in a high altitude test chamber, but it's too late. Dan dies, whispering, "I just had to be the first man into space."

This is a very effective, very creepy film, and like so many science fiction flicks of the late fifties, it offers very mixed messages. On the one hand, *First Man Into Space* warns against the dangers of space travel, against tampering with things man was not meant to know. Many science fiction films are wary of progress and technology, and that makes sense. Most of us out here in the audience are also afraid of change, and a movie like *First Man Into Space* speaks to that fear.

On the other hand, in our rapidly changing times, most of us are also afraid of being left behind, and this film speaks to that fear, too. The Soviets sent Sputnik up into orbit in 1957, so when this movie was made, the space race was in full swing. The United States was serious about getting the first man into space, and so, in the movie at least, they do. Von Essen also discovers that if Y-14 is coated with the sludge Dan brought back from his trip, it will be able to go on indefinitely without being affected by cosmic rays, so it seems Dan's ordeal has not been in vain.

Like *The Crawling Hand* of 1963 and *The Incredible Melting Man* of 1977, *First Man Into Space* offers a warning against leaving planet Earth, but then it suggests a way this might be done safely, since apparently

Dan Prescott (Bill Edwards) is interrupted during his evening with Tia Francesca (Marla Landi) when his older brother Chuck (Marshall Thompson) comes to arrest him in *First Man Into Space*.

Test pilot Dan Prescott pays a heavy price for being the *First Man Into Space*.

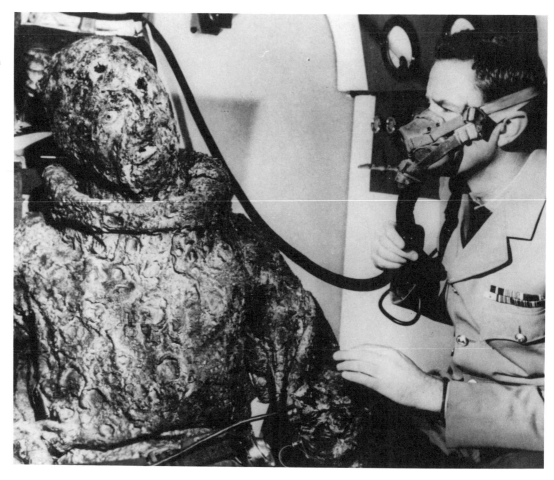

Dan Prescott, the *First Man Into Space*, spends his last moments in a pressure chamber with his brother Chuck (Marshall Thompson).

space travel is necessary in order to keep up with the Soviets.

The bad news for American viewers of the film in 1958 was that not long after *First Man Into Space* was released, the first man really did go into outer space—and he was a Russian.

# FRANKENSTEIN'S DAUGHTER

1958

**DIRECTOR:** Richard E. Cunha
**PRODUCER:** Marc Frederic
**SCREENPLAY:** H. E. Barrie
**CAST:** John Ashley, Sandra Knight, Donald Murphy, Sally Todd, Harold Lloyd, Jr., Felix Locher, Wolfe Barzell

**ORIGINAL RELEASE:** Layton/Astor Pictures
**VIDEO:** Rhino Home Video, Sinister Cinema, and Scorched Earth Productions

Ah, another no-budget sci-fi/horror gem made in the days when it looked as if John Ashley's career as a teen idol was really going to take off. This was before he started making all those terrible movies in the Philippines. Still, this one is wacky enough to be fun, as Dr. Frankenstein's grandson (Murphy) tries to keep the family business going in the America of *Lassie* and *Leave It to Beaver*.

Oliver Frankenstein, who wisely goes by the name of Oliver Frank, has fallen on hard times, however. He can't even afford his own lab, so he works as an assistant to Dr. Carter Morton (Locher) and carries on his experiments on his own time in Morton's basement with the help of Elsu (Barzell), the Morton gardener, who coincidentally used to work for Oliver's father.

The story really centers on Dr. Morton's niece Trudy (Knight) and her teenage friends. One evening Suzy (Todd), the town slut, is frightened by an ugly woman in a nightie, and that very night Trudy dreams of the same woman. In fact the woman is Trudy herself. Oliver has been spiking her fruit punch with a new serum that is supposed to preserve human cells but that just seems to make Trudy ugly for a few hours before she returns to her normal self, remembering nothing. Fortunately the serum seems to affect only her face, so that later, when she runs amok in a bathing suit, most of her still looks pretty good.

Of course the ugly serum is just a sideline for Oliver. What he really wants to do is create another monster just like Grandpa's, only female, because, according to him, female brains are more used to following orders than male brains—feminists in the audience should love that theory. Elsu has been supplying him with parts, but they have yet to find just the right head.

No one believes Suzy's story about the monster lady, even though other people report seeing her, too, and the cops start to investigate. Her sometime boyfriend Don (Lloyd, Jr., son of noted comedian Lloyd, Sr.) thinks she's just trying to get attention, and Johnny (Ashley) thinks his girl Trudy is off the wall because she believes that somehow she *is* that monster.

Anyway, Oliver hits on Suzy and they go for a ride in his convertible, but when she won't put out, he kills her for her head: "We have to graft this head on the other body."

Oliver and Elsu bring Frankenstein's daughter to life, but she doesn't look particularly feminine—rumor has it that Harry Thomas, who designed the makeup for the monster, wasn't told it was supposed to be a female until it was too late. In any case, she escapes and kills some locals before Oliver and Elsu manage to catch her again and tie her up in the basement.

To take her mind off her nightmares, Trudy throws a pool party featuring music by the legendary (?) Page Cavanaugh and his trio. Don joins in to sing "Special Date" and "Fly Away Tonight," providing some of the worst music ever heard in a fifties teenage sci-fi/horror/rock 'n' roll movie.

Now, for no particular reason, Elsu—who has faithfully served two generations of Frankensteins—has a

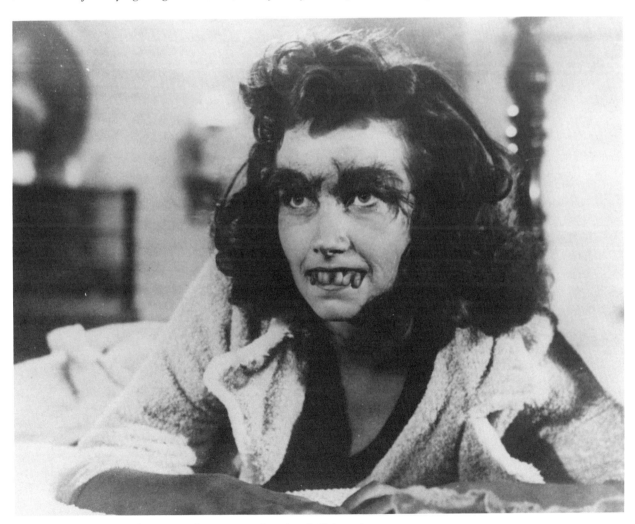

Trudy Morton (Sandra Knight) isn't *Frankenstein's Daughter*, but she'll do until a better monster comes along.

Oliver Frank (Donald Murphy), a.k.a. Frankenstein, introduces his assistant Elsu (Wolfe Barzell) to *Frankenstein's Daughter*.

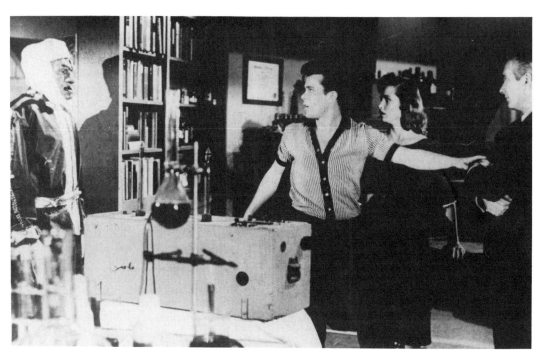

Johnny Bruder (John Ashley) and Trudy Morton are shocked when the evil Dr. Frank orders *Frankenstein's Daughter* to kill them.

change of heart and objects to Oliver's plans to turn Trudy into a monster because, like Suzy, she won't put out for him either. Oliver orders his monster to kill Elsu, but the cops are closing in, and the creature has to slaughter Detective Dillon, played by Robert Dix, who would become a regular in a string of awful Al Adamson films in the sixties and seventies.

Eventually Trudy and her boyfriend are cornered by the monster-with-Suzy's-mangled-head, but resourceful Johnny manages to douse Oliver with acid and set fire to the creature. Now everyone is happy again, even Don, who doesn't seem particularly disturbed to learn about the fate of his girlfriend Suzy—well, she wouldn't put out for him either.

This is a very optimistic film, because it suggests that evil science is transmitted genetically from father to son to son—from the original Dr. Frankenstein to his kid and then to Oliver. Now, if we could just isolate the gene for evil science, or better yet, keep evil scientists from reproducing themselves during their off-hours, we could rid the world of bad science forever, and there would never again have to be movies like *Frankenstein's Daughter*—though, personally, I think that would be a real loss to humanity.

# THE FROZEN DEAD

1966

**DIRECTOR/PRODUCER/SCREENPLAY:** Herbert J. Leder
**CAST:** Dana Andrews, Anna Palk, Philip Gilbert, Karel Stepanek, Kathleen Breck, Alan Tilvern
**ORIGINAL RELEASE:** Goldstar Productions
**VIDEO:** Sinister Cinema

Some time between *The Best Years of Our Lives* and his appearance as a regular on TV soap operas, Dana

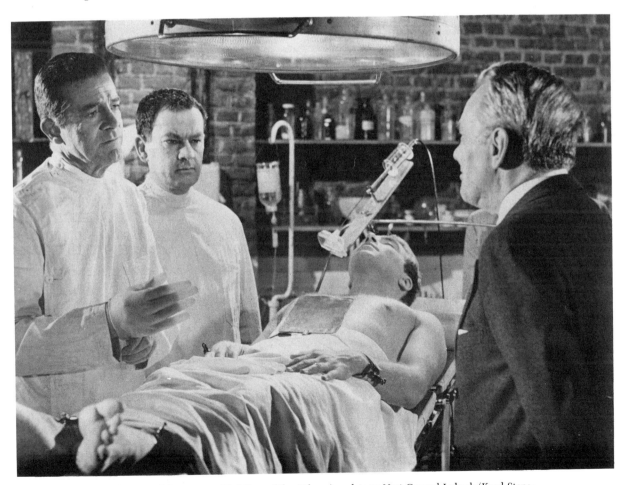

Dr. Norberg (Dana Andrews) and his assistant Karl Essen (Alan Tilvern) explain to Nazi General Lubeck (Karel Stepanek) about the problems they've been having in bringing *The Frozen Dead* back to life. (Courtesy Hollywood Book and Poster)

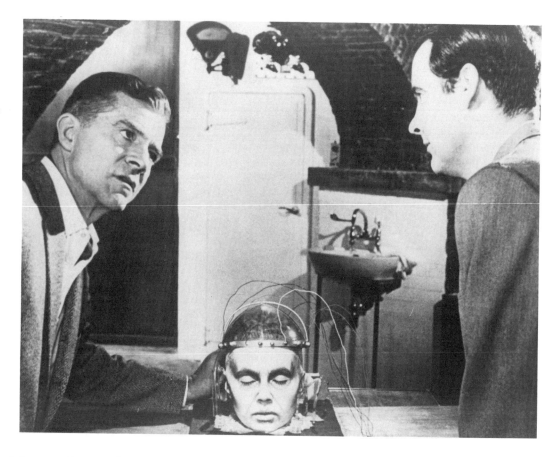

Dr. Norberg introduces young Dr. Ted Roberts (Philip Gilbert) to the talking head of Elsa (Kathleen Breck) in *The Frozen Dead*.

Andrews played the part of Dr. Norberg, a former Nazi scientist now living in London, who is trying to figure out how to freeze living people and bring them back to life. In fact, he's got a freezer full of Nazis, all still in uniform and frozen at the end of the war. There are also about 1,500 more of the Nazi elite stashed in secret iceboxes in other countries, and as soon as Norberg can figure out how to revive them, they will once again launch their plan for world conquest.

The problem is that Norberg can't quite get it right. He has revived several of his charges so far. One died, and the rest—including Norberg's brother—are hopeless mental cases, kept tucked away in a cell in the basement of his London home. The Nazi high command, represented by General Lubeck (Stepanek), is not pleased. "We need our leaders now, immediately," he explains, but Norberg cannot figure out how to jumpstart the frozen brain. What he really needs is a living, unfrozen brain to experiment on.

He gets his chance when his niece Jean (Palk) returns from school in America with her friend Elsa (Breck). Of course Jean knows nothing about her uncle's involvement with the Nazis or the true nature of his experiments, and she thinks her father died in the war.

Norberg's demented assistant, Essen (Tilvern), kills Elsa, blames Norberg's crazy brother for the murder, and explains his actions thus: "There is your live head." Norberg is shocked by the suggestion that he experiment on his niece's friend, but oh, what the heck! He decapitates her, cuts off the top of her skull, and puts it in a clear plastic window so he can watch her brain as it works. Then he hooks her head up to a bunch of tubes and wires and keeps it in a wooden box on the table in his lab.

He and Essen tell Jean that her friend decided to return home, but the niece doesn't buy it. Meanwhile, Norberg has invited young Dr. Ted Roberts (Gilbert), a brain expert, to help with his research. Ted arrives, knowing nothing about the real purpose of Norberg's work, and he and Jean hit it off right away. Norberg shows Ted around the lab, and the young scientist is particularly impressed by a wall of human arms Norberg can move by way of electrical impulses.

As it turns out, Elsa is telepathic, and she begins sending signals to Jean, invading her dreams, so Jean becomes convinced that her friend is still nearby. She and Ted investigate, and when they start getting too close to the truth, Norberg decides to tell Ted some of what happened—that Jean's father is alive but crazy, that he killed Elsa, and that Elsa's head is living in the

Ted (Philip Gilbert) and Jean (Anna Palk) have a little tête-à-tête with Elsa in *The Frozen Dead*.

Jean is almost killed by her defrosted father (Edward Fox), who used to be one of *The Frozen Dead*.

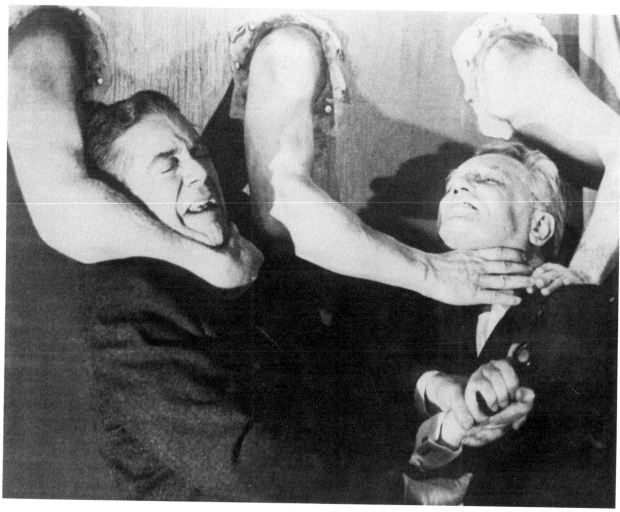

In the climactic moments of *The Frozen Dead*, Dr. Norberg and General Lubeck are strangled to death by a wall of disembodied arms.

cabinet. He even shows Ted the head, which is not very happy about the whole setup. Ted agrees to help Norberg in his research on Elsa's brain.

Eventually Jean finds Elsa's head in the lab and Lubeck decides to kill her: "She knows too much." Norberg objects, and while he and Lubeck struggle, Elsa's head animates the wall of arms, which strangle both Nazis. By now Ted is sorry for having collaborated with Norberg, and he brings the cops, who shoot Jean's father and clean up the mess. Now all they have to do is figure out what to do with Elsa's head, which keeps saying over and over again: "Bury me. Bury me."

*The Frozen Dead* is not a high point in the history of film, but it isn't the worst living-head movie around—check out *The Brain That Wouldn't Die* and *They Saved Hitler's Brain* by way of comparison. Of course evil science is the basis of most sci-fi movies, and we all know that Nazi scientists are the worst. But what is

amazing in this movie is that Ted, the good scientist, is willing to go along with Norberg as far as he does. He doesn't know that Norberg is a Nazi, but he does know that Elsa is the friend of the woman he loves, and he also knows that what he is doing is illegal, immoral, and downright nasty. So why does he participate? Well, as he explains to Jean, "You know how we scientists are—a new concept and we're carried away."

Yeah, we know how Nazi scientists are, but we've come to expect better things of handsome, good-guy scientists like Ted. And admittedly, he does change his mind later: "I made a mistake." But what *The Frozen Dead* suggests is that all scientists are dangerous fanatics, no matter how moral and upright they seem to be. Apparently all it takes is a "new concept" to turn a good, decent brain expert into a Nazi collaborator.

In other words, there is no need to revive a bunch of frozen Nazis to make the world a miserable place. We already have plenty of apparently good and neighborly scientists around, who according to this movie would be more than willing to do that at the first opportunity.

# THE GAMMA PEOPLE

1955

**DIRECTOR:** John Gilling
**PRODUCER:** John Gossage
**SCREENPLAY:** John Gilling and John Gossage
**CAST:** Paul Douglas, Eva Bartok, Leslie Phillips, Walter Rilla, Philip Leaver, Martin Miller, Michael Carridia
**ORIGINAL RELEASE:** Columbia Pictures
**VIDEO:** Goodtimes Home Video

American journalist Mike Wilson (Douglas) and British photographer Howard Meade (Phillips) are on their way to cover the Salzburg Music Festival when their railroad car becomes disconnected from the rest of the train and they find themselves stranded in Godavia, an Eastern European nation so small it isn't even on the map. They are promptly arrested by Commandant Koerner (Leaver) as spies.

But Koerner is only a cop; he doesn't run Godavia. That honor belongs to Dr. Boronski (Rilla), who is conducting experiments in the castle on the hill. Boronski is bombarding children's brains with gamma rays, a process that can produce geniuses but which also produces idiots if the dosage isn't exactly right. His assistants Bikstein and Paula Wendt (Bartok) don't agree with his methods, but apparently everybody in Godavia must do what Boronski wants or else.

The evil doctor orders Mike and Howard released but informs Koerner that they are not to leave the country, so they are told there are no cars available and the country lacks telegraph and long distance phone service. They take a room at the hotel run by Herr Lochner (Miller) and immediately begin to suspect that something is wrong when the hotel maid gives them a note from Bikstein asking for their help in destroying Boronski. Shortly afterward, Bikstein is found dead.

Mike and Howard are taken to meet Boronski and

Journalists Howard Meade (Leslie Phillips) and Mike Wilson (Paul Douglas) study the grotesque sculpture created by the evil little Hugo (Michael Carridia), who is one of *The Gamma People*. (Courtesy Hollywood Book and Poster)

recognize him as the former Dr. Mackland, a biologist who used to be known for his experiments in longevity. "Today I am a humble schoolmaster," Boronski claims as he tries to convince the journalists that everything is fine in Godavia. The guys meet Paula, the head teacher, who works with Hedda Lochner, a brilliant young pianist, and Hugo (Carridia), an officious little brat with a genius IQ who spies for Boronski and who would have been a sterling member of the Hitler Youth a decade or so earlier. Mike sees a huge mask that Hugo is making for the upcoming Godavia festival—the very image of the idiots who roam the streets of the country in packs and who seem to do all of Boronski's dirty work.

Eventually Mike and Howard learn about Boronski's experiments and about how the country is run. When their friend Herr Lochner and his daughter Hedda try to escape to Vienna, Boronski's goons kill the father and take Hedda prisoner, and Mike tells Paula that he will help find the child. He wants to expose Boronski in the world press. "I can show what's being done to these children . . . I'll bring this horror out into the open."

For no particular reason, Boronski cancels the upcoming festival, but when Wilson announces to the people of Godavia that Lochner has been murdered, they rebel and hold their celebration anyway. After a while, Mike and Paula manage to sneak into the castle to get Hedda while Howard rounds up support from the villagers. But Hugo becomes aware of their plan and rats to Boronski. Mike, Paula, and Hedda are captured, and Boronski plans to destroy their brains with gamma rays.

It is now that Paula tells Hugo the truth—he is her brother, and Boronski murdered their father. Suddenly Hugo has a change of heart and pushes Boronski into his own high-tech machinery, causing a fire that kills the evil scientist and eventually destroys the entire castle. Mike, Paula, Hugo, and Hedda escape, of course, while outside, Howard and the locals defeat Boronski's goon squad. Finally Godavia is safe for democracy.

Obviously, Godavia is supposed to be an Eastern Bloc country under the control of the Soviet Union, and Mike and Howard are the representatives of Western democracies. Unfortunately Mike Wilson, as played by aging tough guy actor Paul Douglas, comes off as the typical ugly and obnoxious American who goes to a European country and makes fun of the way the people talk and of the fact that they lack American luxuries. Still, he is the hero of *The Gamma People*, so I guess we're stuck with him. Howard is a stereotypical Englishman—proper and stuffy, effeminate, superficially cultured, not very bright, and prone to wearing smoking jackets—which is surprising, given that *The Gamma People* is a British production. The problem with this

movie is that the heroes are so lame, it's hard to get behind them or to believe that they would give a damn about what happens to the people of Godavia.

The point of this flick is that the presence of an American private citizen and his British buddy should be enough to topple even the most dictatorial Eastern Bloc government. After all, when the people of Godavia invade Boronski's castle at the end of the movie, you realize that they could have done this all along. It just never occurred to them to seize control of their own lives until an American came along to show them the way.

This notion is wrongheaded and naive, of course, but when you watch *The Gamma People*, you get the feeling that with more attention and care, it could have been pretty good. You also get the feeling that big chunks of it must have ended up on the cutting-room floor, because there are holes in the story big enough for the entire country of Godavia to fit through. For example, early in the movie, Mike makes a big deal out of Boronski's

being the former Dr. Mackland, but then this is never mentioned again. So who was Mackland? A Nazi scientist? A Harvard professor? Former head of the Federal Drug Administration? And why has he changed his name to Boronski? The implication is that he was a good guy who has turned bad, but beyond this, nothing is ever made clear.

Even more confusing is the issue of the Godavian festival. The whole movie seems to turn on this special event, but we never find out what it means. At first, Boronski encourages his gamma-induced geniuses to participate by making masks for the occasion. And there must be something secret about the whole thing, because when Howard takes a photo of Hugo's sculpture, the little brat and Boronski's band of morons go to great lengths to get the print and the negative. Then without any explanation, Boronski cancels the festival, which seems to cause the final rebellion of the Godavia people. And when the peasants decide to celebrate in spite of

In the final scenes of *The Gamma People*, Mike Wilson saves the life of Hugo, even though the little creep doesn't deserve it. (Courtesy Hollywood Book and Poster)

Boronski's army of brats nearly runs down Mike Wilson and Howard Meade in *The Gamma People*. (Courtesy Hollywood Book and Poster)

Boronski's orders, the scientist's pet stooge Hugo takes part in the festivities, too, wearing the same mask that he worked so hard to conceal. But why? And what do the festival and the masks have to do with anything?

In the end, *The Gamma People* makes no sense except as an example of cold war propaganda. Of course, there's nothing unusual about that—most American and British science fiction films of the 1950s have the same political agenda. It's enough to make you think that if the Soviets had spent less time persecuting their own people and more time cranking out low-budget sci-fi movies, the Soviet Union might still be around today.

# THE HANDS OF ORLAC

1960

**ALTERNATE TITLES:** *Hands of a Strangler, Les Mains d'Orlac*
**DIRECTOR:** Edmond T. Gréville
**PRODUCERS:** Steven Pallos and Donald Taylor
**SCREENPLAY:** John Baines and Edmond T. Gréville
**CAST:** Mel Ferrer, Christopher Lee, Dany Carrel, Lucille Saint-Simon, Sir Donald Wolfit, Donald Pleasence
**ORIGINAL RELEASE:** British Lion Films
**VIDEO:** Sinister Cinema

This is the third film based on the novel by French science fiction writer Maurice Rénard—the first two were *Orlacs Haende* (1924) and *Mad Love* (1935). Here Stephen Orlac (Ferrer) is a concert pianist who is involved in a plane crash on his way to see his fiancée, Louise (Saint-Simon), in Paris. His hands are destroyed, but she takes him to Professor Volcheff (Wolfit), a brilliant experimental surgeon. Volcheff manages to save Stephen's hands, but in time Orlac realizes that something is wrong. He has violent urges, and his hands no longer seem to obey him: "These hands don't feel as if they belong to me." He can't play the piano, and his gloves and rings are too small.

Orlac begins to suspect that Volcheff has grafted onto his wrists the hands of the strangler Louis Vasseur, who was executed in Paris the night of Stephen's accident. Stephen and Louise go away to the country for a rest, but when a cat turns up strangled and Orlac almost chokes Louise during a kiss, he runs off to hide in a nearby town.

There he runs into Nero (Lee), a stage magician, and his beautiful assistant Li-Lang (Carrel). Nero is a sleazy guy who figures Orlac is in trouble and decides there might be some blackmail money to be made. By using Li-Lang to seduce Stephen, Nero gets the whole story

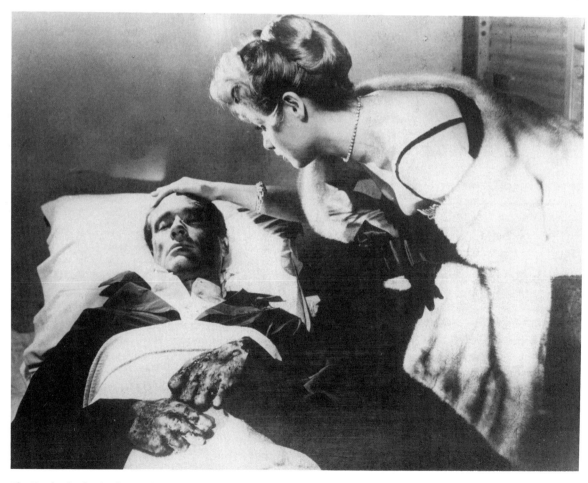

*The Hands of Orlac* (Mel Ferrer) are horribly injured in an airplane crash, much to the concern of the pianist's fiancée, Louise (Lucille Saint-Simon).

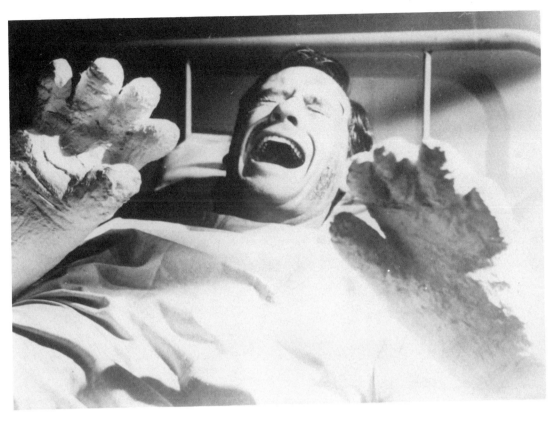

Stephen Orlac is horrified to realize that he might now have the hands of a murderer in *The Hands of Orlac*.

and begins to torment Orlac by sending him gloves marked with the name Louis Vasseur and pulling other dirty tricks calculated to drive the unbalanced Stephen over the edge.

Eventually Stephen returns to London and marries Louise, but Nero and Li-Lang follow. Orlac is becoming dangerous, and Louise's uncle, Sir Francis, agrees to get some information on Louis Vasseur, which he hopes will force Stephen to recognize that the problem is all in his mind.

Louise learns what Nero is up to and gets Li-Lang, a tramp with a heart of gold, to go to the police. But Nero finds out about this, and when they perform their famous swords in the cabinet trick before a London audience, Nero fails to unlock the secret trapdoor to release his assistant before jamming the swords into the box, thus murdering Li-Lang before a packed house.

The police seize Nero and present Stephen with proof that Louis Vasseur was innocent of the crimes for which he was executed. The real killer has confessed. This doesn't do Louis much good, but it does let Stephen off the hook, and he goes back to his piano and the concert halls of Europe.

The performances and the camera work in this film are excellent, but there are problems, too. We never get to know what Stephen was like before the accident, so it's hard to know how much he has changed because of his ordeal. Even so, his breakdown comes much too quickly to be convincing.

*The Hands of Orlac* does raise some interesting issues, though. The science fiction aspect of the film is the transplanting of the hands of a dead man onto a living person, but in fact we're never sure that this is what has really happened—it might all be a delusion on the part of Stephen and in the end it doesn't make any difference anyway, since the hands are innocent.

The question the film seems to pose, however, is this: Where is the human personality, the self—the soul, if you will? Is it in the brain or in the heart? Is it distributed throughout the body? Or does the location of the soul differ from one person to the next? Is it in one person's brain, in another's eyes, in another's hands?

If these questions make any sense, then they have some bearing on the possibilities of transplant surgery, which was in its infancy when *The Hands of Orlac* was filmed but which has made enormous progress since then. Certainly we can foresee a time when any organ or limb will be replaceable, but at what point in this process would I, as the recipient of the organs and limbs of others, cease to be myself? Is any healthy heart, hand, or liver really the equivalent of any other? And who is to decide who receives the eyes of an artist, the hands

The Great Nero (Christopher Lee) and his assistant Li-Lang (Dany Carrel) demonstrate one of their famous stage illusions in *The Hands of Orlac*.

of a sculptor, or the heart and lungs of a long-distance runner?

If these questions were worth asking in the early sixties, they are certainly worth asking again today.

# HERCULES AGAINST THE MOON MEN

1 9 6 5

**ALTERNATE TITLE:** *Maciste e la Regina di Samar*
**DIRECTOR:** Giacomo Gentilomo
**PRODUCER:** Luigi Mondello
**SCREENPLAY:** Giacomo Gentilomo, Arpad De Riso, Nico Scolaro, Angelo Sangarmano

**CAST:** Alan Steel (Sergio Ciani), Jany Clair, Anna-Maria Polani, Jean-Pierre Honoré, Delia D'Alberti
**ORIGINAL RELEASE:** Nike Cinematographica/ Comptoir Français du Film
**VIDEO:** Goodtimes Home Video

Whatever happened to all those Italian sword-and-sandal movies, anyway? Back in the sixties, it seemed that thousands of those films were coming out of Europe, and any guy with half a bicep could get a part as a mythological hero. Now that moment of cinematic history has passed. And out of all those movies, there was only one sword-and-sandal alien invasion flick, and this is it. Perhaps it's one too many.

But wait a minute, I'm being unfair. Sword-and-sandal movies were not intended to be intellectually stimulating, and as the genre goes, *Hercules Against the Moon*

*Men* isn't too bad. There are plenty of good fights, amazing feats of strength, and attractive women. What more could you want?

As you can tell from the original Italian title, this is not really a Hercules movie—it's a Maciste movie. But, no doubt to cash in on the success of the original Steve Reeves films of the late fifties—the ones that started it all—Maciste had his name changed to Hercules for the American release, as Sergio Ciani had his name changed to Alan Steel. Oh, well, it really doesn't matter. If you've seen one muscle-bound hero, you've seen 'em all.

Once upon a time long, long ago, something landed on a mountain near Samar, and since that time, apparently for centuries, the people of the region have had to sacrifice their young folk to the monster of the Mountain of Death.

Now, though, the Samarians are getting tired of the whole thing. Claudius, the elderly adviser to the throne, sends for Hercules (Steel/Ciani) to put a stop to the sacrifices, but Queen Samara (Clair) is opposed to the idea and tries to have Hercules killed. The monster of the mountain is actually a man from the moon who commands an army of living rock creatures and who plans to conquer the world once he can manage to bring his dead queen, Selena, back to life. Samara is in league with him because he has promised to make her the most powerful woman on Earth after the takeover.

Hercules makes it to Samar anyway and joins the rebels led by Samara's cousin the prince (Honoré), who is in love with the queen's half sister, the princess (D'Alberti). Claudius is killed in a trap meant for Hercules, but his daughter, Arga (Polani), continues the fight, and she and Hercules fall for each other.

During the course of the flick, Hercules gets captured and escapes and gets captured and escapes and gets captured and escapes. When he isn't busy doing that, he's freeing Arga or the prince from Samara's evil clutches. Eventually he finds out that the moon man plans to use the princess to revive Selena, so he and the rebels storm the Mountain of Death.

Hercules (Sergio Ciani/Alan Steel) displays his great strength—and he's going to need it in *Hercules Against the Moon Men.*

The lovely Princess Billis (Delia D'Alberti) is threatened by the leader of the moon men, who plans to sacrifice her in order to revive Selena, the moon queen, in *Hercules Against the Moon Men*.

When the plan for world conquest begins to fall apart, the moon guy has Samara killed by his rock creatures. He then begins to drain the princess's blood to revive Selena: "Drop by drop, this blood will bring you back to life, my queen." Of course Hercules arrives just in time, destroys the rock creatures, saves the princess, and kills the moon man. Selena disintegrates into dust, and Hercules and Arga ride off into the sunset.

Despite the fact that sword-and-sandal movies were aimed at an adolescent male audience, this one is a cautionary tale for women. It says that a good woman—Arga, for example—stands by her man, while an evil woman—Samara, for instance—who is more interested in personal power than in marriage must be destroyed. This is why Samara is crushed by rock people while Arga goes off with Hercules to become his bride. As a good woman she will devote herself to her husband and forget about her own interests.

What Arga doesn't seem to know at the end of the film is that according to Greek mythology, Hercules killed his wife and children in a fit of insanity. So much for happily ever after.

Queen Samara (Jany Clair) gets what she deserves when the rock people squash her to death in the final moments of *Hercules Against the Moon Men*.

92

# HORROR EXPRESS

1972

**ALTERNATE TITLE:** *Pánico en el Transiberiano*
**DIRECTOR:** Eugenio Martin
**PRODUCER:** Bernard Gordon
**SCREENPLAY:** Arnaud D'Usseau and Julian Halvey
**CAST:** Christopher Lee, Peter Cushing, Telly
 Savalas, Silvia Tortosa, Jorge Rigaud
**ORIGINAL RELEASE:** Scotia International
**VIDEO:** Congress Video Group, Sinister Cinema,
 and others

This Spanish-British production is one of my personal favorites because it is so very bizarre and yet so remarkably well done.

Professor Saxton (Lee) is a British anthropologist who discovers the frozen body of the missing link in Siberia in 1906. He books passage on the trans-Siberian railway

to take his specimen home to England, and on board he meets his old rival, Dr. Wells (Cushing), Polish countess Irina Petrovski (Tortosa) and her husband (Rigaud), their mad Russian monk-in-residence, and a host of others.

Saxton's missing link defrosts and begins killing off the passengers. Autopsies performed by Wells show that the victims die by having their brains boiled; it seems the killer sucks the knowledge and memories out of every person it kills. Eventually a police inspector tracks the apelike creature down and kills it, only to be taken over by the super-mind of the thing that now inhabits his body.

Here comes the good part. The killer is not really the apelike thing. The missing link was merely the host for an alien being that was stranded on Earth by accident millions of years ago and that has survived inside other living organisms since then. Now it can simply move from person to person on the train—"It's like some contagious disease," says Wells—and there is no way to tell the monster from the normal folk.

Meanwhile, the fanatical monk has become convinced that the alien is Satan, and he decides that it is time to switch sides for his own good. "Come into me, Satan," he proposes to the police inspector/alien. "*Thine* is the Kingdom and the Power and the Glory." The creature is happy where it is, however, and doesn't take the monk up on his offer—at least not yet.

The train is boarded by a troop of Cossack soldiers led by Colonel Kazan (Savalas), who has been assigned to discover who is committing the murders. Savalas is wonderful as the maniacal officer who clearly has been in Siberia too long. The Cossacks find out that the policeman is really the alien and Kazan kills him, but not before the thing manages to leap into the monk. From his new body, the alien wipes out the Cossacks, then brings them back to life as zombies to slaughter the others on board the train.

Everything comes to an end when the train gets sidetracked over a cliff. Saxton, Wells, Irina, and most of the other passengers manage to survive, but it seems the alien has been caught in the monk's body and killed for good. But of course, in movies like this one, you never know.

This is a wonderful film because it simply never lets up. There is something going on every minute, and the plot is complicated enough to keep you involved and guessing. Lee, Cushing, and Savalas are very good, and the movie as a whole has the claustrophobic feeling you find in classics like *The Thing From Another World* or *Night of the Living Dead*. As in those films, *Horror Express* sets up a situation in which a group of people are trapped in a confined area with a monster, and then it pumps that circumstance for all it's worth.

The film also reminds me of the original *Invasion of the Body Snatchers* because it too raises the unanswerable question: Who can you trust? Saxton says of the alien: "It's alive . . . in someone on this train." But who is it? There is no way to tell, so there is nowhere to turn for help.

Most science fiction films exhibit a traditional Christian morality: Goodness is stronger than evil and wins out in the end, and we know that that's going to happen right from the opening credits.

*Horror Express*, though, subverts the usual moral lesson by suggesting, as *Carrie* would a few years later, that religious fanaticism is as dangerous and as evil as satanism. The representative of Christianity here is the fanatical monk who goes on and on about God, sin, and the immortal soul in the early stages of the movie but who is more than willing to side with the devil the first chance he gets. He even argues that evil is stronger than good when he says, "Where evil is, there is no place for the cross."

But of course the monk is wrong on all counts. There is no devil here, only an alien from outer space. There is no good or evil involved. The alien is simply there and must be dealt with as an alien. As Saxton says, "It's a fact, and there's no morality in a fact."

*Horror Express* is an interesting and intelligent movie because it first raises traditional Christian issues, then wipes them away in favor of the simple question of

The missing link from outer space attacks Natasha (Helga Line), the lovely thief riding on board the *Horror Express*.

The thing on the *Horror Express* threatens the Polish countess (Silvia Tortosa).

Countess Irina Petrovski is menaced by a living dead Cossack in the final moments of *Horror Express*.

survival—the alien wants to survive, the humans want to survive, and in the end, sheer dumb luck determines who wins and who loses. This is not a particularly comforting thought.

# HORROR OF THE BLOOD MONSTERS

1970

**ALTERNATE TITLES:** *Creatures of the Prehistoric Planet, Horror Creatures of the Prehistoric Planet, Vampire Men of the Lost Planet*
**DIRECTOR/PRODUCER:** Al Adamson
**SCREENPLAY:** Sue McNair
**CAST:** John Carradine, Robert Dix, Vicki Volante, Joey Benson, Jennifer Bishop, Bruce Powers, Fred Meyes, Britt Semand
**ORIGINAL RELEASE:** Independent International
**VIDEO:** Super Video and VidAmerica

In his novel *Image of the Beast*, Philip José Farmer toys with the idea that our legendary monsters are not legends at all but real beings who have come to our world from another dimension. In *The Space Vampires*, Colin Wilson explores similar territory. *Horror of the Blood Monsters* seems to begin with the same promising idea, but by the time director Al Adamson and the gang at Independent International get finished with it, the result is a complete mess.

Here's the problem. Adamson came upon a movie shot in the Philippines about vampire cavemen and incorporated a good bit of that film into *Horror of the Blood Monsters*, filling it in with his own footage featuring Carradine, Dix, et al. He also lifted dinosaur footage from the silent version of *The Lost World* and *One Million B.C.* of 1940, as well as outer space shots from a variety of sources—Adamson is a firm believer in recycling. Of course Independent International wanted to be able to say in its ads that *Horror of the Blood Monsters* was in living color, but the Filipino film was in black and white, so somebody tinted the black-and-white footage a variety of colors—red or blue or green or yellow—and advertised this exciting new process as Spectrum X, a process that in fact has been in use since the earliest days of silent movies.

So does this patchwork quilt of a film actually have a plot? Well, you judge. The opening sequences show vampires attacking people in various situations while a voice-over narrative featuring the worst Bela Lugosi

*Horror of the Blood Monsters* purports to tell us about the origin of vampirism. Pretty scary, huh? (Courtesy Hollywood Book and Poster)

Dr. Rynning (John Carradine) loses his balance during a tense moment on board the rocket ship that is heading toward the planet of the vampire people in *Horror of the Blood Monsters*.

imitation ever explains the premise: "The infected blood of the vampire was carried to Earth millions of years ago by the Tuberton vampire men of a distant galaxy far beyond this solar system." Got it? Okay.

Now it's some time in the not-too-distant future, and Dr. Rynning (Carradine) and his crew are taking off in rocket ship XB-13 for the Spectrum solar system, but a radioactive disturbance throws them off course and damages their vessel. They are forced to land on a nearby planet to make repairs, and when they do, they find that the place is awash with "spectrum radiation," which means that everything there is tinted a single color—sometimes red, sometimes green or blue or yellow. In fact, the whole planet looks exactly like old black-and-white footage that has been artificially colored by that ancient process Spectrum X.

Rynning stays on board while the others go out to explore, and they discover dinosaurs from *The Lost World* and *One Million B.C.* and warring cavemen from the Filipino film I told you about before. Actually, there are a number of different tribes on the planet: some normal human types; some more or less humans who have snakes growing out of their bodies; some lob-

stermen who live in the river; some bat people who live in a cave; and of course, the Tuberton tribe, which is made up of vampire people with long scary fangs.

The Earthlings meet a cavewoman (Bishop) from the normal-looking tribe and implant an electronic communicator in her brain so she will speak and understand English—though apparently it doesn't work so well, because she ends up talking like Tonto. In any case, her name is Lian Malian, and she immediately falls for Willy (Benson), the comedy relief member of the landing party. Commander Bryce (Powers) already has a girlfriend, Linda (Semand), and that leaves only Bob Scott (Meyes) and Dr. Rynning unattached.

Well, everybody has a lot of adventures—Rynning

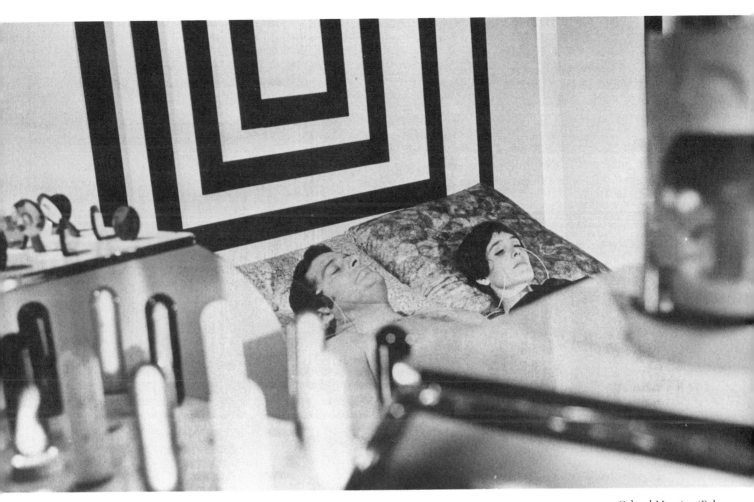

Colonel Manning (Robert Dix) and Valerie (Vicki Volante) take a sex machine break and reminisce about how couples used to do it in the good old days in *Horror of the Blood Monsters*.

97

The astronauts in *Horror of the Blood Monsters* discover vampire people, snake people, lobster people, and even some little bat people on the alien planet.

Another scene from the Philippines that director Al Adamson used to pad out his ridiculous *Horror of the Blood Monsters*.

has a minor coronary, Bob gets run through with a spear, Willy says good-bye to Lian Malian ("I find a girl I could really like, and it has to be a million miles from Earth"), and all of them find out that they've been infected by the spectrum virus, which is what has caused the inhabitants of the planet to mutate into lobster people, bat people, snake people, and vampire people. Not to worry, though. As Rynning explains, "We'll be all right.

The virus can't live in Earth's atmosphere." So with XB-13 repaired, they take off for home.

But wait a minute. I have a couple of problems with all this. I thought the movie was supposed to explain how vampirism appeared on Earth, right? In the beginning of this flick, I was told that the Tubertons carried the vampire virus to Earth millions of years ago, but since the Tubertons are cave people who don't even seem to

Director Al Adamson dons the vampire cape for a brief moment in *Horror of the Blood Monsters*, proving that he wouldn't ask anyone to do something he wasn't willing to do himself.

understand how fire works, it's a bit hard to believe that millions of years ago, they were capable of traveling the distance between their planet and ours. Besides, if the vampire virus can't live in Earth's atmosphere, how was anyone on Earth ever infected? And if the virus arrived here millions of years ago, then there weren't any human beings around to be infected by it.

Am I being too picky?

# HUMANOIDS FROM THE DEEP

1980

**DIRECTOR:** Barbara Peeters
**PRODUCER:** Martin B. Cohen
**SCREENPLAY:** Frederick James
**CAST:** Doug McClure, Ann Turkel, Vic Morrow, Cindy Weintraub, Anthony Penya

**ORIGINAL RELEASE:** New World Pictures
**VIDEO:** Warner Home Video

There's a cannery coming to the Pacific fishing village of Noyo. Some of the residents are happy about it and some aren't. It'll mean jobs; it'll also mean pollution of the water—a very modern dilemma. In fact, *Humanoids From the Deep* is a pretty typical example of the ecological disaster films that started to appear in the 1970s and that have since become a solid subgenre of science fiction.

Morrow, who died tragically in 1982 during the filming of *Twilight Zone: The Movie,* is Hank Slattery, the leader of the pro-cannery forces and a racist who hates all Indians and blames them for everything. Johnny Eagle (Penya) heads the environmentalists and is threatening to sue for the return of Native American lands to stop the cannery from being built. Jim Hill (McClure) favors the cannery but stands up for the Indians.

These various forces have to join together, however, when Noyo is attacked by mutant amphibious fish, the humanoids of the title who look sort of like the big-brained insect mutants from *This Island Earth* but are

Dr. Susan Drake (Ann Turkel) explores the beach near the fishing village of Noyo, looking for *Humanoids From the Deep*.

colored green and covered with seaweed. The monsters go around killing the men and raping the young women, and eventually, in the climactic scene of the flick, they invade the Salmon Festival, messing up what little tourist trade Noyo has and ruining everyone's good time.

It seems that Canco, the cannery people, have been experimenting with ways to make salmon grow larger and reproduce more quickly. Dr. Susan Drake (Turkel) worked on the project, and she explains that salmon treated with DNA-5 escaped from the research lab some time ago. Apparently these salmon were eaten by more primitive fish, and the DNA-5 has caused them to evolve into humanlike creatures at an accelerated rate. Now they feel compelled to mate with human women in order to evolve further—it's a bizarre and wrongheaded

notion of how evolution works, but what the hell, how smart are mutant fish supposed to be anyway?

Drake has been warning Canco for some time that such a thing could happen, but the cannery people refused to allow her to contact the authorities and covered the whole thing up. In *Humanoids From the Deep*, then, science isn't evil, big business is, and that is a pretty typical message for an ecological disaster film. Thus scientist Drake is depicted as a good person, even though she never apologizes for indirectly creating the humanoids in the first place and never explains why she just didn't quit her job at Canco if she thought the company was so immoral.

Eventually Hill, Eagle, Drake, and the others shoot, hack, and burn the mutants, and even Slattery turns out

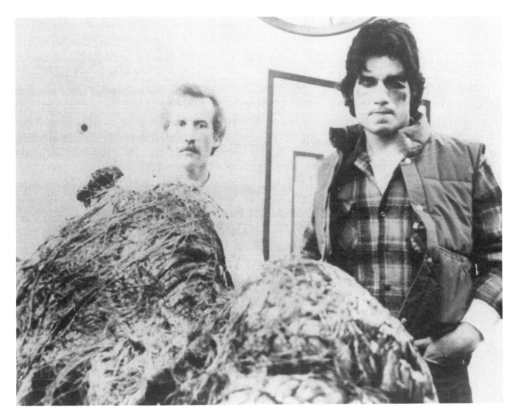

A battered Johnny Eagle (Anthony Penya) and a Canco employee look on as Dr. Drake begins an autopsy on the body of one of the *Humanoids From the Deep*.

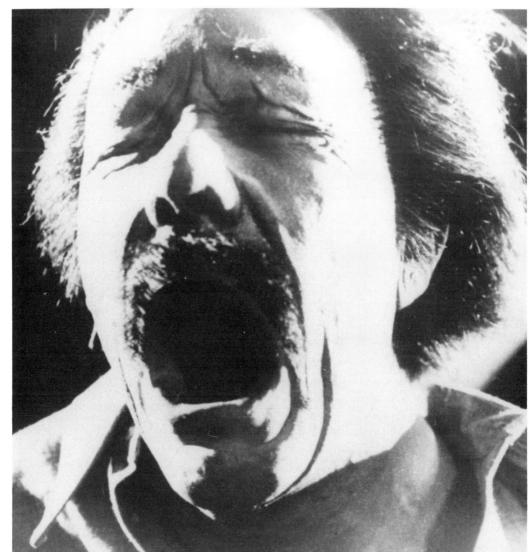

Just another victim of the *Humanoids From the Deep*.

about big-breasted women being brutally and graphically raped by mutant fish. The character of Dr. Drake is a nod in the direction of some kind of feminist message—when the boss of Canco calls her "a great little scientist," we know he's a jerk—and yet clearly this is anything but a pro-woman film. Don't be fooled by the fact that the director of *Humanoids From the Deep* is a woman. Like Dr. Drake, Peeters has blamed the end product of her efforts on her boss—in this case, the legendary exploitation director and producer Roger Corman of New World Pictures—but that doesn't alter the fact that the treatment of women here is simply repellent. Again, like Dr. Drake, Peeters has a lot to answer for.

# THE INCREDIBLE MELTING MAN

1977

**DIRECTOR/SCREENPLAY:** William Sachs
**PRODUCER:** Samuel W. Gelfman
**CAST:** Alex Rebar, Burr DeBenning, Myron Healey, Michael Aldredge, Ann Sweeny
**ORIGINAL RELEASE:** American International Pictures
**VIDEO:** Vestron Home Video

When the monsters attack her home, Carol Hill (Cindy Weintraub) must defend herself and her baby until help arrives in the climactic moments of *Humanoids From the Deep*. (Courtesy Hollywood Book and Poster)

to be a hero by rescuing a little girl from the humanoids, showing that racists aren't really so bad after all.

*Humanoids From the Deep* is an effort to make a fifties bug-eyed monster flick for the eighties, and at that level it's a lot of fun. The film also borrows liberally from other science fiction and horror movies, using the handheld camera technique from *Halloween,* the underwater tracking shots from *Jaws,* and even the "birth" scene from *Alien,* when at the end of *Humanoids* a baby mutant erupts from the stomach of a woman impregnated by one of the monsters. Sci-fi fans always get a kick out of such "quotations," and at least they show that the film knows where it comes from.

But this is not an easy movie to come to terms with. On the one hand, it's a film about the dangers of ecological tampering and racism. On the other hand, it's a film

This is the kind of movie we've come to expect from AIP—cheaply made, nasty, and lots of fun.

Astronaut Steve West (Rebar) and his crew are on a flight to Saturn, but something goes wrong. When the rocketship returns to Earth—and how this happens is never explained—Steve is the only member of the crew left alive, and he is in bad shape. In the hospital, he rips off his bandages to reveal that his entire body is melting—hence the title of the film. He then kills and partially eats a nurse and escapes. Dr. Ted Nelson (DeBenning) and General Mike Perry (Healey) of the space program are called in to solve this little problem.

The government and the military are trying their best to cover up the whole mishap, but this gets harder and harder to do, because Steve needs to ingest human cells in order to survive, and he seems to get stronger and more violent as he melts. He keeps drawing attention to himself by ripping off the head of an innocent fisherman, frightening the local kids, and slaughtering Nelson's mother-in-law and her boyfriend. Eventually even Sheriff Blake (Aldredge) begins to notice that something is not quite right in his community.

There is a lot of footage of Steve wandering around and melting—the special effects makeup is by Rick Baker, and it is impressive. West's feet kind of stick to the ground as he walks, and bits of him keep dropping off. At one point Nelson is hot on Steve's radioactive trail when he comes upon a bit of slime in a bush. Studying it more closely, the good doctor whispers, "Oh, God, it's his ear."

Steve spends some time lurking around Nelson's house, checking out his wife, Judy (Sweeny). He also enters the home of a young couple and kills the husband, though the wife manages to chop off one of his melting arms with a meat cleaver. Like I said, this is a nasty film.

It's also a very funny film. After Steve kills General Perry, Nelson and the sheriff find the body. Blake notices something weird in Perry's hand and thinks it might be part of Steve. But when Nelson examines it, it turns out to be a turkey leg, the remnants of the general's midnight snack.

Anyway, near sunrise, Steve finds his way to a refinery. Nelson and Blake follow him there, but Steve kills the sheriff. Remarkably, though, he recognizes Ted and even saves the good doctor from a deadly fall. Then, unfortunately, a couple of bewildered security guards shoot Nelson by mistake, and Steve kills them in turn.

At dawn, Steve suffers a final meltdown in an amazing scene that reduces him to a disgusting pile of sludge. The maintenance guy at the refinery finds him and sweeps him into the trash as a radio newscaster reports on the new Saturn launch taking place that morning. Oh, no, not again!

This is, of course, a throwback to the sci-fi films of the 1950s, right down to the presence of Myron Healey, a prominant heavy of fifties movies and TV, in the role of General Perry. The movie cribs its title from the classic *Incredible Shrinking Man* of 1957, but in fact it is a virtual remake of 1958's *First Man Into Space*, one of many fear-of-space-travel flicks of the era. The only difference is that in the fifties we were willing to believe that governmental cover-ups were really for our own good. By the late seventies it had become clear that our military and government leaders often had their own agendas and weren't always very concerned about what happened to us as a result. *The Incredible Melting Man* reflects that sensibility.

In some ways, this movie owes as much to Mary Shelley's *Frankenstein* as it does to fifties sf. Dr. Ted Nelson has created a monster—accidentally, of course, but then Dr. Frankenstein never really expected to cre-

ate a monster either. Nelson tries to solve the problem himself, but in the process of hunting down his creation, Ted's family is destroyed—well, at least his mother-in-law is destroyed, and there is every indication that his pregnant wife, Judy, will lose their baby as a result of this ordeal. Ted is the only human being Steve still responds to, and when Nelson dies, West is pretty much finished, too. In its own way, *The Incredible Melting Man* follows the novel *Frankenstein* more closely than any of the movies supposedly based on the book.

This movie also gave a boost to a couple of younger

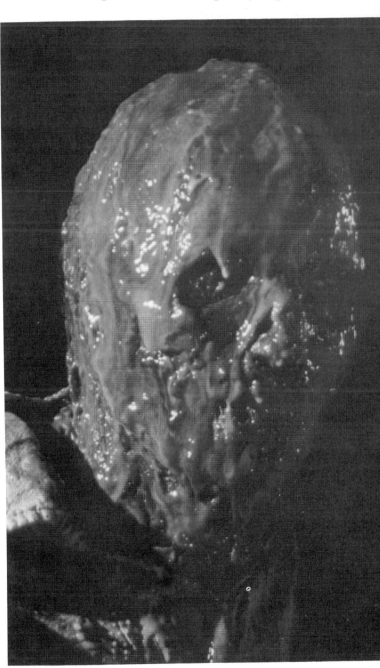

Astronaut Steve West (Alex Rebar) returns to Earth from a space mission a bit worse for wear, now that he is *The Incredible Melting Man*. (Courtesy Hollywood Book and Poster)

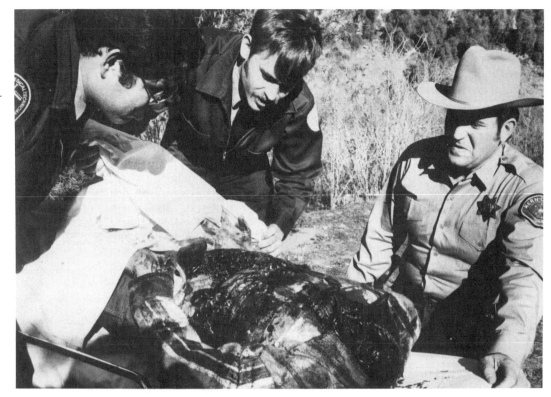

Sheriff Blake (Michael Aldredge) and his men examine a headless corpse, the work of *The Incredible Melting Man*. (Courtesy Hollywood Book and Poster)

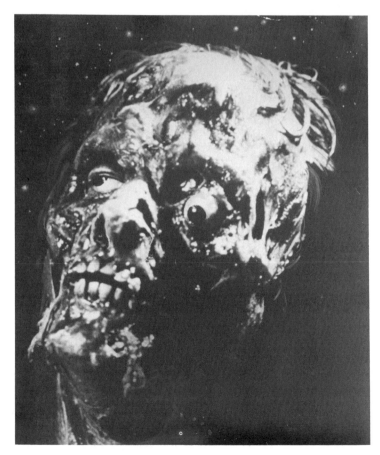

It's meltdown time for *The Incrdible Melting Man*, thanks to the incredible makeup of Rick Baker. (Courtesy Hollywood Book and Poster)

directors. Michel Levesque, who made the women-in-prison film *Sweet Sugar* and the legendary lycanthropic biker flick *Werewolves on Wheels,* heads up the second unit. And Jonathan Demme appears in a bit part. If for no other reason, it's worth watching *The Incredible Melting Man* just to see if you can spot the future director of *Silence of the Lambs.*

# THE INCREDIBLE TWO-HEADED TRANSPLANT

1 9 7 0

**DIRECTOR:** Anthony M. Lanza
**PRODUCER:** John Lawrence and Wolodymyr Kowal
**SCREENPLAY:** James Gordon Whie and John Lawrence
**CAST:** Bruce Dern, Pat Priest, Casey Kasem, Berry Kroeger, Albert Cole, John Bloom

**ORIGINAL RELEASE:** American International
Pictures
**VIDEO:** Trans-Atlantic Video

This is one of the stupidest movies I have ever seen—
and believe me, I've seen plenty of stupid movies. The
plot is insipid, the special effects are terrible, and the
casting doesn't help. Dern is the mad doctor—I'll bet
he doesn't list *this* movie on his resume. Casey "Top
Forty" Kasem is the good doctor, and Pat Priest—
formerly Marilyn on TV's *The Munsters*—is Dern's frus-
trated wife. At least she gets to sport much sexier outfits
than she ever got to wear on television. The movie also
introduces John Bloom as one of the two heads, but his
performance is hopelessly inept. Even the theme song,
"It's Incredible"—sort of a "Love Theme from *The Incredible Two-Headed Transplant*"—makes no sense.

There might have been some hope for this atrocity if
it had a bit of humor, but everyone seems to be perfectly
serious about the whole thing. Well, it just goes to show
you that two heads are not necessarily better than one.

Roger Girard (Dern) is a surgeon who has had a
nervous breakdown and lost his job at the hospital. Fortunately he is rich enough to be able to construct a
lavish laboratory in his home, and he spends almost all
his time there with his weird assistant Max (Kroeger),
ignoring his lovely wife, Linda (Priest). Ken (Kasem),
an old med school friend, shows up to try to get Roger
out of the lab and back to his spouse, but Girard is
involved in a series of important experiments. He shows
Ken a whole menagerie of two-headed animals and explains what he is trying to do. The goal is to transplant
the heads of valuable dying people onto the bodies of
worthless healthy people. Once the transplant takes, the
old head would be removed, and the valuable person's
head would have a new chance at life. "I'm trying to

Roger (Bruce Dern) tries to stop escaped maniac Manuel Cass (Albert Cole) from spiriting
away his wife, Linda (Pat Priest), in *The Incredible Two-Headed Transplant*.

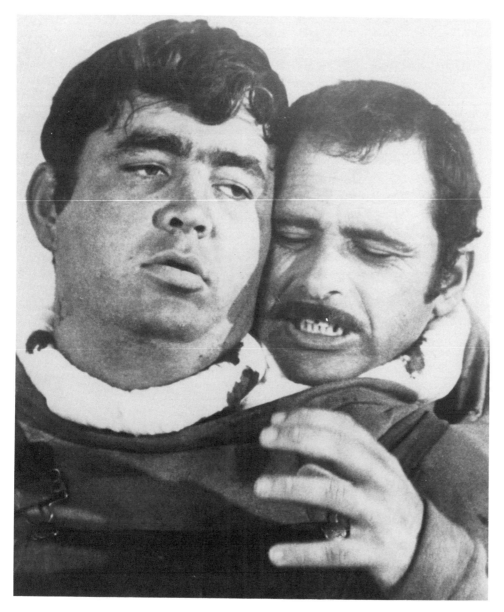

Danny (John Bloom) and Cass awaken after surgery to find that they have been transformed into *The Incredible Two-Headed Transplant*.

show those doctors," Roger says, "those antiquated old men, that I am really doing something with my life. . . . I want to give something of myself to science."

Well, everybody needs a hobby.

Roger's caretaker Andrew has an enormous and powerful son, Danny (Bloom), who though fully grown has the mind of an eight-year-old as the result of an accident in a nearby mine when he was little. Harmless Danny helps out around the place by pulling up tree stumps with his bare hands and saying "Yes, Daddy" a lot.

One day rapist/murderer Manuel Cass (Cole) escapes from a local asylum, invades Roger's home, kills Danny's dad, and kidnaps Linda. Roger and Max take off after him, and Max stops Cass with a blast from a shotgun. Danny is so unbalanced by his father's death that Roger

*The Incredible Two-Headed Transplant* attacks a couple of young lovers necking in a parked car.

has to sedate him. With Cass dying and Danny unconscious, Max points out: "Don't you realize we have here two perfect specimens? . . . Such an opportunity may never come again." Of course, what Max wants to do is put the head of a homicidal maniac onto the body of a super-strong giant.

Sure, that seems like a good idea.

Roger feels a bit guilty about using poor Danny as a guinea pig, but hey, what the hell! He and Max do the operation, and when Danny/Manny wakes up, he/they are the incredible two-headed transplant. Needless to say, they escape. Because Danny is weak of mind, Manny manages to get control of their shared body, and he sets off for lovers' lane to kill a couple of teenagers while Danny merely shakes his head and says, "No, no, no"—he doesn't want to be a bad boy, but there doesn't seem to be anything he can do about it.

Roger locks Linda up in a cage in the lab for her own

*Danny and Cass hide in a nearby cave in the closing moments of The Incredible Two-Headed Transplant. (Courtesy Hollywood Book and Poster)*

*Two-Headed Transplant* does not show too much imagination. There's nothing here that you haven't seen a million times before—with the possible exception of Marilyn Munster in a skimpy bikini.

Of course transplant surgery does pose some difficult ethical questions. Ken offers one of them himself when he asks Roger, "Who's going to judge who should live and who should die?" But the only answer this flick can come up with is: not Roger.

This one, folks, is a loser.

# INVASION OF THE SAUCER MEN

### 1957

**ALTERNATE TITLE:** *Invasion of the Hell Creatures*
**DIRECTOR:** Edward L. Cahn
**PRODUCERS:** James H. Nicholson and Robert J. Gurney, Jr.
**SCREENPLAY:** Robert J. Gurney, Jr. and Al Martin
**CAST:** Steve Terrell, Goria Castillo, Frank Gorshin, Raymond Hatton, Lyn Osborn
**ORIGINAL RELEASE:** American International Pictures
**VIDEO:** Columbia TriStar Home Video

good, and he and Max pursue their creation, which is now on a killing spree. When they aren't slaughtering people, Danny/Manny hide out in the mine where the big guy had his tragic accident years before. At about this time Ken returns to Roger's house, frees Linda, and gets the whole story. Then they set out to look for Roger, who is looking for Danny/Manny. The sheriff's posse is looking for everybody.

Finally Roger and Max track Danny/Manny to the mine, where all of them are killed in a cave-in. To cover up for Roger, Ken tells the sheriff that Danny was the killer and that Roger died trying to capture him. Then he adds, "Sometimes too much imagination can destroy a man."

If that's the case, then nobody who worked on this film has anything to worry about, because *The Incredible*

By 1957, newspaper headlines were so full of reported UFO sightings and theater screens were so full of alien invasion movies that a parody like *Invasion of the Saucer Men* was inevitable. In fact this film pokes fun at some of AIP's own efforts, particularly the teen sci-fi and horror movies that were perfect for the drive-in audience. *Invasion of the Saucer Men* is a well-made film that effectively balances a number of plots and subplots and delivers some laughs at the expense of more serious ventures such as *The Blob* and *The Crawling Hand*.

The narrator is a drifter named Artie (Osborn, who played Commander Buzz Corey's sidekick Happy in an early fifties Saturday-morning sci-fi adventure show), who is stranded in the small town of Hicksburg without a job or any prospects. His partner Joe (impressionist Gorshin, who later had enormous success as the Riddler in the sixties *Batman* TV series) goes for a ride one night after a few drinks and sees a flying saucer land. Some of the kids in town see it, too. So does the local army recruiter. Meanwhile, teenagers Johnny (Terrell) and Joan (Castillo) are off to get married secretly because Joan's father, the local district attorney, does not approve of her boyfriend.

Joe hurries back to his apartment to tell Artie of what he has seen—he has plans to exhibit the UFO and make a fortune—but Artie doesn't believe him. At the same time, the army recruiter reports the UFO landing to his commanding officer. It seems that the military has known about flying saucers all along, and the only thing they want to do is to keep the public from getting the facts.

On their way to get married, Johnny and Joan run over one of the little green saucer men and kill it. While they're trying to decide what to do, the alien's severed hand comes back to life and punctures their tire with its needle-like fingernails. The kids call the police, but of course the cops think it's just a teenagers' prank. Returning to the scene, Joe finds the car and the dead alien and sees a real opportunity to make a few bucks. By now Joe has been drinking pretty heavily, so he doesn't have much chance to escape when he is attacked by a whole gang of little green men, who use their

fingernails to inject him with what seems to be some kind of poison.

Eventually the cops come out to investigate and find Joe dead under Johnny's car. Johnny is arrested, though he insists that he did not run Joe down—"It was little green men, I tell you." But Johnny can't prove his story. The aliens have taken their dead buddy away, and meanwhile, in its efforts to break into the UFO to study it, the army has managed to blow the spacecraft to smithereens.

Johnny and Joan escape from the cops and steal a police car, hoping to return to the scene of the accident and find some evidence to clear themselves. While they are looking around in the woods, the severed alien hand gets in their car and later tries to attack them, but they manage to trap it inside the vehicle. Now they have the proof they need, and they go in search of Joe's roommate, Artie, because by now they know that none of the adults in town will help them.

Artie comes to believe their story and goes with them to see the alien hand, but when they throw a spotlight on the thing to get a better look, it dissolves into nothing. Moments later, they are surrounded by aliens, and they

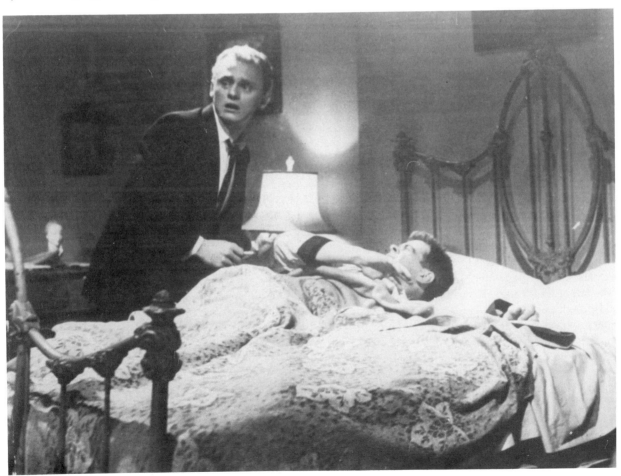

Joe (Frank Gorshin) awakens his friends Artie (Lyn Osborn) to tell him about the UFO that has just landed, bringing with it the *Invasion of the Saucer Men*.

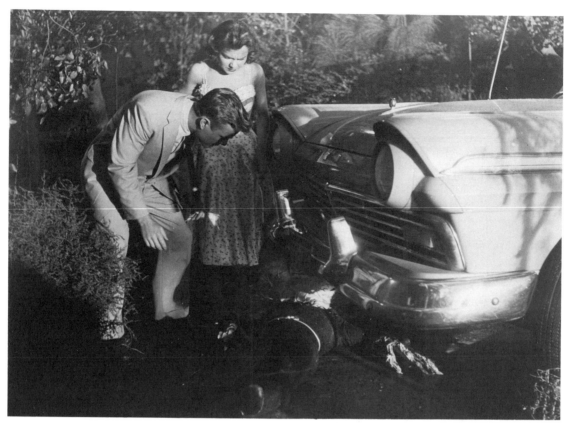

Teenagers Johnny (Steve Terrell) and Joan (Gloria Castillo) are running away to get married when they drive over one of the ugly little creatures in *Invasion of the Saucer Men*.

discover that the creatures are sensitive to light. Artie gets cornered, and the aliens inject him with their venom, but Johnny and Joan manage to get away.

The kids call the cops again, but the chief of police informs them that they are off the hook. An autopsy showed that Joe did not die from being hit by a car—he died of a massive overdose of alcohol. The chief's theory is that Joe was already dead when Johnny's car hit him, so the case is closed.

Johnny and Joan finally decide that the only help they can get is from other teenagers, so they round up their friends in lovers' lane and go after the aliens themselves. The kids manage to surround the creatures with their cars. Then they turn their headlights on, and the saucer men explode, thus ending the threat to Earth.

The teens find Artie in the woods, alive but drunk, and Johnny figures out what must have happened. Apparently the aliens inject pure alcohol into their victims, though not enough to kill a human being—unless, like Joe, that person has also been drinking heavily. Anyway, the kids know that no one in authority will ever believe them, but the world has been saved, and now Johnny and Joan can get married and live happily ever after.

In most 1950s alien invasion films, those in authority

The aliens attack Johnny's car in *Invasion of the Saucer Men*. (Courtesy Hollywood Book and Poster)

Johnny and Joan try to convince the police that they are witnesses to the *Invasion of the Saucer Men*.

Young lovers Joan and Johnny are threatened by a disembodied alien hand—and this isn't even the worst of their problems during the *Invasion of the Saucer Men*.

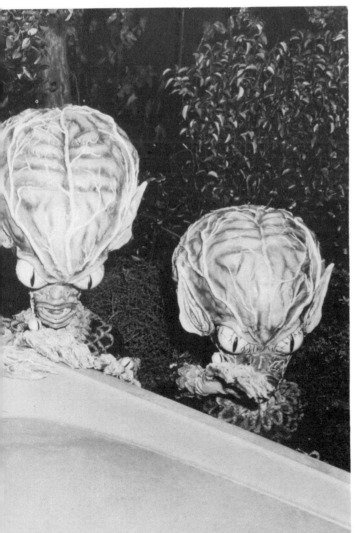

111

must solve the problem, and this is true even in teen flicks like *The Blob*, where the kids first discover the threat but eventually manage to convince the police and the military to deal with it. In *Invasion of the Saucer Men*, however, the police are totally incompetent. The military *already* knows about the aliens but only wants to cover everything up. And so, like the torch-wielding villagers of the 1930s and '40s, the teenagers have to take matters into their own hands.

In this sense, *Invasion of the Saucer Men* overturns most of the basic assumptions of fifties sci-fi, and that in itself makes this an interesting movie. The final message, of course, is that the kids are okay, and during the fifties, with all the media hype about juvenile delinquency and the evils of rock 'n' roll, that was something teens really needed to hear.

# THE ISLAND OF DR. MOREAU

1 9 7 7

**DIRECTOR:** Don Taylor
**PRODUCERS:** John Temple-Smith and Skip Steloff
**SCREENPLAY:** John Herman Shaner and Al Ramrus

**CAST:** Burt Lancaster, Michael York, Nigel Davenport, Barbara Carrera, Richard Basehart, Nick Cravat
**ORIGINAL RELEASE:** American International Pictures
**VIDEO:** Goodtimes Home Video

H. G. Wells's novel *The Island of Dr. Moreau* is one of the classics of the genre and still one of the best science fiction works I have ever read. The first screen version, *Island of Lost Souls* (1933), is also a classic, and this 1977 movie owes a lot to it, though it departs in important ways from both the book and the first movie.

Personally, if I had been casting this film, I never would have considered Burt Lancaster for the role of the mad scientist, and it's very tempting to compare his performance with that of Charles Laughton in the original, but that would be a bit unfair. To my mind, Lancaster's take on Moreau is wonderful—usually understated, though when he flips out from time to time, he's very convincing. The *Island of Dr. Moreau* is a good, solid movie, and Lancaster is clearly the star.

Sailor Andrew Braddock (York) is shipwrecked on an island in the middle of nowhere, the sole survivor from the sinking of the *Lady Vain*. He is rescued by Montgomery (Davenport), who runs the estate of Dr. Moreau (Lancaster), an eccentric scientist who has retired from the world. Andrew also meets the beautiful Maria (Carrera), who lives in the mansion with Moreau amid a

The sinister Dr., Moreau in his study—Burt Lancaster makes a wonderful mad scientist in *The Island of Doctor Moreau*.

collection of very strange looking servants, including the animalistic M'Ling (Cravat).

Needless to say, Andrew and Maria hit it off, and Moreau seems nice enough as he explains that his experiments in genetics drove him out of the medical community to this island, where he can work in peace. Once Andrew starts looking around, however, he becomes aware of strange creatures living in the jungle beyond the compound. Entering the doctor's lab unexpectedly one day, he finds animals in cages and a creature that is half man and half bear strapped to an operating table.

At this point Moreau explains what he is really up to. He has developed a serum that, along with surgery and transplants, makes it possible for him to control heredity and change animals into humans. The things in the jungle are his creations.

The beast men on *The Island of Doctor Moreau*—actors Richard Basehart, Fumio Demura, Gary Baxley, John Gillespie, and David Cass.

Later Andrew discovers a cave in which the animal-men have their new society, which exists according to laws set forth by their god, Moreau. As the Sayer of the Law (Basehart) says to Andrew, "His is the hand that makes. His is the hand that hurts." Any animal-man caught breaking the law—walking on all fours, eating meat, spilling blood—is taken back to the lab, to the House of Pain, for reconditioning. Moreau rules this

The lovely Maria (Barbara Carrera) and friends, all residents of *The Island of Doctor Moreau*.

114

The evil doctor checks on one of his experiments in *The Island of Doctor Moreau*.

Castaway Andrew Braddock (Michael York) becomes the subject of a weird experiment after he lands on *The Island of Doctor Moreau*.

Braddock is midway between man and beast as he and Maria attempt to escape from *The Island of Doctor Moreau.* (Courtesy Hollywood Book and Poster)

little society through fear and torture, but his experiments do not seem to be working. "Always, almost always, they revert to what they once were."

Andrew decides to escape from the island in the lifeboat that brought him there, taking Maria with him. Before this can happen, however, the bull-man runs amok and kills a tiger, spilling and tasting blood, and Moreau fears a revolution. The bull-man is captured, but when he begs not to be taken back to the House of Pain, Andrew takes pity and shoots him.

The animal-men are disturbed about what happened to the bull-man, but Moreau is more concerned with a new experiment he has in mind. He captures Andrew and injects him with a serum that will turn him from a man into an animal. Montgomery, who has put up with a lot from Moreau, objects to this, but the good doctor explains: "If one is to study nature, one must become as remorseless as nature." Montgomery isn't convinced, so Moreau kills him. The murder is witnessed by some of the animal-men, and the Sayer of the Law notes: "He tells us not to kill, and yet he kills."

Andrew's transformation begins, and though he struggles against it, he begins to take on the physical and some of the emotional qualities of a beast. Meanwhile, the revolution is in full swing, and the animal-men set fire to the compound and kill Moreau. Maria lets Andrew out of his cage, and together they escape to the boat while the fire seemingly destroys the island. Not long after, Andrew reverts to himself once more, and they spot a ship on the horizon.

Dr. Moreau gets what's coming to him in the final scenes of *The Island of Doctor Moreau.*

116

The movie ends as they are about to be rescued. But what about Maria? If you've seen *Island of Lost Souls*, you know that Lota, the love interest of the young castaway, is also one of Moreau's creations, a panther woman, and his crowning achievement. In *Island of Dr. Moreau*, there are some indications that Maria may not be the sweet young thing she seems to be. She makes cryptic comments about never having been anywhere else except the island, though Moreau claims to have found her in Panama, and she seems totally innocent of the ways of the world. Remember, too, that Moreau tells Andrew that his creations "always, *almost always*, revert to what they once were." Is Maria the one who has not yet gone back? This issue is never resolved, and in some ways it weakens the end of the film. It certainly weakens the character of Maria, who really seems to serve little purpose in the movie.

Even so, this is a strong film that goes beyond the

usual mad scientist flick about a guy who tampers with things man was not meant to know. Unlike Laughton's Moreau in the 1933 version, Lancaster's doctor does not seem to be a weirdo. In fact most of the time he seems sophisticated and charming, completely in control of himself and his environment. His tragic flaw is his belief that there is a fundamental difference between human beings and animals, but by his behavior he demonstrates that if such a difference exists, animals, who live without laws, are actually morally superior to humans. *The Island of Dr. Moreau* raises the possibility that by becoming civilized, we have abandoned the best in ourselves—hardly an original notion, but one addressed here effectively and with intelligence.

# ISLAND OF TERROR

1 9 6 6

**ALTERNATE TITLE:** *Night of the Silicates*
**DIRECTOR:** Terence Fisher
**PRODUCER:** Tom Blakely

**SCREENPLAY:** Edward Andrew Mann and Alan Ramsen
**CAST:** Peter Cushing, Edward Judd, Carole Gray, Eddie Byrne, Sam Kidd
**ORIGINAL RELEASE:** Planet Productions
**VIDEO:** Sinister Cinema

On an island off the east coast of Ireland, Dr. Philips and his crew of lab assistants are working on a cure for cancer, but something goes wrong. One night Constable Harris (Kidd) discovers the body of a local man near the grounds of the lab and reports to Dr. Landers (Byrne), the island physician, that as far as he can tell, "the body doesn't seem to have any bones."

I love movies that start like this!

Landers goes to the mainland to round up Drs. Brian Stanley (Cushing) and David West (Judd), who return to the island to investigate this strange death. Tagging along is West's socialite girlfriend, Toni (Gray)—they use her dad's private helicopter to get there—though what she's really doing in this movie is anybody's guess.

After doing an autopsy on the dead man, Stanley and West take off for Philips's lab, hoping he can shed some light on the situation. There they find more boneless

Dr. David West (Edward Judd) and Toni Merrill (Carole Gray) are lovers in peril on the *Island of Terror*.

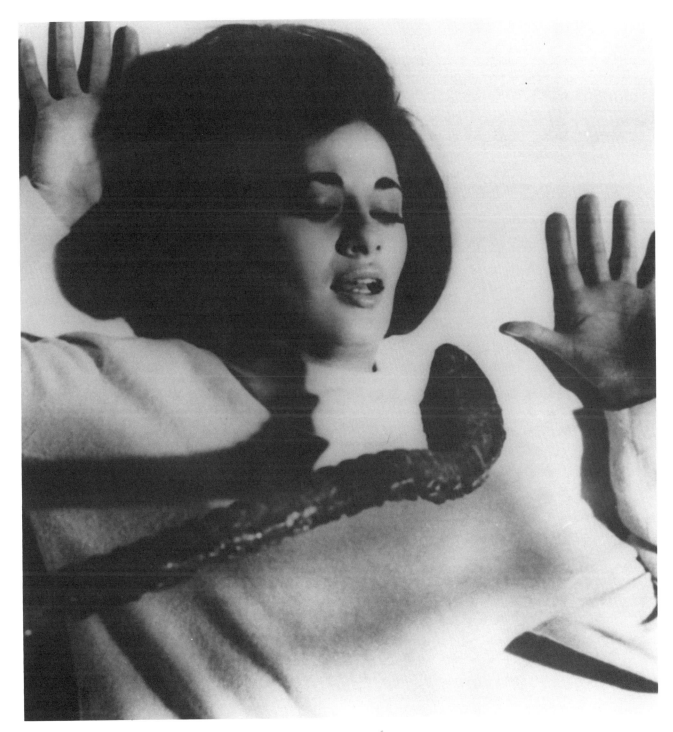

Toni is attacked by one of the silicates on the *Island of Terror*.

bodies. "Whatever it was," Stanley exclaims, "it must have started in this lab."

The doctors study Philips's notes and discover that their colleague was trying to create a new life-form designed to combat cancerous cells. Meanwhile, local horses and even Constable Harris turn up boneless, and when Landers, West, Stanley, and Toni return to the lab for another look-see, they encounter the monsters themselves—large turtle-like things with armored shells and long scary tentacles, one of which sucks the bones out of poor Landers. These are Philips's new life-forms. The monsters have a silicon rather than a carbon base—

Dr. Stanley (Peter Cushing) loses a hand to a silicate in one of the most striking scenes from *Island of Terror*.

Stanley calls them silicates—and they survive by draining the calcium out of living bodies. Even worse, they reproduce like single-cell animals, by dividing, and they divide every couple of hours. As David explains, "If the multiplication continues till the end of the week, there'll be about a million of them."

Needless to say, the islanders are on the verge of panic, but Stanley and West put together a hunting party and try guns, fire, and even dynamite to kill the things. Nothing seems to work. Then one of the things turns up dead. It seems that this one tried to suck the bones out of Philips's dog, which had received an accidental overdose of radiation. Since radioactivity seems to be the best weapon they have, West and Stanley decide to contaminate the local cattle and feed them to the silicates.

They need the isotopes from Philips's place to do the trick, but when they go back to the lab to get them, a silicate tentacle grabs Stanley's hand. In the most memorable scene of the movie, West chops Stanley's hand off with an ax and saves his colleague, who quips, with a stiff British upper lip, "I might have to sue you for malpractice."

The plan works. The silicates eat the cattle, then break into the town hall, where the people of the island are hiding out, and kill a few locals before dying from radiation poisoning. West breathes a sigh of relief and points out: "We were lucky this is an island. If it had happened anywhere else, I don't think we would have been able to destroy them."

Here, surprisingly, the scene shifts to a lab in Tokyo where scientists seem to be doing cancer research, too. A technician opens the door to the laboratory and enters. Then we hear his scream, followed by the closing credits. Apparently, Tokyo is in for it—again! And eventually, so is the rest of the world.

This is a very slick, very effective film, and it should be. Director Terence Fisher is a horror and sci-fi legend. Peter Cushing is, of course, Peter Cushing, one of Britain's finest character actors ever. Given the following that Fisher and Cushing have, it's amazing that *Island of Terror* is virtually unknown, and that's a shame, because it is certainly worthy of attention.

This is another scathing attack on science and a very disturbing movie. Of course science fiction films are supposed to shake us up a bit, but *Island of Terror* shakes us more than most. Perhaps it's because Dr. Philips and his crew of researchers are not mad scientists trying to create monsters or take over the world—we'd expect that to turn out badly. But these guys are trying to cure cancer! If a noble pursuit like that can result in the end of carbon-based life on this planet, then we really are in bad shape.

# IT! THE TERROR FROM BEYOND SPACE

1 9 5 8

**DIRECTOR:** Edward L. Cahn
**PRODUCER:** Robert E. Kent
**SCREENPLAY:** Jerome Bixby
**CAST:** Marshall Thompson, Shawn Smith, Kim Spalding, Ray "Crash" Corrigan, Ann Doran, Dabbs Greer
**ORIGINAL RELEASE:** Vogue Pictures
**VIDEO:** MGM/UA Home Video

It's the future—1973—and the space program isn't going at all well. Six months before, Colonel Edward Carruthers (Thompson), the first man ever to travel into

John Purdue (Robert Bice), Captain Van Huesen (Kim Spalding), Edward Carruthers (Marshall Thompson), and Dr. Eric Royce (Dabbs Greer) discuss what is to be done now that *It! The Terror From Beyond Space* is on board their ship on its return flight from Mars.

Mary Royce (Ann Doran) and Ann Anderson (Shawn Smith) study the body of their comrade Gino Finelli (Richard Hervey) while the other crew members search for the killer It! The Terror From Beyond Space.

outer space, crash-landed on Mars with his crew. Now he is the sole survivor, and a rescue ship is picking him up to take him back to Earth, where he is to stand trial for murdering his colleagues for their rations in the attempt to sustain his own life. Of course he says he didn't do it: "Those people were killed by something— not me." No one believes him, but we do, because as the rescue ship is about to take off for home, we see something enter an open air lock and come on board.

Flight commander Van Heusen (Spalding) has it in for Carruthers from the beginning, but geologist Ann Anderson (Smith) sort of wants to believe his story that he and his men were attacked during a sandstorm by a monster he never really saw. Meanwhile, on a lower level of the ship, something attacks and kills crewmen Keinholz and Gino Finelli, and when Van Heusen and the others search for their missing colleagues, they finally come face to face with It!—an enormous guy in an ill-fitting rubber monster suit (played by former cowboy and serial star Crash Corrigan).

The rest of the movie follows the crew's efforts to stay alive and to kill It! before It! kills them by sucking all the moisture out of their bodies. They try guns, grenades, poison gas, electricity, even radioactivity, but nothing seems to work. During one of the battles with It!, Van Heusen is wounded and contracts a virulent alien infection. Then John Purdue, one of the other crew members, gets it, too. Meanwhile, Bob Finelli, Gino's brother, is mauled to death, and soon It! has taken complete control of the ship except for the command center in the top level.

Eventually, just as the creature is tearing its way through the last hatch, Carruthers figures out that It! needs an enormous amount of oxygen to survive, so the remaining crew members get into their space suits and open one of the doors, thus draining the air out of the ship. It! dies in a matter of minutes. We never find out whether Van Heusen and Purdue recover from the alien bacteria or whether the rest of the crew members contract the infection, but for the moment anyway, everyone is safe, and Carruthers is in the clear.

If this sounds familiar, it should, because this is the plot of Ridley Scott's enormously successful *Alien*, made some twenty years later. The basic elements of both films are virtually identical, from the idea of a crew of humans being trapped on board their own ship with a monstrous, unstoppable creature to the final scene in which an air lock is popped open to destroy the thing. And both films use the visiting alien as a means of focusing attention on the relationships among the crew members—if anything, *It!* does this even better than *Alien* by setting up Carruthers, Van Heusen, and Ann Anderson in a triangle that becomes more and more complicated as the monster puts on the pressure.

I don't want to take anything away from *Alien*—it's a remarkable film. But within the limits of its obviously low budget, so is *It! The Terror From Beyond Space.* The cast is solidly professional, featuring Thompson (*First Man Into Space, Friend Without a Face*), Doran, Greer, and other fixtures of fifties B movies and televi-

*It! The Terror From Beyond Space* (Ray Corrigan) puts an end to crewman Bob Finelli (Richard Benedict).

123

In fact, this scene never happens in the movie *It! The Terror From Beyond Space* but it sure makes a snappy photo for fans of Ray Corrigan and Shawn Smith. (Courtesy Hollywood Book and Poster)

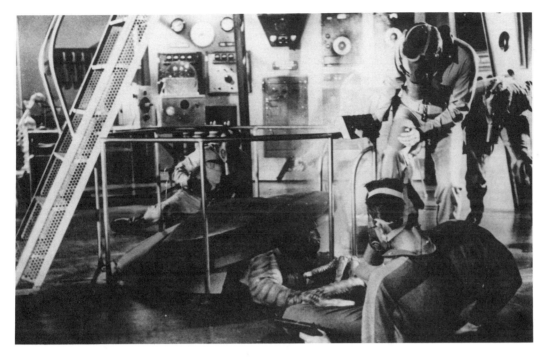

By letting the air out of their ship, the members of the crew finally manage to put an end to *It! The Terror From Beyond Space*.

sion, and the movie skillfully generates a feeling of claustrophobia that doesn't let up until the final scene.

*It!* is very much a sci-fi film of the 1950s, expressing a fear of anything or anyone who is different from us and urging us to stay with what we know and not venture too far into new territory. It's interesting that *Alien* was released in 1979, on the brink of the Reagan-Bush era, which in some ways marked an effort to return to a fifties sensibility, an effort that Ridley Scott's film reflects and also opens to question.

Of course *Alien* started a new wave of sci-fi/horror that is still with us. Fans of the genre who haven't seen *It! The Terror From Beyond Space* should check it out, if for no other reason than to trace the roots of today's films. And if you have seen it before, try it again. It's worth the time.

# JESSE JAMES MEETS FRANKENSTEIN'S DAUGHTER

1965

**DIRECTOR:** William Beaudine
**PRODUCER:** Carroll Case

**SCREENPLAY:** Carl H. Hittleman
**CAST:** John Lupton, Estelita, Cal Bolder, Narda Onyx, Steven Geray, Raymond Barnes, Jim Davis
**ORIGINAL RELEASE:** Embassy Pictures
**VIDEO:** Scorched Earth Productions

In fact, Jesse James does *not* meet the daughter of the original Baron Frankenstein in this movie. He meets the evil doctor's granddaughter, but the people who made this flick probably thought that *Jesse James Meets Frankenstein's Granddaughter* was a stupid title for a movie. In any case, Maria Frankenstein's father was obviously a Frankenstein, too, so the title holds true— she is the daughter of *a* Frankenstein, though not the daughter of *the* Frankenstein.

But enough bickering. On with the plot!

Villagers in Arizona are abandoning their homes and running away in terror, leaving behind only the Lopez family, who are looking for their son. Young Francisco has been working at the Frankenstein house, where other young villagers have died, supposedly of some sickness. Now Papa and Mama Lopez and daughter Juanita (Estelita) fear Francisco might be dead, too. "It's because of *them*," Juanita sobs.

She is talking about Maria Frankenstein (Onyx) and her brother Rudolph (Geray), who have come to the New World from Europe and taken over a local abandoned mission for their experiments. Maria has popped an artificial brain into Francisco's skull, and now she

Jesse James (John Lupton) and his big, stupid partner Hank Tracy (Cal Bolder) win a bet from one of the locals (Nestor Paiva) in the opening moments of *Jesse James Meets Frankenstein's Daughter.*

hopes to energize it and make the kid her slave, a slave who cannot die. Francisco is lying on an operating table, wearing a striped army helmet fitted with neon tubes, and Maria and Rudolph are arguing. Her brother doesn't agree with these experiments—"No one should tamper with the laws of God"—but Maria thinks he is a spineless wimp.

The experiment fails because unknown to Maria, Rudolph injects Francisco with poison instead of digitalis. But Ms. Frankenstein is not willing to give up. Apparently Grandpa made a number of artificial brains before he passed on, but now Maria is down to the last one, so she needs absolutely the right subject. "What we need is a man, a powerful man, a giant."

Meanwhile, Jesse James (Lupton, who starred in TV's *Broken Arrow*) and big, powerful, but dumb Hank Tracy (Bolder) arrive in Arizona to join the remnants of the Wild Bunch in a stagecoach robbery. But Lonny (Barnes), one of the gang members, decides it's safer to turn Jesse in and collect the reward, so he rats to Marshal McFee (Davis, who had a less-than-distinguished career in movies and TV, then gained international fame as Jock Ewing on *Dallas*).

Jesse and Juanita (Estelita) are an item in *Jesse James Meets Frankenstein's Daughter.*

Hank (Col Bolder), now transformed into a monster by the evil Ms. Frankenstein, kills her brother Rudolph (Steven Geray) in *Jesse James Meets Frankenstein's Daughter*.

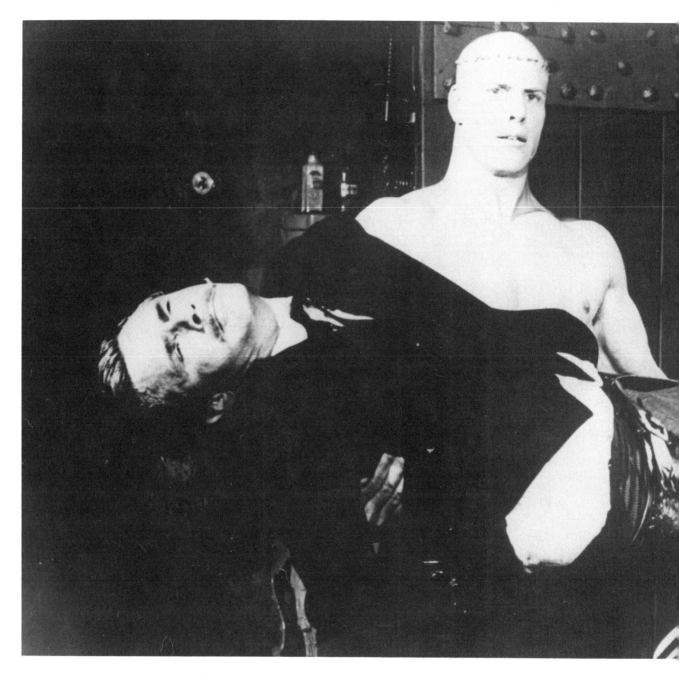

McFee sets an ambush, and though Jesse and his sidekick escape, Lonny manages to wound Hank badly. The two outlaws come upon the Lopez family, and Juanita says she will take them to doctors who can help. She leads them to the Frankenstein hacienda, where Maria is thrilled to meet them, especially gigantic Hank. "I intend to use him in my next experiment," she informs Rudolph.

The Frankensteins patch Hank up. By this time Juanita and Jesse are an item, though Hank really likes her, too. Maria also has her eye on Jesse, but she gets really angry when the outlaw rejects her for a Mexican peasant.

For revenge, Maria sends Jesse to town with an envelope that she says contains a prescription for Hank but which actually holds a note saying that the bearer is Jesse James.

While Jesse is gone, Maria and Rudolph put the artificial brain into Hank, then put the striped army helmet on his head. Maria wears another helmet so she can inject her brain waves into her new creation, and she informs him: "You are no longer Hank Tracy! You are Igor!" Apparently she thinks Hank is a stupid name for a monster.

Rudolph tries to put a stop to the experiment by way

Hank carries his former pal Jesse off to the operating room where *Jesse James Meets Frankenstein's Daughter*.

of a poison injection, but Maria catches him at it and orders Igor/Hank to kill her brother, which he does. Juanita witnesses the whole thing and runs to tell Jesse.

Jesse almost gets caught in town, but he manages to put an end to that dirty rat Lonny. When he realizes that Maria tried to turn him in, he heads back to the old mission. On the way he runs into Juanita, who fills him in on all that happened in his absence. Jesse rides on to help Hank while Juanita goes to McFee for assistance.

At the Frankenstein house, Igor clobbers Jesse and straps him to the operating table as Maria tells him: "I

In *Jesse James Meets Frankenstein's Daughter*, Maria Frankenstein (Narda Onyx) renames her creature Igor, which seems like a more appropriate name for a monster than Hank. (Courtesy Hollywood Book and Poster)

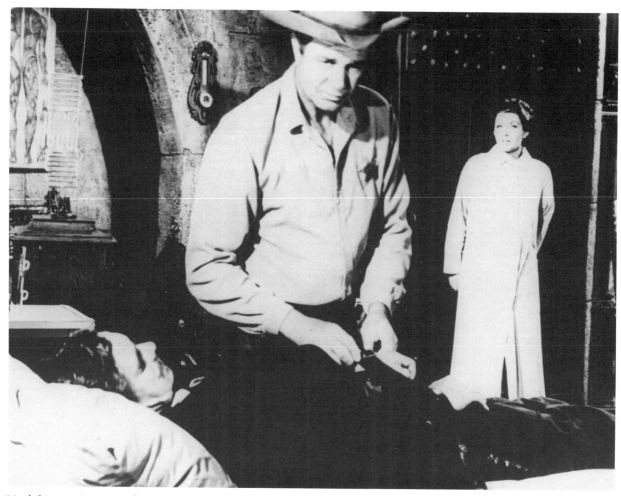

Marshal McFee (Jim Davis) discovers Jesse strapped to an operating table in the laboratory of Dr. Maria Frankenstein in the final moments of *Jesse James Meets Frankenstein's Daughter.*

will use you in my next experiment"—though it's hard to know what she has in mind, since she is now out of artificial brains. Juanita and McFee arrive, but Igor clobbers the lawman, too. Then Maria orders Igor to kill Juanita, but the creature hesitates. It seems that he remembers Juanita, though it's hard to see how this is possible, since Hank no longer has his old brain. Igor kills Maria instead, then attacks Jesse. Juanita is forced to shoot Igor and he dies—despite the fact that earlier in the movie, Maria assured us that Igor was immortal. Oh, well. In the end, Jesse goes off with McFee to pay his debt to society, and Juanita promises to wait for him, so true love triumphs over all.

If there is anything worse than a male mad scientist, it's a female mad scientist, particularly a lady doctor who can't get a guy on her own and so has to create one—and even then, her homemade boyfriend kills her. Well, maybe if Ms. Frankenstein hadn't been so uppity in the first place, if she hadn't insisted on getting all that education and trying to do something with her life,

she might have found the right guy eventually and lived happily ever after. At least she and Rudolph could have kept each other company and cultivated roses or something.

Obviously, *Jesse James Meets Frankenstein's Daughter* is not a great movie, and neither is its double-bill companion *Billy the Kid vs. Dracula,* but these films are distinguished by being the final efforts of director William Beaudine. Nicknamed "One Shot" because he didn't like to do second takes, Beaudine started directing in the silent era and was responsible for movies like *Federal Fugitives, The Panther's Claw, Phantom Killer, The Ape Man, Ghosts on the Loose, Voodoo Man, Black Market Babies, Bela Lugosi Meets a Brooklyn Gorilla, Lassie's Great Adventure,* a number of the Bowery Boys features, and dozens of others.

Some of Beaudine's film are quite good, many are terrible, but the important thing about his long career is that he was a solid professional who had the guts to make movies fast and cheap. So before you thoughtlessly write off a movie like *Jesse James Meets Frankenstein's Daughter*, remember that without people like Beaudine, there could have been no Roger Corman, no Herschell Gordon Lewis, no Russ Meyer, no William Castle—maybe no American film industry at all.

# JOURNEY TO THE CENTER OF TIME

1 9 6 7

**DIRECTOR:** David L. Hewitt
**PRODUCERS:** Ray Dorn and David L. Hewitt
**SCREENPLAY:** David Prentiss

**CAST:** Scott Brady, Anthony Eisley, Gigi Perreau, Abraham Sofaer, Poupee Gamin, Lyle Waggoner
**ORIGINAL RELEASE:** American General Pictures Corporation
**VIDEO:** Academy Home Entertainment and Genesis Home Video

Dr. Gordon (Sofaer), Mark Manning (Eisley), and Karen White (Perreau) have been working on a time machine that will show the past on a large TV screen, but after two years of research, they haven't been able to go back more than twenty-four hours. Meanwhile, their benefactor, Mr. Stanton, has died, and his son, Mr. Stanton, Jr. (Brady), wants to turn the facility over to weapons research unless our heroes can show him something really impressive.

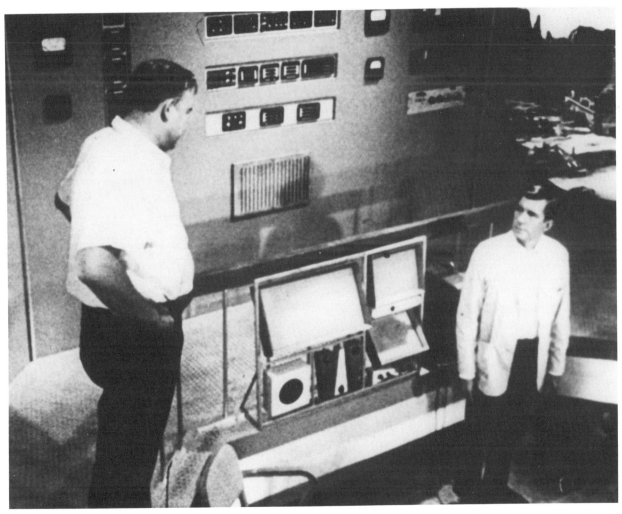

Stanton (Scott Brady), the evil industrialist, and Mark Manning (Anthony Eisley) in the time vault where they are to begin a *Journey to the Center of Time*.

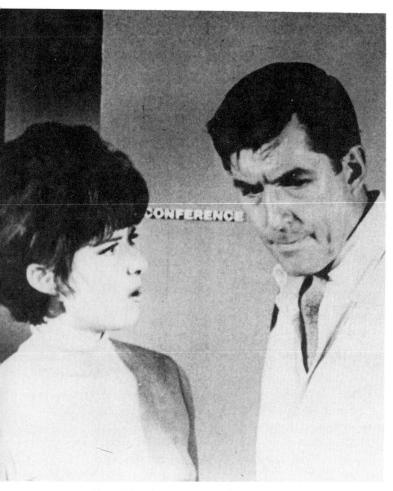

Karen White (Gigi Perreau) and Mark Manning are travelers who embark on a *Journey to the Center of Time*.

witness a lot of stock footage from movies about World War II, the Civil War, wagon trains, pirates, and Roman legions as they travel backward to 1,000,000 B.C.

Jerk that he is, Stanton leaves the time lab to look around; since he's been pretty much of a coward so far in the movie, this is out of character, but I guess the writer needed him to leave the lab to keep the plot moving along. Anyway, the others go after him and are attacked by stock-footage dinosaurs. Gordon falls to his

Stanton in a prehistoric world. He is soon to come to the end of his *Journey to the Center of Time*.

They do. During their demonstration, Mark turns the power up all the way, and the entire time lab is propelled 5,600 years into the future. The time travelers are captured by strange-looking people and taken to a nearby spaceship to meet Dr. Vina (Gamin), a large-breasted alien who explains that this is an exploration vessel from another world which has landed for repairs. The Earth has been destroyed by war, and the spaceship is under attack from Earthling survivors who want alien superweapons so they can continue fighting. During this little chat, the Earthlings break through the aliens' defenses. Vina is killed, and Stanton, Gordon, and the others run for it back to the time lab.

They try to get back to their own time, but on the way they find themselves on a collision course with someone who is also traveling in time in the opposite direction. Jerk that he is, Stanton uses a laser discharge to destroy the other time traveler. This discharge throws the time lab off course, and Gordon and the others death in a lava pit, and reverting to cowardice, Stanton panics, runs back to the time lab, and takes off for the future, leaving Mark and Karen behind.

On the way, though, he finds out that he is on a collision course with another time traveler. That's right, the traveler he zapped earlier in the flick was himself moving forward in time when he and the others were going backward. Stanton is laser-discharged out of existence, but somehow the time lab returns to 1,000,000

B.C.—how this happens is never explained—and Mark and Karen get on board. They return to their own time but arrive twenty-four hours before they left. Now they are unstuck in time, existing parallel to themselves in the present but at such an accelerated rate that they will age and die in a few minutes. So they hop back into the time lab and head off again for who knows where. "We may be the Adam and Eve of a brave new world," Mark says as they disappear into eternity.

In many ways, this movie is an unacknowledged remake of *The Time Travelers* from 1964, though it offers a few nice twists. For example, the idea that 5,600 years in the future, aliens on Earth will be the good guys and Earthlings will be the bad guys is interesting.

*Journey to the Center of Time* has problems, though. In good science fiction, no matter how outlandish the premise of a story might be, what follows from that premise must be presented logically. But the logic here is pretty murky, and though there's a lot of talk about lasers and photons and such, all the scientific chatter never really makes any sense.

Despite the problems and contradictions inherent in time travel, the idea is attractive, even as it is presented in the most mindless films and stories. As a kid waiting for the school bell to ring, waiting for summer vacation, waiting for Christmas, I realized that time was my enemy because it stood between me and what I wanted. Later on, I also realized that while I was waiting for what I wanted, time was killing me. Most of us feel the same way, I'm sure.

If time is the enemy, then we ought to be able to avoid it, possibly by traveling through it, skipping over the boring parts and looking at the future as it will be beyond our own life spans. Time travel seems as if it should be possible. After all, we're always traveling in time anyway but slowly, minute by minute. But if we can travel through time slowly, then why not quickly? And if we can travel in one direction, why not the other? In our memories and fantasies, we can move around in past and future time whenever we want to, recalling what life was like years ago, then imagining what it might be like years from now. If it's that easy to travel through time in our heads, shouldn't we be able to figure out some way to do the same thing in real life?

Unfortunately, time travel—at least as it's shown in novels and the movies—probably isn't possible, and that's too bad, because for me the idea of traveling in time is even more exciting than the prospect of traveling in outer space. I mean, going to Mars might be fun, but I'd really like to know what next week's winning lottery numbers are going to be.

# KILLERS FROM SPACE

1954

**DIRECTOR/PRODUCER:** W. Lee Wilder
**SCREENPLAY:** Bill Raynor
**CAST:** Peter Graves, Barbara Bestar, James Seay,
Frank Gerstle
**ORIGINAL RELEASE:** RKO
**VIDEO:** Rhino Home Video and Star Classics

This is what low-budget filmmaking is all about. Directed by Billy Wilder's brother, W. Lee (who also di-

rected *Phantom From Space*, among others), *Killers From Space* is 30 percent footage from other sources—stock atomic bomb tests, military and police scenes, nature documentaries, even segments lifted from William Cameron Menzies's classic *Things to Come* of 1936. It also repeats its own footage endlessly—you'll love watching star Peter Graves run through the same cave again and again and again.

Graves is Dr. Doug Martin, nuclear physicist, who disappears in a plane crash after an A-bomb test and shows up later with amnesia. After he tries to steal some atomic secrets, the military and the FBI fear he has turned commie, but when he is given truth serum, he tells of being kidnapped and hypnotized by aliens from the planet Astron Delta who are living in caverns beneath the test site at Soledad Flats, Nevada, and who are preparing to take over the Earth. Astron Delta must be a low-budget planet, because its inhabitants can only afford uniforms made up of sweatshirts with hoods, mittens, and the Ping-Pong ball eyes that have made

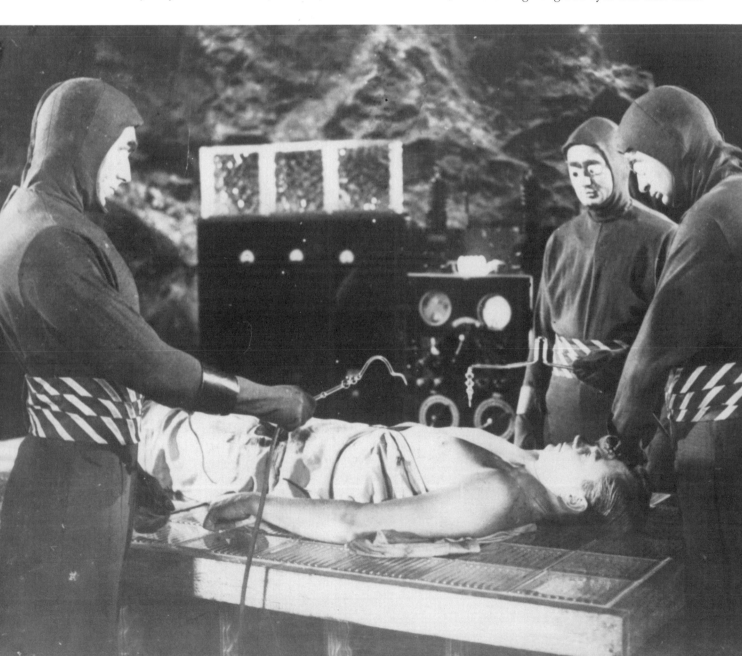

Deneb-Tala (John Merrick), one of the *Killers From Space*, shows Doug Martin around the alien installation.

Doug Martin on the run from the *Killers From Space*.

135

Bug-eyed aliens restore Doug Martin (Peter Graves) to life in their underground lair in *Killers From Space*.

*Killers From Space* famous ("Their eyes, those horrible eyes. . .").

The aliens have been accumulating energy from the A-bomb tests and using it to develop giant mutant creatures—spiders, cockroaches, lizards, grasshoppers, etc.—which they plan to turn loose on the Earth's population. They need more information about the next test, and they hypnotize Martin so they can force him to turn it over.

Nowadays with this story Dr. Martin could appear on the talk show of his choice, but amazingly, his coworkers don't believe him. He realizes, however, that the Astron Deltans are using electricity stolen from the local power plant to contain the tremendous energies they have been gathering. Martin shuts off power to the area for ten seconds, enough time to create an overload, which results in an atomic blast in the aliens' subterranean lair, finishing them off and saving the Earth.

The mixed message here is typical of 1950s pop culture. On the one hand, the atomic bomb is clearly a threat: Its power can be used against us. On the other hand, atomic power can also be used to destroy our enemies, so maybe it isn't really so bad after all. There were no easy answers to this dilemma in the postwar era, but even low-grade sci-fi/horror films like *Killers From Space* managed to pose the question with remarkable force.

# KINGDOM OF THE SPIDERS

## 1977

**DIRECTOR:** John "Bud" Cardos
**PRODUCERS:** Igo Kantor and Jeffrey M. Sneller
**SCREENPLAY:** Richard Robinson and Alan Caillou
**CAST:** William Shatner, Tiffany Bolling, Woody Strode, David McLean
**ORIGINAL RELEASE:** Dimensions Pictures
**VIDEO:** Goodtimes Home Video

Given the enormous popularity and influence of the *Star Trek* series, the movies, and the spin-offs, it's hard to remember that the original show was on for only three seasons back in the sixties. It's also hard to imagine William Shatner in any role other than the intrepid

James T. Kirk. In a way, that's too bad, because Shatner really is a versatile actor—see his pre-Kirk performance as Alyosha in *The Brothers Karamazov* of 1957, for example. In any case, *Kingdom of the Spiders* is fun, if only to see Shatner doing something a little different.

Veterinarian Rack Hansen (Shatner) of Verde Valley, an Arizona desert town, is baffled by the death of farmer Walter Colby's (Strode) prize calf. He sends some samples of the animal's blood to Arizona State University, and entomologist Diane Ashley (Bolling) shows up with the news that the calf was killed by a massive dose of tarantula venom.

Colby shows Dr. Ashley and Rack a gigantic spider hill on his property, home to thousands of the creepy crawlies. Obviously something is wrong. As Ashley explains, tarantulas usually don't attack in groups and aren't aggressive toward any creatures other than their usual insect prey. But these spiders are nasty, they attack in waves, and their venom is five times more toxic than normal. They manage to kill Colby's dog and his prize bull before he, Hansen, and Diane set fire to the hill and destroy them.

But the next day, twenty or thirty more hills appear on Colby's land. Verde Valley's mayor is upset. The county fair is coming up, and that means tourists and money for the town, as long as nothing goes wrong. Over Diane's objections, he orders a crop duster to spray the fields with insecticide, but the spiders get inside the plane and kill the pilot before the mass extermination can even begin.

In rapid succession, the tarantulas knock off Colby, his wife, Rack's widowed sister-in-law, and a bunch of other people in town. Bodies are discovered wrapped in cocoons—"That's how they store their food," says Diane. Eventually, Hansen and his little niece, Ashley, a couple of tourists, and Emma, the local innkeeper, take shelter in her lodge, where they try to fight off the zillions and zillions of spiders who are closing in on them. At the same time, in one of the best scenes in the film, a couple of zillion more spiders invade downtown Verde Valley and pretty much wipe the place out.

Back at the lodge, Hansen and the gang are fighting the beasties off as best they can. Rack gets attacked and badly bitten, but he survives, and come the dawn, all of the people in the lodge are still alive. But when they unboard the windows and look outside, they find that the inn and the entire town have been wrapped in a gigantic cocoon. It looks like the end for Verde Valley and maybe for all of humankind.

In 1963, just about the time that the big bug craze in movies was winding down, Alfred Hitchcock made *The Birds*, and the whole thing started all over again. *Kingdom of the Spiders* owes a lot to Hitchcock's classic,

Walter Colby (Woody Strode) and his wife survey their farm, which has become the *Kingdom of the Spiders*.

Rack Hansen (William Shatner), Dr. Diane Ashley (Tiffany Bolling), and other guests in Emma Washburn's (Lieux Dressler) inn huddle together against the tarantula invasion in *Kingdom of the Spiders*.

137

Some of the destruction caused by the mutant tarantulas in *Kingdom of the Spiders*.

but it owes more to *Jaws* of 1975—you might say it's sort of a *Jaws* of the desert, with lots of spider-point-of-view shots, a money-hungry mayor, and other borrowings from the Spielberg blockbuster.

Bud Cardos has a knack for making his directorial efforts look like made-for-TV movies even when they're not. There just isn't a lot of imagination here. Even so, thanks to performances that make you really care about the characters, the movie is a convincing and scary ecological disaster flick.

The disaster here is the overuse of insecticides. As Dr. Ashley explains, "Through the excessive use of insecticides like DDT, we are inadvertently killing off the spider's natural source of food." Which means that we're next. The message is not new, but it's effective.

And so are the spiders. There are literally hundreds of them gathered together by spider wrangler Lou Schumacher—what some people won't do for a living! They are big and fuzzy and ugly, and the actors seem to be genuinely grossed out to have these monsters crawling all over them.

I would be, too.

# THE LAST MAN ON EARTH

1964

**ALTERNATE TITLE:** *L'Ultimo Uomo della Terra*
**DIRECTOR:** Sidney Salkow
**PRODUCER:** Robert L. Lippert
**SCREENPLAY:** Logan Swanson and William P. Leicester
**CAST:** Vincent Price, Franca Bettoia, Emma Danieli, Giacomo Rossi-Stuart
**ORIGINAL RELEASE:** Associated Producers and La Regina
**VIDEO:** Scorched Earth Productions

Based on Richard Matheson's novel *I Am Legend* and remade in 1971 as the heavy-handed *Omega Man,* this Italian production starring Vincent Price—a legend in his own right—is supposedly one of the sources for George Romero's *Night of the Living Dead,* a film that would change the history of horror and science fiction movies forever.

stakes through the hearts of anyone he finds. Morgan returns to his home fortress by dark, and *they* come, pounding on the door and calling out to him by name.

*They* are the living dead, and it seems that Morgan is the only person in the world who is not one of them. In a flashback, we learn that Morgan and his friend Ben Cortland (Rossi-Stuart) were once scientists in a research lab, working on a cure for a plague that was devastating Europe. Ben feared the disease would soon infect everyone on Earth, and he also believed the rumors that those who had died of the plague were coming back from the dead. Morgan, always the hardheaded scientist, refused to consider such notions.

Eventually, though, people in the city began to die by the thousands, including Morgan's own daughter and wife, Virginia (Danieli). By law, the dead are to be burned, but Morgan buries his wife instead. That night she returns to their home for him in a scene that is really terrifying.

Plague victims are like vampires—they drink the blood of the living, they can't stand the light, they are

Robert Morgan (Vincent Price) is a vampire hunter and perhaps *The Last Man on Earth*.

The year is 1965—the near future, given that *The Last Man on Earth* was released in 1964—and the world has been destroyed. Cities are littered with dead bodies and debris, and it seems that only one man, Robert Morgan (Price), is still alive.

The film begins with a typical day in Morgan's life. He lives in a boarded-up house with his own generator, and garlic and mirrors hang on all the doors and windows. Morgan spends his morning turning out wooden stakes on a lathe, then heads off in his station wagon to get gasoline, dump some dead bodies in an enormous firey pit on the outskirts of the city, and pick up some provisions at a local abandoned grocery store. He then moves through the city from house to house, driving

Morgan delivers another dead plague victim to the pit in *The Last Man on Earth*.

repelled by garlic, and though they can see their reflections in mirrors, they can't stand the sight of their own faces. Stakes through the heart kill them permanently. Morgan has made it his personal mission to search the city and destroy all of them, especially their leader, the now-dead Ben Cortland.

Back in the present, Morgan finds a dog and takes it in, but when a blood test shows that it is infected, he kills and buries it. Then he sees a living woman who runs from him. He chases her and convinces her to return to his home before dark. Her name is Ruth Collins (Bettoia), and she seems well, but when he thrusts garlic into her face, she becomes sick. "You are infected," he exclaims.

Ruth explains that she is a member of a new society of people who are all infected but still alive. To this new order, Robert Morgan is a figure of legendary evil, even worse than the living dead who prey on them. "You're a monster to them," she says. "Many of the people you destroyed were still alive." For their own protection, her people are on their way to kill him.

Robert tells Ruth that he is immune to the disease, though he has never figured out exactly why. Still, he tries an experiment and manages to cure her with his own blood. Realizing that Robert is their salvation, Ruth goes out to stop her people, but Ben attacks and bites her, infecting her again. Ruth's friends arrive and chase Robert to a nearby church, where they shoot him. With his dying breath, he shouts, "Freaks, all of you! I'm a man. The last man."

At first glance, the ending seems to suggest that humankind is doomed after the people of the new society murder the only person who can help them—which is the kind of thing we humans have been prone to do over the years. There is another way to read the end of the movie, however.

Morgan is a tragic figure who suffers from the sin of pride. All along, he assumes that he knows exactly what is going on, though in fact he doesn't. He also assumes that his definition of what it means to be human is the only possible one, and for him, to be human is to be completely free of the disease. By this definition, he is

The vampire people try to invade the fortified home of Robert Morgan in *The Last Man on Earth*. (Courtesy Hollywood Book and Poster)

Morgan gives Ruth (Franca Bettoia) the garlic test to see whether she is infected by the vampire plague in *The Last Man on Earth*.

*The Last Man on Earth* is killed by plague victims in an abandoned church.

the only real human being left on Earth—his willingness to drive a stake through anything that moves and his final words seem to show that this is what he believes. But perhaps he is wrong there, too. Perhaps Ruth and her people—infected but alive—are the future of hu-

mankind, and Morgan is the obsolete past. They have, after all, formed a new community, while Morgan is merely a hermit, an outsider, and a danger. Perhaps there simply is no place for him in this new world, and his death is not the end of humankind but the beginning of something else.

No matter how you decide to read it, *The Last Man on Earth* is a remarkably effective and intelligent film and well worth a look.

# THE LAST WOMAN ON EARTH

1960

**DIRECTOR/PRODUCER:** Roger Corman
**SCREENPLAY:** Robert Towne
**CAST:** Antony Carbone, Betsy Jones-Moreland, Edward Wain
**ORIGINAL RELEASE:** Filmgroup
**VIDEO:** Sinister Cinema

Question: Is Roger Corman a schlockmeister or a genius?

Answer: Both.

As director and producer, Corman is responsible for some of the worst movies ever released—*Monster From the Ocean Floor, Voyage to the Prehistoric Planet,* and *Teenage Caveman,* to name only a few. He is also responsible for some classic films—the original *Little Shop of Horrors, Bucket of Blood,* and more recently, *Frankenstein Unbound.* In addition, the list of actors and directors who owe their careers to him is a long one—Jack Nicholson, Bruce Dern, Francis Ford Coppola, Peter Bogdanovich, to name but a few.

*The Last Woman on Earth* is not a classic, but I think it's an impressive movie, given that it was thrown together in Puerto Rico on a budget of about $1.98. Soon after finishing *Little Shop of Horrors,* Corman took a cast and crew to Puerto Rico to make three quickies in about as many weeks—*Battle of Blood Island, The Last Woman on Earth,* and *Creature From the Haunted Sea.* Robert Towne, who later went on to win an Academy Award for his *Chinatown* screenplay, didn't have the script to *Last Woman* finished when it was time to leave. Corman needed to take him along

Harold (Anthony Carbone), his wife Evelyn (Betsy Jones-Moreland), and Martin (Edward Wain/ Robert Towne) may be the only survivors of a global disaster in Roger Corman's *The Last Woman on Earth*.

Evelyn, *The Last Woman on Earth*, comes on to Martin, who is now one of the best-looking guys in the world.

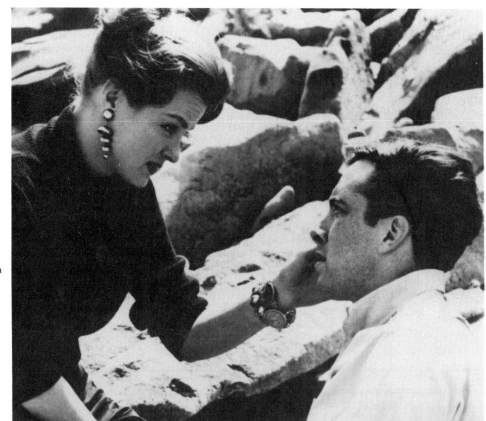

Harold does not appreciate the fact that Martin has taken up with his wife, who is, after all, *The Last Woman on Earth*.

to complete the writing but couldn't afford it unless Towne agreed to double as an actor. He appears in *Last Woman* and in *Creature From the Haunted Sea* under the name Edward Wain, and he does a fine job.

Harold Gern (Carbone) is a wheeler-dealer business-man who operates just this side of the law, and when he crosses the line and gets himself indicted, which happens from time to time, his hotshot lawyer Martin (Wain/Towne) is there to bail him out. Gern, his wife, Evelyn (Jones-Moreland), and Martin are in Puerto Rico to live it up, but only Harold seems to be having a good time. Martin is too cynical to enjoy anything; when Evelyn asks him, "What do you believe in?" he answers, "Nothing, Ev. I'm too civilized." Ev drinks too much and puts herself down for being married to Harold: "I've so little to say and no one to listen."

The three go scuba diving one afternoon, and when they come out of the water, they find they can't breathe, so they put their tanks and masks back on and make their way to shore. Everyone there is dead. "Something took the oxygen out of the air," Martin speculates, though we never find out whether this was caused by a natural disaster or man-made devices. In any case, the lush vegetation on the island restores the oxygen, and Harold, Martin, and Ev can breathe again, but they are, it seems, the only ones left in Puerto Rico and perhaps in the whole world.

They gather food and go to an isolated house to avoid the stench of rotting corpses in the city. Once there, Harold plans how they will survive and eventually make their way north in search of others who might still be alive. Martin and Ev, on the other hand, spend their time moping around, and the lawyer makes fun of his client for believing that anything means anything in the new world.

Eventually, while Harold fishes for food, Martin and Ev make love on the beach and decide to run away together, taking the boat and leaving Harold on his own. Theirs is not a love made in heaven, however. Ev wants children, but Martin doesn't see the point. "All that's left for us," he says, "is to live without pain."

In any case, they make a break for it, but Harold catches up with them, hits Martin in the head with a rock, and takes his wife back. The lawyer goes blind and then dies from his injury, leaving Harold to realize that, even in the new world, people are still killing each other. Now he and Ev must make a life for themselves together whether they want to or not.

145

This is a powerful film because none of the characters is right or wrong. Ironically, the drive that makes Harold a crook and a hustler is also the force that keeps him going after the disaster: "Somebody's gotta take responsibility," he says. On the other hand, the thing that makes Martin a good lawyer—his absolute lack of faith in human beings—is what makes him give up later on. Ev, of course, has no confidence or self-esteem, and so when she decides to turn away from Harold, she can't think of anything else to do but turn to another man who can do no more for her than her husband could. You can understand why these people do what they do, whether you approve or not, and these characters make you wonder what you would do in their situation.

Virtually every end-of-the- world movie from the fifties and sixties asks the same question: In the event of a global holocaust, would it be better to survive or not? And virtually every such film answers that survival is better. *Last Woman on Earth* raises the question, too, but it doesn't answer it. That is left up to us.

# LIFEFORCE

1 9 8 5

**DIRECTOR:** Tobe Hooper
**PRODUCERS:** Menahem Golan and Yoram Globus
**SCREENPLAY:** Dan O'Bannon and Don Jakoby

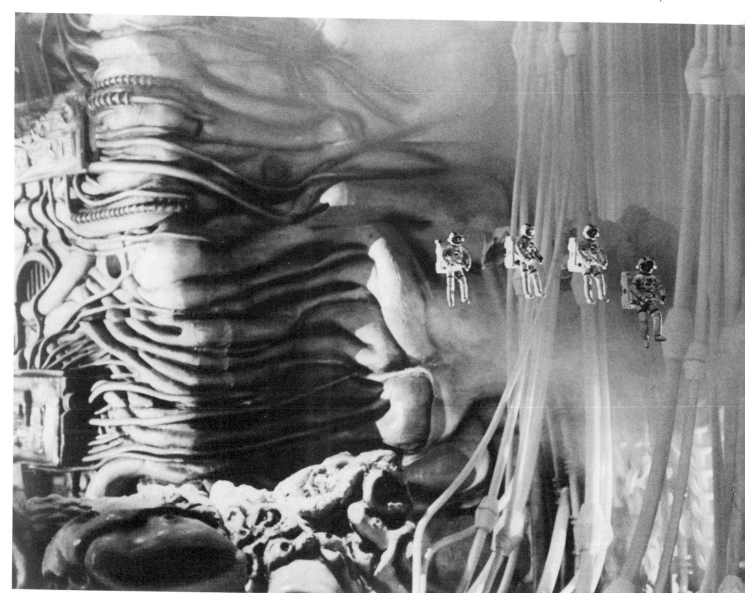

Crew members from the space shuttle Churchill explore the interior of an alien vessel in *Lifeforce*. (Courtesy Hollywood Book and Poster)

The alien umbrella ship sucks up human souls from Earth in Tobe Hooper's *Lifeforce*. (Courtesy Hollywood Book and Poster)

**CAST:** Steve Railsback, Peter Firth, Frank Finlay, Mathilda May, Patrick Stewart, Michael Gothard
**ORIGINAL RELEASE:** TriStar Pictures
**VIDEO:** Family Home Entertainment, Live Home Video, and Vestron Video

A decade after the release of his classic *Texas Chainsaw Massacre* and with *Poltergeist* under his belt, director Tobe Hooper was ready for something different. *Lifeforce* was just the ticket. This classy, effective sci-fi film has everything going for it—fine performances, striking special effects, an intelligent story, and for you Trekkies out there, an early appearance by Patrick Stewart of *Star Trek: The Next Generation* in a small part as the head of a mental institute.

On a joint U.S.-British venture to study Halley's comet, the space shuttle Churchill discovers an enormous alien ship full of dead, human-sized bat creatures and three perfect human beings—two male and one female (May)—encased in transparent capsules and seemingly in a state of suspended animation. The explorers take the three humans back to the Churchill with

the intention of carrying them to Earth. Then quite suddenly, all contact with the shuttle is lost.

Another shuttle goes on a rescue mission and finds the Churchill drifting in space, gutted by fire. All aboard have been burned to death, except for the three from the alien craft, who are still intact in their capsules.

The three are taken to the Space Research Center in London, where Dr. Bukovsky (Gothard), Professor Fallada (Finlay), and secret service officer Colin Caine (Firth) try to figure out who they are and how they happened to be aboard an alien ship. Then one night the woman awakens, kills a guard by draining the life force right out of him, and strolls away, stark naked, into the streets of London.

Shortly thereafter, the two males awaken, too, but they are apparently blown to bits when they try to escape. Meanwhile, the desiccated body of the dead guard comes back to life during his own autopsy, drains the energy out of the attending physician, and seems to be okay. Two hours later, though, now in a holding cell, he needs to feed again, and so does his victim, the doctor who performed the autopsy. It seems that the visitors from space have brought with them a virulent, deadly disease, and one of them—the female—is engaged in

147

spreading it all over London. As Fallada puts it, "Within days, we could all be doomed."

Back in the States, the Churchill's escape pod comes down in Texas, bearing Colonel Tom Carlsen (Railsback), commander of the ill-fated shuttle mission and still alive and well. He hurries to London, where he tells Fallada and the others that what has been happening at the research center happened on board the Churchill as well, until only he was left to burn the ship and escape. Carlsen knows that the space woman is a monster—one of the bat-creatures from the alien ship who can assume any form they wish—but he is obsessed with her. "I feel as if my mind is not entirely my own," he says. In fact he seems to be in telepathic contact with her, and even though she disguises herself by moving from body to body, he is able to help Caine and the others track her down and hold her prisoner for a while.

Unity (Suzanna Leigh) is threatened by a huge tentacle that belongs to one of the many weird inhabitants of *The Lost Continent*. (Courtesy Hollywood Book and Poster)

Unfortunately, the two male space creatures did not die in the research center—they too simply moved to other bodies. They have been out spreading the disease as well, and soon London is the scene of mass destruction and murder, with the infected infecting others, who infect others in turn. Fallada explains: "It is my belief that the vampire of legend came from creatures such as these," and Carlsen agrees. "They've visited Earth before," he says.

The alien ship arrives over London and begins to gather the souls of the dead that drift up to it in a funnel of blue light. This life energy is what the aliens live on, and though eventually the two males and the female are killed—impaled not on wooden stakes but on a lead sword—London is in shambles, the killing and destruction still goes on, and the ship moves off with the promise that it will return someday.

Most alien invasion movies end with the invaders being driven off forever or wiped out, thus proving once again that Earthlings are really the finest and coolest creatures in the universe. *Lifeforce* has the courage to suggest that there might be beings out there who are so superior to us that they feed upon Earthlings like we feed upon hamburgers and fries and that there is virtually nothing we can do to keep this from happening again and again. That's an unpleasant thought, but one worth thinking whenever we Earthlings start believing that we know it all and that the entire universe revolves around us.

# THE LOST CONTINENT

1968

**DIRECTOR/PRODUCER:** Michael Carreras
**SCREENPLAY:** Michael Nash
**CAST:** Eric Porter, Hildegard Knef, Suzanna Leigh, Tony Beckley, Nigel Stock, Neil McCallum, Benito Carruthers, Jimmy Hanley, James Cossins, Dana Gillespie
**ORIGINAL RELEASE:** Hammer Productions
**VIDEO:** Fox Home Video

To my knowledge, there are at least two *Lost Continent*s. One movie was released in 1951 and stars Cesar Romero, a mediocre Latin lover type who proved himself to be a comic genius when he landed the part of the Joker in the 1960s *Batman* TV series. The flick also features Hugh Beaumont (the father on *Leave It to Beaver*) and Whit Bissell, who appeared in virtually every movie made in the fifties. This is one of those twentieth-century-guys-discover-land-of-dinosaurs movies, and though it cops a lot of special effects footage from the silent version of *The Lost World*, it isn't too bad.

*The Lost Continent* of 1968 is very different. In fact it's so different, it's downright wacky, though everybody involved plays it with a straight face. But I wonder what they were thinking as they made this movie.

Captain Lansen (Porter) is taking his ship, complete with crew and some passengers, to Venezuela, secretly carrying a huge cargo of explosives that will go off if they get wet. All of the passengers seem to have something to hide, too. For instance, Eva (Knef) has stolen two million dollars and is skipping the country with it. Ricaldi (Carruthers), Dr. Webster (Stock), his daughter, Unity (Leigh), Harry Tyler (Beckley), and all the others seem

The Inquisitor (Eddie Powell) and his evil followers roam around on the seaweed surface of *The Lost Continent* using homemade snowshoes and helium-filled balloons. (Courtesy Hollywood Book and Poster)

149

Poor Pat (Jimmy Hanley) gets his at the hands (?) of a giant crab on *The Lost Continent*. (Courtesy Hollywood Book and Poster)

pretty shady, too—otherwise why would they be headed for South America aboard this broken-down tub?

The ship springs a leak—not good, given what's down in the hold—and the crew members mutiny and take to the lifeboats, leaving the captain, the passengers, and a few of the crew behind. Then a hurricane hits, and the rest abandon ship, too, taking the remaining lifeboat.

Now the adventure becomes hot and heavy. Dr. Webster is eaten by a shark, and a crew member is devoured by living seaweed. Amazingly, they come upon their own ship again—yes, somehow it managed to stay afloat and not explode, even with no one on it. They climb back on board and discover that the living seaweed is pulling them into the Sargasso Sea.

Now a giant tentacled thing grabs Unity, but when Ricaldi comes to her rescue, he is the one who gets carried off. At last the ship arrives in a kind of oceanic graveyard near a small island where ships from all eras are hopelessly trapped. A woman named Sarah (Gillespie) comes walking toward them across the seaweed, wearing homemade snowshoes and being supported by helium-filled weather balloons attached to her shoulders to keep her from sinking—you really have to see this to believe it. She warns them that the bad guys are coming, and sure enough, they do. Lansen's ship is attacked by a group of guys in pirate and conquistador costumes, all wearing snowshoes and balloons. The good guys manage to drive them off and even to take one prisoner.

The scene changes to the conquistadors' ship, where we meet the boy king, El Supremo, and his companion, the Grand Inquisitor. It seems that these people are the descendants of the original conquistadors who became mired in the seaweed centuries before and who have been living, reproducing themselves, and maintaining their culture on board their ships ever since. Sarah's people are the descendants of peaceful settlers who also became stuck and who for generations have been the slaves of the conquistadors. The pirates work for the Spaniards, too, and everybody wears clothes from his or her own era and cultural group—clothes that apparently have been holding up remarkably well for hundreds of years. It is never explained how these isolated folks of another time learned about helium balloons.

Anyway, Lansen and Eva are an item by now, and Harry and Sarah are hitting it off. Then for no particular reason, Sarah leaves the safety of Lansen's ship, and Harry and a couple of crew members go after her. They find her, but all of them become lost in the fog and end up on the island, where Pat (Hanley), the bartender from the ship, is killed by a giant crustacean, which then battles an enormous scorpion. Talk about excitement!

The bad guys capture Harry and Sarah and take them to El Supremo, who is really just a stupid kid who has been told by the Inquisitor that he is a god. Lansen and the others arrive to save Harry and Sarah and invite the conquistadors to join them in an effort to get free of the seaweed. El Supremo decides he'd like to get out of there, too, so the Inquisitor kills the kid; then Lansen kills the Inquisitor.

Now everything is okay. Apparently it was the Inquisitor and his band of hoodlum monks who were keeping everyone stuck in the past for their own evil purposes, though we never find out what those evil purposes might have been. The conquistadors' ship catches fire and blows up, and Lansen uses his explosives at last to burn the seaweed—apparently, in all those centuries it never occurred to anyone to try to set fire to the stuff. In the end, all the various prisoners of the Sargasso Sea are pals and can leave together.

Maybe when I said before that this movie is wacky, I wasn't doing it justice. Maybe I should have said that

Sarah (Dana Gillespie) doesn't have much of a part in *The Lost Continent*, but for some unknown reason, the advertising people use her a lot in the publicity shots for the film. (Courtesy Hollywood Book and Poster)

it is downright insane. It's hard to know what the people who made this flick might have had in mind. When you watch it, you get the feeling that they were just making it up as they went along, adding more and more stuff until they had about ninety minutes' worth of footage. Fans of science fiction and horror have come to expect more from a Hammer production.

Even so, *The Lost Continent* is worth seeing, if only to catch those scenes that feature groups of people walking across an ocean of seaweed on snowshoes and balloons. Such moments are certainly unique in the annals of cinema.

# THE MAN WHO TURNED TO STONE

1956

**DIRECTOR:** Leslie Kardos
**PRODUCER:** Sam Katzman
**SCREENPLAY:** Raymond T. Marcus
**CAST:** Victor Jory, Ann Doran, Charlotte Austin, William Hudson, Paul Cavanagh, Jean Willes, Frederick Ledebur
**ORIGINAL RELEASE:** Columbia Pictures
**VIDEO:** Goodtimes Home Video

I get a kick out of mixed genre films—you know, the ones that try to appeal to two different audiences at the same time by taking two different subjects or themes and trying to put them together in the same flick. *Billy the Kid vs. Dracula* is a good example—a Western/horror film. Or how about sci-fi/sword-and-sandal, as in *Hercules Against the Moon Men?* All kinds of combinations are possible, but to the best of my knowledge, *The Man Who Turned to Stone* is the only example of a women-in-prison/science fiction film.

It's not easy to understand the appeal of women-in-prison films such as *Caged Heat, Ten Violent Women, Sweet Sugar, Women in Cell Block 9,* and *Girls in Prison,* but the genre has been around for a long time. Perhaps the women-in-prison movie is an expression of a traditional cultural attitude that women ought to be confined, kept out of the mainstream of life. Usually this has meant that women are to be kept in the home, as a man's property, the way a guy might keep his car in the garage. Prison, in the films we're talking about, is only the logical extension of that confinement. Of course, in our time this attitude is changing rapidly as women find their own places out in the real world, but the continued popularity of the women-in-prison flick might suggest that these archaic notions are not yet dead and gone.

In any case, the usual women-in-prison film has a stock set of characters: the tough gal with a heart of gold, the tough gal whose heart is not necessarily of gold but who comes through in a pinch, the new kid, the person who works in some official capacity and who is really trying to help the inmates, and of course the evil authorities who run the institution. *The Man Who Turned to Stone* has all of these, but because this is a sci-fi film, too, the evil authorities who run the prison are also evil scientists.

Women at the LaSalle Detention Home for Girls have been dying under mysterious circumstances for the past two years, and the inmates are often disturbed by screams in the night. But hey, who cares what happens to jailbirds, right? Carol Adams (Austin) cares. She is a social worker who is serious about helping those in her charge. So when Tracy, a good-hearted long-timer, tells Carol about the suspicious number of "heart attacks" that have struck inmates in recent years, she tries to investigate, though she is blocked at every turn by Dr. Murdock (Jory) and his assistants.

Murdock, Mrs. Ford (Doran), and the others head up the prison and are, needless to say, really bad guys. They are all scientists, and as it turns out, all of them are over two hundred years old. Back in the 1700s, they discovered a way to renew human life by transferring life energy from one person to another. Unfortunately, every time one of the scientists has to recharge, the "donor" of life energy dies. Experience has shown that the best donors are women in their child-bearing years. This is why Murdock and the gang have set up their lab in a women's prison, though how they ever managed to secure executive positions with the state penal authority is anybody's guess.

The bad news for Murdock and the others is that if they go too long without recharging, their skin becomes as hard as stone, their heart starts thumping wildly, and they die. This happens to a couple of them during the film, and the thump! sound they make when they hit the floor is really impressive. There's more bad news, too. One of their number, Eric (Ledebur)—a hulking idiot whose brain was damaged in their first experiment, though they've kept him alive for a couple of centuries anyway—is no longer responding to the recharging treatments. "We'll all end up like that," Dr. Cooper (Cavanaugh) warns, and it does seem that time is running out.

The demented Eric (Frederick Ledebur) kidnaps one of the inmates of the LaSalle Detention Home for Girls in *The Man Who Turned to Stone*. (Courtesy Hollywood Book and Poster)

Tracy (Jean Willes) smashes a glass pitcher into the face of Eric, but this doesn't bother him, since he is *The Man Who Turned to Stone*. (Courtesy Hollywood Book and Poster)

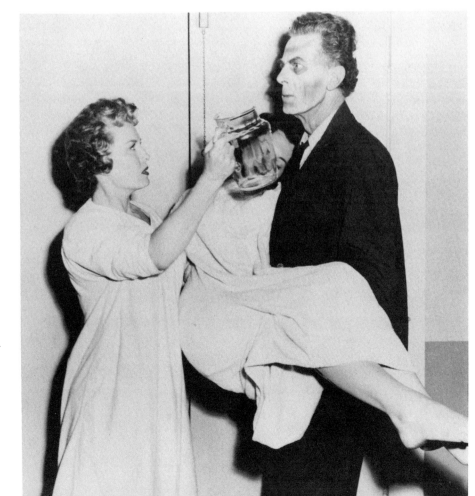

After the "suicide" of one of the new inmates, Dr. Jesse Rogers (Hudson), a psychiatrist with the State Department of Corrections, comes on board to help Carol figure out what's up, and eventually he uncovers the whole story. Murdock and the others try to kill Rogers and Carol several times, but in the end the bad guys die in a fire that burns their lab to the ground, and now things will be better for the inmates at LaSalle.

The amazing thing is that it takes Rogers so long to figure out what's going on. Though they seem to be brilliant scientists, Murdock and the others are constantly making stupid mistakes, saying things like "I bought that painting in 1850—oh, I mean 1950." On top of that, all of them wear eighteenth-century clothes. Wouldn't that make you suspicious? And where do they get these clothes anyway? Have they had them for two hundred years? Or is there a local shop that caters to eighteenth-century tastes?

Well, this one won't spark your intellect, but you might want to include it, along with *Cat-Women of the Moon,* in your next Victor Jory Film Festival.

# THE MANSTER

1959

**ALTERNATE TITLE:** *The Split*
**DIRECTOR:** George P. Breakston and Kenneth G. Crane
**PRODUCER:** George P. Breakston
**SCREENPLAY:** Walter J. Sheldon

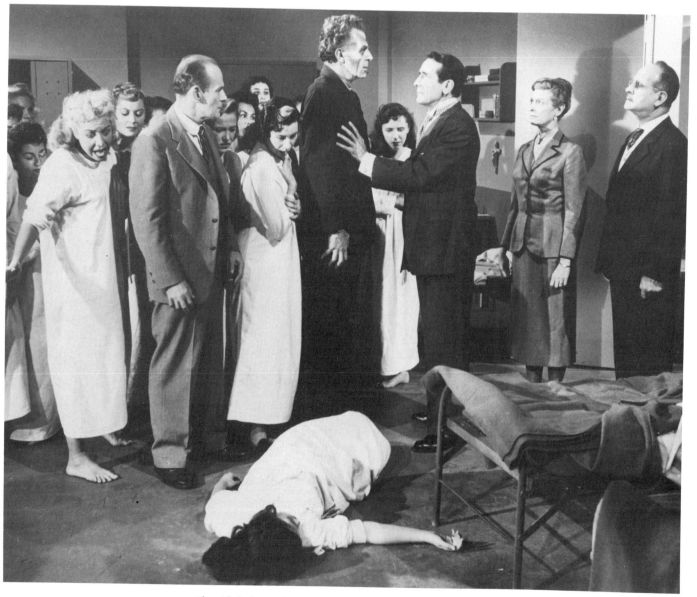

The girls look on in horror as Dr. Murdock (Victor Jory) and his colleagues try to subdue their wayward associate, Eric, in *The Man Who Turned to Stone.* (Courtesy Hollywood Book and Poster)

Ian Matthews (Norman Van Hawley) tries to comfort Linda Stanford (Jane Hylton) as her husband, Larry (Peter Dyneley), walks out with his new love, Tara (Terri Zimmer), in the Japanese-American production *The Manster*.

**CAST:** Peter Dyneley, Jane Hylton, Satoshi Nakamura, Terri Zimmern
**ORIGINAL RELEASE:** United Artists of Japan/ George Breakston Enterprises
**VIDEO:** Al Taylor/Waltersheid Productions and Sinister Cinema

This weird production was made in Japan in English, using American and Japanese cast members, and despite the appalling title, it isn't really as bad a film as you might think.

Dr. Robert Suzuki (Nakamura) is a scientist who works in his mountain lab near a volcano and who is having a bit of trouble with his most recent experiment. Somehow, he has managed to turn his brother Kenji into a hairy apelike creature who has been slaughtering

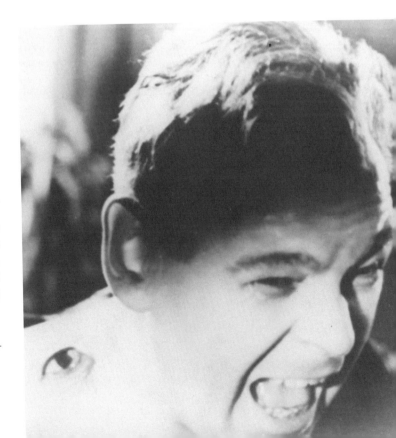

One of the truly great scenes in the annals of cult sci-fi movies— hapless Larry discovers an eye growing out of his shoulder and realizes he is well on his way to becoming *The Manster*.

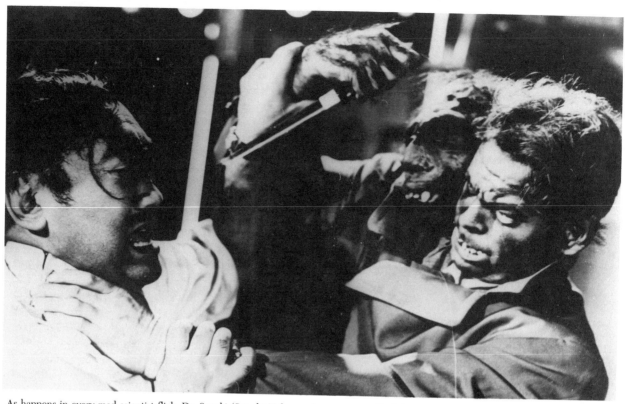

As happens in every mad scientist flick, Dr. Suzuki (Satoshi Nakamura) must eventually duke it out with his own creation, in this case, two-headed Larry Stanford, *The Manster.*

some of the village girls. "You're an experiment that didn't work out," Suzuki tells Kenji just before he shoots him. Like any good mad scientist, Suzuki also has a cage in his lab where he keeps another failed experiment, his wife, Emiko, who is now a very unattractive monster.

The stage is set for the arrival of happy-go-lucky foreign correspondent Larry Stanford (Dyneley). Larry comes to Suzuki's lab for a story, but all he's really thinking about is returning to his wife in New York after a long stay in Japan. To Suzuki, however, Larry looks like a perfect specimen. "This is for science, for human knowledge," Suzuki explains to his gorgeous assistant Tara (Zimmern) as he drugs our hero and injects him with a secret formula.

Back in Tokyo, Larry starts to change. He drinks heavily, runs around with other women, gets surly with his boss, Ian Matthews, and doesn't contact his wife, Linda (Hylton). He also starts getting pains in his shoulder where he got the injection. Suzuki comes to Tokyo to befriend Larry and to keep an eye on his guinea pig, and Tara starts a relationship with him to keep him in town and away from his wife.

Linda comes to Japan from New York, however, to see what's wrong, but Larry tells her to get lost. Then things really start to go downhill. One night Larry's hand

changes into a hairy claw, and he notices a strange growth on his shoulder. He starts having blackouts, and during those times he manages to murder a Buddhist priest and a few local women.

Ian brings a psychiatrist, Dr. Jennsen, around to Larry's place to try to help him out, but Larry chases them away. That same night, though, Larry gets some bad pains in his arm, and when he looks in a mirror, he sees an eye growing out of his shoulder. This is enough to send him to the shrink, needless to say, but in Jennsen's office, Larry suddenly sprouts a second very ugly head and kills the good doctor.

Ian suspects Larry of the wave of murders in Tokyo and tells Police Superintendent Aida all he knows. Meanwhile, two-headed Larry is running amok in the city, knocking people off right and left.

Eventually Larry returns to the mountain lab where Suzuki is waiting, full of regret for what he has done to his brother, his wife, and now an innocent bystander. "Maybe I offended the gods," he says as he shoots Emiko and prepares to kill himself.

Larry arrives and puts Suzuki out of his misery, but not before the doctor gives him a shot of a second serum that will split him into two beings. The cops, Ian, and Linda are in hot pursuit, so Larry grabs Tara and takes her higher up the mountain. There he does indeed split into a normal good Larry and a crazed evil ape creature. The monster throws Tara into the volcano, then Larry pushes the thing in after her just as Linda and the police arrive. Now everyone can live happily ever after—except that Larry is still charged with about a dozen murders.

There are a lot of problems with this flick. For one thing, it's never really clear why Dr. Suzuki does what he does to Larry or what he hopes to prove. He gives a little lecture on evolution at one point, but it's hard to see how Darwin fits into all this. The special effects are mostly pretty bad, too. The second head that grows on Larry in the psychiatrist's office is obviously an ugly balloon that somebody stuck under his coat collar and blew up, but the eye-in-the-shoulder bit is really quite good—it's worth watching the whole movie just to see that scene.

Some writers have seen *The Manster* as a Jekyll-and-Hyde film, and to some extent, that's true. In the end, Suzuki's serum seems to separate Larry's good self and his bad self, just as Jekyll's serum separated the good doctor from the evil Hyde. On the other hand, Dr. Jekyll at least had the decency to experiment on himself. Suzuki seems to use anybody who's handy.

In this sense, then, *The Manster* has a lot in common with the traditional werewolf film. The werewolf is usually an ordinary guy who becomes a monster through no fault of his own. The same thing happens to Larry Stanford, though in his case, the cause is science rather than the supernatural. And Larry is a very ordinary-looking guy with a wife, a potbelly, and big ears who just happened to be in the wrong place at the wrong time. The message of *The Manster* seems clear. Evil scientists are out there waiting, and what happened to an ordinary guy like Larry could happen to anybody.

# THE MEDUSA TOUCH

1978

**DIRECTOR:** Jack Gold
**PRODUCER:** Denis Holt
**SCREENPLAY:** John Briley
**CAST:** Richard Burton, Lino Ventura, Lee Remick, Harry Andrews, Alan Badel, Marie-Christine Barrault, Gordon Jackson, Michael Byrne

**ORIGINAL RELEASE:** ITC Entertainment
**VIDEO:** AVID Home Entertainment

Are psychic phenomena science fiction or science fact? There seems to be plenty of evidence on both sides of that particular argument, but it's safe to say that no psychic around has the powers that John Morlar displays in this British-French coproduction.

Morlar (intensely overperformed by Richard Burton) is murdered in the opening scene—or so it seems. He is watching a news bulletin on TV about an ongoing disaster on a manned spacecraft when somebody smashes his head to a pulp with a small statue. Inspector Brunel (Ventura), visiting from France to study British police methods, conducts the investigation in Morlar's apartment, along with Duff (Byrne), his assistant. The medical examiner has come and gone when, miraculously, Morlar begins to breathe again. He is rushed to a hospital, where they find room for him despite overcrowding due to a recent jumbo jet disaster that has killed 722 people on board and on the ground.

Looking for clues, Brunel interviews Dr. Zonfeld (Re-

An embarrassingly intense Richard Burton plays John Morlar, the man with *The Medusa Touch*.

mick), John's psychiatrist, who explains via flashback that Morlar believes he can will death and destruction: "I have a gift for disaster," as he puts it.

Morlar claims responsibility for the deaths of his parents, a schoolteacher, and several others, including his neighbor's wife, but of course Zonfeld assures Brunel that there is nothing to all this—John is simply a very sick man. At the moment, thanks to his attacker, he is even sicker. At the hospital, Dr. Johnson (Jackson) assures Brunel that Morlar should not be alive, and it is unlikely that he will ever come out of his coma.

The assistant police commissioner (Andrews) tells Brunel that this case is extremely important, though he does not say why, but the inspector needs no encouragement. Morlar is a writer, and Brunel reads his published works and his cryptic private journal; Brunel even discovers a scrapbook John kept of disaster clippings from around the world. Eventually the commissioner explains that certain higher-ups want to get their hands on Morlar's journals and notes. For some reason, they fear he knows too much about potential scandals that could rock the British government.

Brunel keeps returning to Dr. Zonfeld for more information, and she tells him plenty of stories, including the one about John's wife, who left him for another man and who died in a car accident within an hour after walking out the door. Meanwhile, Morlar's brain waves are getting stronger and stronger, though Dr. Johnson cannot explain why or how this is happening. "You're looking at a mind determined not to die," he says.

Eventually Zonfeld confesses to Brunel that she *does* believe in John's powers, that he proved himself to her

John Morlar seeks the professional help of psychiatrist Dr. Zonfeld (Lee Remick), who at first refuses to believe that he possesses *The Medusa Touch*.

As a child, young John uses his unique powers of destruction to start a fire at his old school in *The Medusa Touch*.

by causing that jumbo jet disaster right before her eyes, just by willing it. From notes in Morlar's journal, Brunel comes to suspect that John now plans to destroy Westminster Cathedral during a celebration there that will be attended by the queen and the highest dignitaries in the government. The occasion is an effort to raise money to repair serious cracks in the building.

In time Zonfeld admits that she was the one who attacked John after he caused the space disaster—he was upset because the money spent on the moonshot could have been used to feed the starving. As a political radical, John now plans to wipe out the establishment

159

In *The Medusa Touch*, Dr. Zonfeld is questioned by Inspector Brunel (Lino Ventura) in the attempted murder of her patient, John Morlar.

completely. Brunel believes in Morlar's powers and does not arrest Zonfeld, though she kills herself shortly after her confession.

Brunel and the assistant commissioner try to have the cathedral closed and the celebration canceled, but they can't prove anything. They even fake a bomb threat, but as soon as the gala gets under way, Morlar awakens in the hospital, and the cathedral begins to crumble, killing people right and left.

The inspector races to the hospital, where he pulls the plug on John. Morlar's brain waves stop—he is now dead for sure—and yet his hand writes a single word on a slip of paper: "Windscale." It is the name of a controversial nuclear power plant nearby. Apparently John has a new disaster in mind. His eyes open, his brain waves start up again, and the final credits roll.

Back in the late sixties and the seventies British leaders were as concerned about leftist politics as leaders

Though murdering one's patient is probably not a very professional thing to do, Dr. Zonfeld strikes a blow for humanity as she tries to kill the man with *The Medusa Touch*.

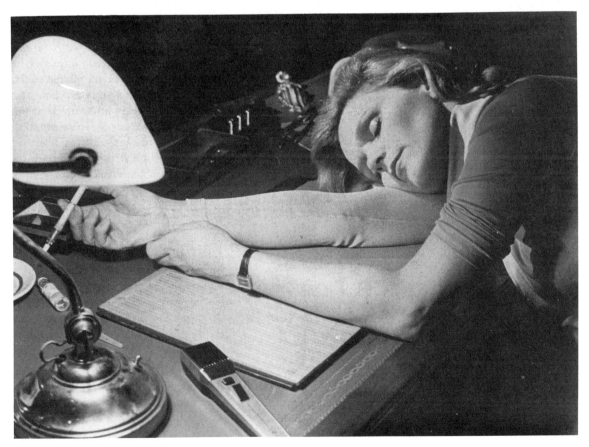

The lovely Dr. Zonfeld prefers to take her own life rather than share the same world with the man who has *The Medusa Touch*.

161

Morlar, a political radical for the seventies, uses his strange powers to bring down a
cathedral on the leaders of the British church and state in *The Medusa Touch*.

in the United States were. Advocates of civil rights and women's rights and members of the antiwar and anti-imperialism movements were often portrayed by government spokespeople and in the media as wild-eyed terrorists out to destroy "our way of life" for no particular reason, though in fact most of the antiestablishment activists at the time were not very far left of center and had legitimate causes to espouse.

John Morlar is a seventies radical who talks about "bringing down the establishment" all the time and who unfortunately has the power to do what the movie suggests every liberal really wants to do—destroy everything. It's surprising, in fact, that a younger man was not cast in the part, given that antiestablishment senti-

ment was part of the youth movement, but the message is still pretty obvious.

*The Medusa Touch* isn't really a bad movie—Burton is overbearing and irritating, but Ventura is charming as the French detective, and Remick is lovely. The title never does make any sense and isn't explained—the Medusa, according to Greek mythology, turned men who looked at her to stone, but what that could possibly have to do with John Morlar's power is anybody's guess. And the mindlessly conservative politics of the film are painfully out-of-date. From our current perspective, the fear of radicals and agitators rampant in many of the world's industrialized nations in the sixties and seventies seems pretty silly, and so does *The Medusa Touch*.

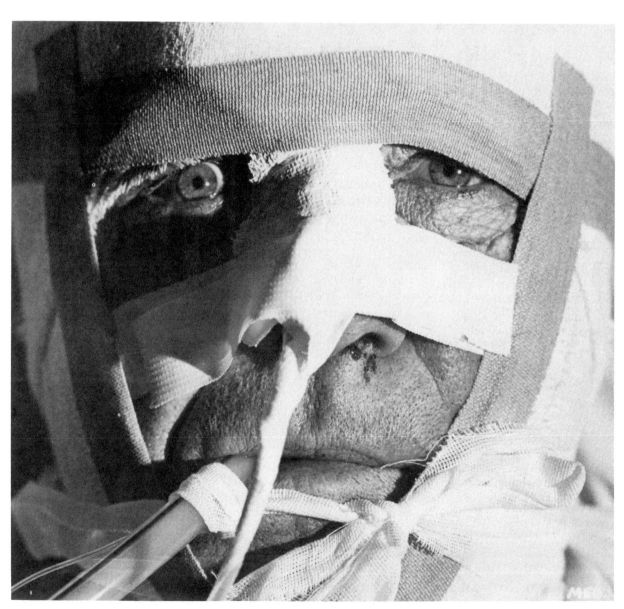

John Morlar, the man with *The Medusa Touch*, is not in good shape, but it appears that he cannot die.

# MESA OF LOST WOMEN

1953

**ALTERNATE TITLES:** *Lost Women, Lost Women of Zarpa*

**DIRECTORS:** Herbert Tevos and Ron Ormond

**PRODUCERS:** Melvin Gale and William Perkins

**SCREENPLAY:** Herbert Tevos

**CAST:** Jackie Coogan, Richard Travis, Allan Nixon, Mary Hill, Robert Knapp, Tandra Quinn, George Barrows, Lyle Talbot, Samuel Wu, Niko Lek

**ORIGINAL RELEASE:** Howco Productions

**VIDEO:** Scorched Earth Productions and Sinister Cinema

This is one of the weirdest science fiction movies ever made. In fact, it is one of the weirdest movies ever made, period. Some time after his career as a child star ended but before he took on the role of Uncle Fester on *The Addams Family* TV show, comedian Jackie Coogan somehow found himself cast in this mess as the mad scientist. But at least Coogan went on to have a career. Lyle Talbot, who does the narrative voice-over for this movie, has the distinction of appearing later in *Plan 9 From Outer Space*, which some would argue is the worst film ever made—though in all likelihood they have never seen *Mesa of Lost Women*. George Barrows, who appears here in his regular skin, gained something like fame as the guy in the ape suit in countless films—he was the Robot Monster in the awful film of the same name and Anatole the gorilla in *Hillbillys in a Haunted House*. Fans of bad cinema might want to watch *Mesa of Lost Women* just for the chance to see what Barrows really looks like.

An oil surveying team discovers Grant (Knapp) and Doreen (Hill) wandering through the desert in Mexico. Back in the oil company's medical room, Grant rants and raves about giant bugs, Zarpa Mesa, and somebody named Dr. Arana (Coogan)—that's Spanish for spider. Company employees Doc (Nixon) and Don (Travis) try to figure out what Grant is talking about and urge him to tell his story, but before he can do that, the narrator (Talbot) takes over in a flashback to the day when Dr. Leland Masterson arrives at Zarpa Mesa at the request of Dr. Arana.

Meet Tarantella (Tandra Quinn), one of Dr. Arana's lovely and immortal creations who lives on the *Mesa of Lost Women*. Her companion is that giant spider who appears in virtually every science fiction movie made in the 1950s. (Courtesy Hollywood Book and Poster)

Cult star Angelo Rossitto, a dwarf companion, and Wu (Samuel Wu) carry off Doreen (Mary Hill) in the thrill-packed *Mesa of Lost Women*. (Courtesy Hollywood Book and Poster)

Arana has a lab built inside a mountain, and Masterson sees lots of women and dwarves running around in there. Masterson is a big fan of Arana's published papers—that's why he came down to Mexico in the first place—so Arana explains that at long last he has isolated a growth hormone that he can use to create giant telepathic spiders—which is fine, if that's what you want to do. It seems a shame to stop there, though, so he then transplants the giant telepathic spider hormones into women, who become indestructible as a result. His crowning achievement is the lovely Tarantella (Quinn), who really does look good but who probably can't act, because she never says a word. The dwarves in Arana's lab are spidermen. In the insect kingdom, the female is usually strong and the male is not, so the same hormones that turn women into superwomen turn grown men into little guys. Arana's plan is to have his superwomen gain control of the world, "subject to my will," of course.

"No, no, you can't do these things," Masterson cries, and that marks the beginning of a very bad time for the good doctor. He is (a) turned into one of Arana's experimental subjects, (b) goes crazy, (c) somehow manages to escape from Zarpa Mesa, (d) is confined in a mental institution, and (e) somehow manages to escape from there, too, all in about six seconds of screen time.

But hey, what about Grant and Doreen? Well, if you want to get their story, you'll have to be patient.

166

indestructible, remember? If you're wondering why Dr. Arana's supreme creation is not out conquering the world but rather dancing in some cheap Mexican dive— good question.

Masterson and the others go to Jan's waiting plane, and guess what? The dashing young pilot is Grant. The airplane is very small, but somehow Grant, Leland, George, Jan, Doreen, and Jan's servant Wu (Wu) manage to jam themselves inside. Shortly thereafter the plane crashes, as coincidence would have it, on Zarpa Mesa.

Well, that night George is killed by a giant spider, and Doreen learns that her fiancé—who is extremely rich—is really a coward and a wimp, so she hooks up with Grant. Now it turns out that Wu is really working for Arana, who wants Masterson back as his colleague and who would like to do some experimenting on Grant and Doreen. For no particular reason, Wu objects to this idea, so Arana has him killed by the spiderwomen.

Later Jan gets killed by a giant spider, too, and some dwarves and superwomen capture the others. Inside the mountain lab, Arana gives Masterson an injection that cures his insanity instantly. Now in his right mind, Leland mixes a couple of chemicals together, tells Grant and Doreen to run for it, then uses the bomb he has made to destroy the lab and everyone in it.

Remember that this was all a flashback, right? In the present, at the oil company, Grant finishes telling his story, but no one believes it. Now the camera moves back to Zarpa Mesa, where we still see one superwoman left alive, so I guess whatever has been going on in this movie isn't over yet.

*Mesa of Lost Women* is proof that if you can manage to fill eighty or so minutes' worth of film with something or other, you can say that you've made a movie. It is senseless, clumsy, and badly acted; in fact it's impossible to believe that it actually took two people to direct this thing.

But students of bad cinema will love it. I know I do.

Masterson arrives at a Mexican cantina, where as coincidence would have it, Tarantella also hangs out. There he meets an older foreign guy named Jan (Lek) and his young fiancée, who turns out to be Doreen from the beginning of the film—see, we all knew she'd be back. Masterson is acting very weird—he's still crazy, of course. Soon the trio is joined by George (Barrows), an attendant at the asylum who has been sent to return Leland to his padded cell.

Tarantella does an awful little dance that is one of the high points of the film, after which Masterson pulls a gun, shoots her, and takes Jan, Doreen, and George hostage. After Leland and his prisoners leave the cantina, Tarantella comes back to life, unharmed—she's

# THE MONSTER FROM GREEN HELL

1957

**DIRECTOR:** Kenneth Crane
**PRODUCER:** Al Zimbalist
**SCREENPLAY:** Louis Vittes and Endre Bohen

**CAST:** Jim Davis, Robert E. Griffin, Barbara Turner, Eduardo Ciannelli, Vladimir Sokoloff, Joel Fluellen

**ORIGINAL RELEASE:** Grosse-Krasne Productions

**VIDEO:** Rhino Home Video, Scorched Earth Productions, and Sinister Cinema

*The Monster From Green Hell* is another one of those big bug movies of the 1950s. This time it's giant wasps in Africa.

Dr. Quentin Brady (Davis of TV's *Dallas*) is a scientist in charge of sending animal and insect specimens into outer space to see what effects cosmic radiation might have on living things. He and Dan Morgan (Griffin), his assistant, lose track of a rocket that contains wasp specimens, and it comes down in Central Africa.

Dr. Lorentz (Sokoloff) and his daughter (Turner) operate a mission hospital near the crash site, and a week or two after the accident, Arobi (Fluellen), the doctor's assistant, brings in a dead man who was killed in a part of the jungle called Green Hell, where the locals believe there are monsters. Lorentz doesn't believe in evil spirits or monsters, but his autopsy shows that the man died of a massive dose of some sort of venom he cannot identify.

Arobi tells Lorentz that he has seen the animals and birds leaving Green Hell—obviously something is driving them out. At the same time, natives who live near Green Hell are attacked by giant wasps.

Six months after the loss of the rocket, Quent reads a newspaper report about monsters in Central Africa and decides that the creatures there might be his wasps, mutated by cosmic rays. He and Dan figure they'd better go there to investigate.

Lorentz, Arobi, and a couple of bearers go into Green Hell to investigate, too. Wasps kill the bearers, and Lorentz and Arobi split up to find out what is going on. The good doctor never returns.

Quent and Dan arrive in Africa, equipped with new super-powerful grenades, which they are sure will take

Africa is invaded by mutant wasps in *Monster From Green Hell.*

168

Quent Brady (Jim Davis) finds out that it isn't easy to kill a *Monster From Green Hell*.

care of any problems they might encounter. They set out on a safari to Green Hell, led by Mahri (Ciannelli), an Arab guide. The trip to Green Hell covers four hundred miles and takes up a lot of screen time, with plenty of stock African footage and the usual safari problems— hostile natives, a shortage of water, a poisoned water hole, a torrential downpour. Finally Quent develops a fever and collapses.

He comes to in Lorentz's hospital and meets Lorna. Arobi returns from Green Hell at about this time and reports that Lorentz is dead: "A monster found him and killed him."

Quent, Dan, Mahri, Arobi, and Lorna go into Green Hell and come upon a village that has been wiped out

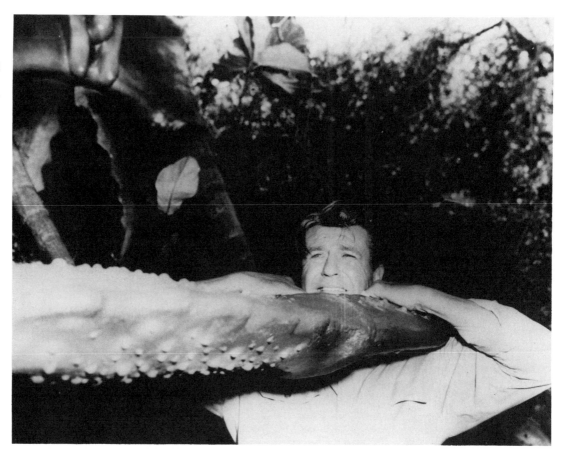

Quent, our hero, is in real trouble when he meets a *Monster From Green Hell*.

by the giant insects. At this point the bearers run off, leaving our four heroes and one heroine on their own.

They soon find the entire colony, including the queen, in a valley in Green Hell. They bombard the wasps with the grenades, which don't work. One of the wasps traps them in a cave, and again a lot of screen time passes while they wander around, looking for a way out.

Finally they arrive at the top of a nearby mountain in time to see a volcano erupt and destroy the wasps. Arobi speaks for everybody when he says: "The gods have been kind. They've taught us as Dr. Lorentz taught us—to have faith."

Despite the boring parts, the stock footage, and the painfully cheap special effects, this movie is kind of fun, and the fact that the scientists who are responsible for the whole mess can't manage to solve the problem is very interesting. In most fifties sci-fi films, science is at the root of the trouble, but the solution is almost always more science. Here it takes a natural disaster to wipe out the giant wasps, suggesting that nature can be counted on to take care of human mistakes.

That's a nice idea, but unfortunately, those of us who live in an age that is far more ecologically aware than people were in the fifties can no longer have that kind of faith.

# THE MONSTER THAT CHALLENGED THE WORLD

1 9 5 7

**DIRECTOR:** Arnold Laven
**PRODUCERS:** Arthur Gardner and Jules V. Levy
**SCREENPLAY:** Pat Fiedler
**CAST:** Tim Holt, Audrey Dalton, Hans Conried, Harlan Warde, Casey Adams, Mimi Gibson, Gordon Jones
**ORIGINAL RELEASE:** United Artists
**VIDEO:** MGM/UA Home Video

In fact there isn't only one monster that challenges the

170

world—there are almost a dozen. And the monsters don't really challenge the whole world, only a little part of California. Even so, this is a very nicely done little picture that goes well beyond the ordinary fifties sci-fi flick.

The setting is a U.S. navy base near the Salton Sea in the California desert, which is disturbed one day by a minor earthquake. Later on, navy parachutists jump into the lake on a routine test mission and disappear. The two men on board the boat that was sent to pick them up are killed. Something is wrong.

As the head of naval intelligence on the base, Lieuten-

ant Commander John Twillinger (former cowboy star Tim Holt, clearly past his prime) is called in to investigate. Twill—as he is known to his friends—is a by-the-book, no-nonsense kind of guy who has been on duty in California for only a week, and he finds himself in the middle of a mystery. He discovers some weird slime on the rescue boat and a shriveled body in the water nearby, and he goes to Dr. Jess Rogers (Conried) of the base science lab for some help.

At the lab, Twill meets Gail MacKenzie (Dalton), a young widow and Rogers's secretary, along with her little daughter, Sandy (Gibson). At first Twill suspects

Dr. Jess Rogers (Hans Conried), Lieutenant Commander John Twillinger (Tim Holt), and Tad Johns (Casey Adams) battle *The Monster That Challenged the World*. (Courtesy Hollywood Book and Poster)

John Twillinger, Dr. Rogers, and Sheriff Josh Peters (Gordon Jones) show military authorities and scientists the giant snail egg they have found. Before long, it will hatch another *Monster That Challenged the World*. (Courtesy Hollywood Book and Poster)

It's *The Monster That Challenged the World*. (Courtesy Hollywood Book and Poster)

that Rogers's experiments with radioactivity might have caused the deaths, but the good doctor assures him that this could not be the case. "Science fiction and science fact are not the same thing," he argues.

When some local swimmers also turn up missing, Rogers and Twill lead an expedition to see what's down there in the water. The divers discover an enormous new cavern at the bottom of the sea, apparently opened up by the earthquake; they also come upon a gigantic egg, which they bring to the surface. Then one of the divers is killed by something, and before Twill and Rogers can figure out what's going on, a huge snail comes up out of the water and attacks the boat. Twill manages to poke its eye out, and it retreats. But their problems have only just begun.

The navy uses depth charges to kill the things—Rogers thinks there may be about ten of them—and the egg goes back to the lab for study, where it is kept in a tank of water at a controlled temperature to prevent it from hatching. Rogers gives a lecture and shows a film about mollusks—the little ones—and speculates that the giants were freed from their underground cavern by the earthquake. He fears that if any managed to survive, they might get into the local canal system, and that would mean *real* trouble, because they seem to like to feed on the local populace, and they breed like crazy.

As it turns out, the mollusks *do* survive the depth charges and get into the canal system through an underground river. Now Twill, Rogers, and their men have to start hunting for them all over again. Everything turns out well, though. The monsters knock off a couple more townsfolk, but the good guys manage to track the snails back to their lair and destroy them with explosives before any more eggs can hatch.

Ah, but the movie isn't over yet. Remember the egg back at the lab? Well, Gail's bratty little kid turns up the temperature of the tank—it's amazing how many spoiled little baby boomers there are in fifties sci-fi movies—and the egg hatches, spawning another monster, which tries to eat mother and daughter. Twill arrives just in time and holds it off until guards from the base come to shoot it down. By this time, it's clear that Twill and Gail are made for each other, and they and Sandy walk off into the sunset together.

Like so many science fiction films of the cold war era, *The Monster That Challenged the World* shows scientists and the military working well together to protect us ordinary citizens from the evils of the world. In most of those movies, however, science and the military had created the problem in the first place by nuclear testing and general carelessness. That isn't the case here. At first Twill is mistrustful of the scientists and thinks that maybe they are at fault, but as it turns out, Mother Nature is to blame this time. So in *The Monster That Challenged the World,* there are no mad scientists or thoughtless experiments; Rogers and his people are intelligent, dedicated, and decent guys. The message here is that science and the military really do have our best interests at heart, even though they usually don't tell us what's going on "to prevent a panic." We are simply to live our lives in blissful ignorance and trust in our leaders to take care of us. Of course we've become too suspicious to fall for this kind of line nowadays, but it was an important notion in the 1950s and early '60s.

*The Monster That Challenged the World* seems a bit dated, but it is still an impressive piece of work. What sets the movie apart from others in the genre is the ordinariness of the characters. There is no dashing heroic male lead here. Twill is short, middle-aged, and a bit overweight, and though Tim Holt is certainly no Laurence Olivier, he looks absolutely terrified as he battles the newly hatched monster in the final scene—as scared as you or I would be under the same circumstances. Gail is attractive, but she isn't a Hollywood glamour girl—she's a widow and a mother. Dr. Rogers is a brilliant man, but he obviously cares more about the people around him than he does about scientific research, and he worries for their safety.

In other words, these are regular people trying to keep it together under extreme circumstances, and that aspect of the film makes *The Monster That Challenged the World* a lot more convincing than most sci-fi movies of its day or ours.

# THE MYSTERIANS

1957

**ALTERNATE TITLE:** *Chikyu Boeigun*
**DIRECTOR:** Inoshiro Honda
**PRODUCER:** Tomoyuki Tanaka
**SCREENPLAY:** Takeshi Kimura
**CAST:** Kenji Sahara, Yumi Shirakawa, Momoko Kochi, Akihiko Hirata, Takashi Shimura, Susumu Fujita
**ORIGINAL RELEASE:** Toho Productions
**VIDEO:** VCI and Star Classics

The legendary Inoshiro Honda and his cohorts at Toho Productions have probably had a more profound effect on American culture than most of us suspect or are willing to admit. After all, Toho gave us Godzilla, whose name is certainly a household word. Honda recognized early on that kids love monsters, a realization Jim Henson also came to, though years later. The influence of Toho can be found in lots of our most popular kiddie TV shows, from *Sesame Street* to *Barney and Friends* to *Mighty Morphin Power Rangers,* and whatever influences the children influences the culture.

Curiously enough, though the United States and Japan were enemies during World War II and though in many ways the two cultures are strikingly different, from about the mid-fifties on, both nations have shared many of the same concerns. If this had not been true, popular culture from Japan would not have translated so well into our own. *The Mysterians* is a good example of how a Japanese film from 1957 could speak quite clearly to an American audience of the same era.

*The Mysterians* begins at a traditional festival where Joji Atsumi (Sahara), Etsuko Shiraishi (Shirakawa), her

Advertising art for director Inoshiro Honda's effective venture into science fiction, *The Mysterians.* (Courtesy Hollywood Book and Poster)

brother Ryoichi (Hirata), and Hiroko (Kochi) are moving among the crowd. Ryoichi, a noted physical astronomer, has recently broken off his engagement to Hiroko, and he has been acting very strange.

Later, Joji goes to talk to Dr. Adachi (Shimura), Ryoichi's old professor, about his friend's behavior. Adachi explains that his former student has been obsessed with his theory of Mysteroid. According to Ryoichi, Mysteroid was once a planet between Mars and Saturn that exploded eons ago, though Ryoichi also believes that survivors of the dead planet are living on other bodies in the solar system. Of course no one in the scientific community takes these theories seriously.

There is an earthquake in the village where Ryoichi has been staying, and Joji goes there to find the area destroyed. His friend is reported dead. Suddenly a giant robot appears, destroys a power plant, and attacks a nearby town. The army fights the thing and eventually manages to destroy it, but Joji sees UFOs zooming away through the sky after the battle. Earth's problems are only beginning.

From his observatory, Adachi also sees UFOs going behind the moon—exactly as Ryoichi had predicted. Then a giant alien dome appears out of the ground, and Adachi, Joji, and other scientists are invited inside by the inhabitants. Once there, they meet the Mysterians, who confirm everything Ryoichi has said—Mysteroid was destroyed 100,000 years ago by a nuclear war, and the survivors migrated to Mars. They admit that their robot was responsible for the recent destruction, but they claim to want only the three kilometers of Earth they already occupy as a base for scientific study: "We do not wish to colonize." Also, because radioactivity has gradually made their females sterile, they want to mate with Earth women, and Etsuko and Hiroko are among those who have been chosen. The Japanese scientists and government leaders do not trust the Mysterians and are determined to resist.

Joji, Etsuko, and Hiroko are watching TV one evening when Ryoichi appears—alive—on the screen in a Mysterian uniform. He is now living in the dome as their official spokesman, and he assures his friends that the aliens are trustworthy. Meanwhile, the army attacks the dome, but flying saucers and a weird ray drive them off. Earth scientists and the military begin working on an electronic cannon which they hope will work against the Mysterians' superior technology.

The truth, of course, is that the Mysterians are building an underground fortress and plan to conquer the Earth. Eventually Ryoichi admits this, but he says: "The Mysterians are only trying to keep mankind from destroying itself. . . . The Earth cannot be left in the charge of man."

With the new electronic cannon and a reflector that

The giant robot from the planet Mysteroid attacks Japan to prepare for the arrival of *The Mysterians*. (Courtesy Hollywood Book and Poster)

can send the Mysterians' ray back at them, the military launches a major assault. In the meantime, Mysterians grab Etsuko and Hiroko, but Joji manages to sneak into the dome to rescue them. He destroys a lot of equipment there before he is captured, but when Ryoichi sees his best friend, his sister, and his beloved as prisoners of the aliens, he realizes that he has been wrong: "I was betrayed by the Mysterians." Ryoichi sets the Earthlings free, then blows up the dome, destroying the Mysterians and himself.

In the 1950s, the Japanese had even more to fear from nuclear weapons and the spread of communism than we did. After all, Japan was and is the only nation ever to suffer the direct effects of the atomic bomb, and after World War II, the Japanese were intimidated by communist governments in nearby China, Vietnam, and Korea. It shouldn't be surprising, then, that Japanese sci-fi of the fifties reflects those concerns, the same concerns we find in American sci-fi pictures of the same period.

*The Mysterians* is a story about seduction and collaboration. Like the communists, the Mysterians plan to conquer the Earth for the Earth's own good, and Ryoichi is seduced into believing that Mysterian rule would be better than the world as it is under human direction, a world perpetually at war. In other words, Ryoichi is a good man who means well and who sees his collaboration with the Mysterians not as a betrayal but as an effort to bring peace to Earth. Fortunately, he comes to understand the error of his ways before it is too late.

Ryoichi, of course, is a scientist, and the movie warns us that intellectuals with liberal leanings are dangerous because they can be seduced into betraying us to the enemy without even knowing what they are doing. The source of Ryoichi's error is that he studied the Mysterians, just as other intellectuals study the works of Marx and Lenin. Knowledge, then, is a dangerous thing, and the less we know about other cultures or political theories, the less likely we are to be seduced by them.

*The Mysterians* is a very conservative and isolationist film, and though its politics don't hold up very well in our time, it spoke eloquently to audiences of the late fifties in Japan and in the United States, because it said what people needed it to say.

# MYSTERIOUS ISLAND

1 9 6 1

**DIRECTOR:** Cy Endfield
**PRODUCER:** Charles H. Schneer
**SCREENPLAY:** John Prebble, Daniel Ullman, and Crane Wilbur

The guests on *Mysterious Island* manage to deal with a giant crab, but other horrors await.

As far as Captain Harding (Michael Craig) is concerned, Lady Mary Fairchild (Joan Greenwood) is a welcome addition to the company on the *Mysterious Island*—at least she can cook.

**CAST:** Michael Craig, Joan Greenwood, Michael Callan, Gary Merrill, Herbert Lom, Beth Rogan
**ORIGINAL RELEASE:** Ameran Productions
**VIDEO:** Columbia TriStar Home Video

Based on Jules Verne's sequel to his classic *Twenty Thousand Leagues Under the Sea, Mysterious Island* is distinguished by the special effects of the legendary Ray Harryhausen. Even in our day of ultrasophisticated fx and computer-generated graphics, Harryhausen's painstaking model animation is a joy to watch.

In 1865, near the end of the Civil War, a group of Union soldiers and a journalist named Gideon Spilett (Merrill) escape from a Confederate prison in an observation balloon. They crash on—you guessed it—a mysterious island that seems to be uninhabited, though there are also signs that someone or something is looking out for them. For example, someone saves Captain Cyrus Harding (Craig) from drowning after the crash landing of the balloon and lights a campfire so his men will find him. Very mysterious.

While the men are still adjusting to life on the island, two shipwrecked women wash ashore—what incredible luck! Lady Mary Fairchild (Greenwood) and her niece Elana (Rogan) pitch right in with the cooking and the

cleaning, and soon our castaways are doing rather well. They begin plans to build a boat that will take them back to civilization.

One day a chest washes ashore containing weapons, a compass, charts, tools, pots and pans, and even a copy of *Robinson Crusoe*. Herbert Brown (Callan), one of the young soldiers, remarks, "Whoever packed this sure knew what we needed." How mysterious.

The arrival of the chest solves some of their problems, but every now and then the gang is attacked by a giant thing—first an enormous crab, then a huge chicken, then colossal bees. Where did these mysterious creatures come from? Then pirates land on the island, but someone blows a hole in their ship and sinks it before they can do harm to the castaways. What is going on in this mysterious place?

The answers aren't long in coming when Herbert and Elana discover a huge metal ship in a cave under the island. It is the submarine *Nautilus*, creation of famed antiwar activist Captain Nemo (Lom), and though the sub seems deserted, Nemo himself shows up shortly thereafter to explain what's been going on.

Yes, Nemo is the one who has been secretly helping them out. He is the last surviving member of his crew, and the *Nautilus* is hopelessly damaged, so he has more or less retired to this island to try some experiments that will put an end to war once and for all.

According to the captain's theory, war is caused by

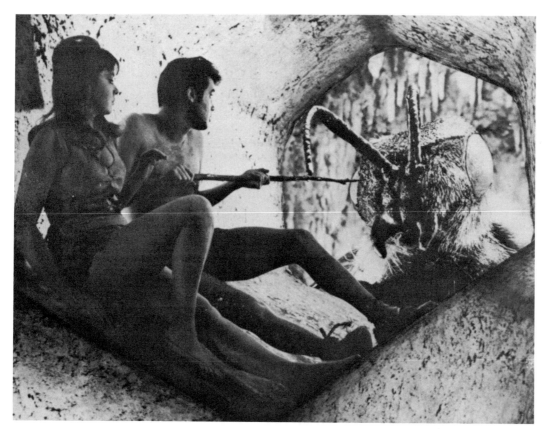

Elana (Beth Rogan) and
Herbert Brown (Michael
Callan) are trapped by a gigantic bee, provided by special effects wizard Ray Harryhausen in *Mysterious
Island.*

Lady Fairchild and Elana
suffer what is perhaps the
only giant chicken attack in
the history of the science fiction cinema in *Mysterious
Island.*

Lady Fairchild hits it off with crusty journalist Gideon Spilett (Gary Merrill), a fellow castaway on the *Mysterious Island*.

Members of the cast come together on the beach of the *Mysterious Island*—from left to right, Sergeant Pencroft (Percy Herbert), Lady Fairchild (Joan Greenwood), Elana (Beth Rogan), Captain Harding (Michael Craig), Captain Nemo (Herbert Lom), Neb (Dan Jackson), Herbert Brown (Michael Callan), and Gideon Spilett (Gary Merrill).

shortages of land and food. He has therefore developed a way to make animals and other creatures grow to gigantic size—this explains the monsters on the island. His discovery will mean an end to human need and an end to war. Now, however, the island's volcano is due for a cataclysmic eruption, and they all must escape as soon as possible, taking Nemo's notes and results with them so they can save the world when they get back.

The castaways manage to repair and raise the sunken pirate ship, using Nemo's underwater gear, but, unfortunately, when the volcano erupts, Nemo and the *Nautilus* are lost, and so are all his notes. Still, the survivors

Beneath the ocean near the *Mysterious Island,* the castaways are attacked by yet another of Ray Harryhausen's masterful creations.

pledge that, when they return to civilization, they will work for peace, as Captain Nemo would have wanted.

This movie should be a lot better than it is. Unfortunately, it has no interesting characters and virtually no plot. Mostly, it's just one gigantic thing after another. The antiwar message is well taken, but all *Mysterious Island* really has going for it are the Harryhausen special effects, which all by themselves make the film worth seeing.

# THE NAVY VS. THE NIGHT MONSTERS

1 9 6 6

**DIRECTOR/SCREENPLAY:** Michael Hoey
**PRODUCER:** George Edwards
**CAST:** Anthony Eisley, Mamie Van Doren, Walter Sande, Bobby Van, Bill Gray, Phillip Terry, Pamela Mason

A scientist who has seen better days—he's fallen from an airplane, then been attacked by an omnivorous plant in *The Navy vs. the Night Monsters.* (Courtesy Hollywood Book and Poster)

A pilot is devoured by one of the plant creatures in *The Navy vs. the Night Monsters*. (Courtesy Hollywood Book and Poster)

Dr. Beecham's assistant and her escorts (Bobby Van and Anthony Eisley) search for the killer plants—unfortunately, one will soon find her in *The Navy vs. the Night Monsters*.

**ORIGINAL RELEASE:** Standard Club of California
**VIDEO:** Paragon Video Productions

I have a particular affection for movies with "vs." in their titles—*King Kong vs. Godzilla, Gammera vs. Goas, Billy the Kid vs. Dracula, Earth vs. the Spider*. In fact, I much prefer "vs." to, say, "meets"—as in *Jesse James Meets Frankenstein's Daughter* or *Frankenstein Meets the Wolfman*. "Vs." is simply more combative. When I see a "meets" movie such as *Frankenstein Meets the Space Monster*, I know that Frankenstein and the Space Monster aren't going to shake hands and say hi—they're going to have a colossal battle that'll be the climax of the picture. Calling this a meeting seems almost like false advertising. At least with a "vs." movie, you know what you're getting into.

Maybe this explains why I get a kick out of *The Navy vs. the Night Monsters*, even though it has virtually nothing going for it.

The movie features a number of notables, among them Anthony Eisley, who appeared in a lot of flicks like this in the fifties, sixties, and seventies but who also had a fairly successful career in television. It co-stars Mamie Van Doren, the busty 1950s sex kitten who ap-

pears in profile in almost every shot; comedian Bobby Van, who went on to TV game shows; and Bill Gray, better known as Billy Gray, who played Robert Young's one and only son, Bud, on *Father Knows Best*. A cast like that has to be worth something.

In Antarctica, scientists gather plant and animal specimens from the warm lakes region and board a plane to take their finds back to the States. Meanwhile, at a navy base on an island in the South Pacific, Lieutenant Charles Brown (Eisley) and his right-hand man, Ensign Rutherford Chandler (Van), are temporarily in charge while Commander Simpson is away, but that's okay because things are pretty quiet. Dr. Beecham (Sande) is doing meaningless experiments in the lab, and civilian meterologist Bob Spalding (Terry) is getting ready to go back to the States. Spalding is the bad guy in the movie—all he does is complain about the island, the Navy, Lieutenant Brown, the food, the heat. In fact the only thing he likes is nurse Nora Hall (Van Doren), but of course she doesn't like him. Brown is more her type.

Back on the plane from Antarctica, something goes wrong, and when the aircraft crash-lands on the island, only Miller the pilot is left on board, and he is in deep shock. The crew and the eight scientists are gone, and there are signs of a terrific struggle. Dr. Beecham examines the specimens, particularly some very unusual trees,

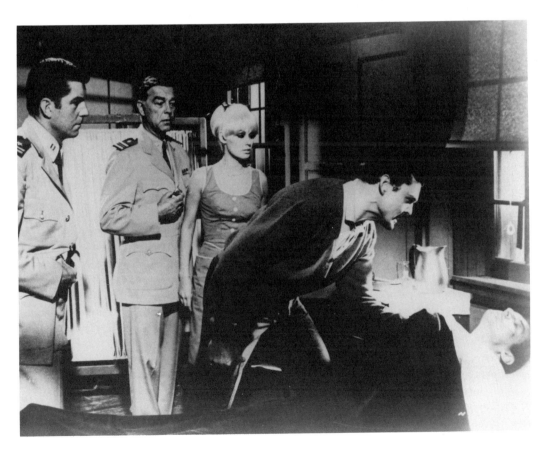

Lieutenant Charles Brown (Anthony Eisley), the base doctor, and his nurse Nora Hall (Mamie Van Doren) look on as meteorologist Bob Spaulding (Philip Terry) questions an injured pilot about what is happening on the island in *The Navy vs. the Night Monsters.*

Dr. Arthur Beecham (Walter Sande), nurse Nora Hall, and their colleagues watch for the jets that will napalm the deadly plant creatures out of existence in the thrill-packed ending of *The Navy vs. the Night Monsters.*

and decides to plant them near the hot springs temporarily to keep them alive.

A hurricane is coming, so Spalding is trapped on the island for the moment, and this gives rise to more complaining on his part. Pilot Miller is still catatonic, though several times he comes out of it long enough to attack someone or try to escape, but he still can't tell the others what happened on board the plane.

Now more people start to disappear, and a search party finds the body of one of the Antarctic scientists. The scientist obviously fell from the plane and his body has been burned almost beyond recognition by acid of some sort. Who or what is doing this?

Well, whatever it is, it eventually gets Beecham's assistant Marie, pilot Miller, Ensign Chandler, and Chandler's dog. Before too long, Brown and the others figure

out that their people are being killed and eaten by the Antarctic trees, which secrete a corrosive, deadly acid and which, while immobile during the day, have the ability to uproot themselves and walk around at night. They also look remarkably like guys in tree suits.

The trees keep killing off the servicemen on the island, including poor radar operator Fred Twining (Gray); in fact, one of the monsters rips Fred's arm out by the roots (those of you who found young Bud irritating on *Father Knows Best* might get a real charge out of this scene). Fire destroys the creatures, however, so Lieutenant Brown and his men get busy with Molotov cocktails. Even so, the things are multiplying at an alarming rate, and it won't be long before they overrun the entire island.

Then just when things seem hopeless, Commander

Simpson orders navy ships to evacuate the island while planes blast the trees with napalm. They pick up survivors. Interestingly, in this scene the tree monsters are out strolling around in broad daylight, even though, earlier in the movie, Dr. Beecham assured us that they could move only in the dark. The problem is now solved—no thanks to our hero, Lieutenant Brown, who does virtually nothing throughout the entire flick, even though he still ends up with the girl.

*The Navy vs. the Night Monsters* is a sixties movie with a fifties message. Obviously, the Antarctic scientists should have known better than to take strange life-forms out of their natural environment and bring them to ours, and Dr. Beecham, a pretty good guy, should have known better than to plant those trees. But scientists are careless because they care only about science, and so it is up to the military—in this case, the Navy—to put the world into order again, despite the interference of loud-mouthed antimilitary civilians like Spalding.

These ideas played well enough during the early years of the cold war, but *The Navy vs. the Night Monsters* was made in the Vietnam era, when Americans were beginning to suspect that the top military brass really didn't have a very tight rein on things. In this sense, *The Navy vs. the Night Monsters* turns out to be a conservative, prowar film, a movie that doesn't particularly like either civilians or the ordinary uniformed guys in the trenches.

Bob Spalding is the civilian protester who doesn't really trust the military, and he is portrayed as a rat, a fool, and a man clearly out of touch with reality. Brown,

Chandler, and the other men on the island are foot soldiers who simply get killed off and who in the end must look to the admirals and commanders to get them out of trouble with superior wisdom and firepower. In this movie, the only people who really know what's going on are the top brass, though they aren't even where the action is, and it seems that we—civilians and grunts alike—are being asked to trust them and to let them take care of the world as they see fit. Nowadays, in the post-Vietnam era, it's hard, if not impossible, to muster that kind of faith.

Even so, I get a kick out of this movie. Is it the weird monsters? Mamie Van Doren? Billy Gray getting his arm ripped off? I wonder what I'd think of this flick if they'd called it *The Navy Meets the Night Monsters.*

# NIGHT OF THE BLOODY APES

---

1968

**ALTERNATE TITLES:** *La Horriplante Bestia Humana, Gomar—The Human Gorilla, Horror y Sexo*
**DIRECTOR:** René Cardona, Sr.
**PRODUCER:** G. Calderon Stell

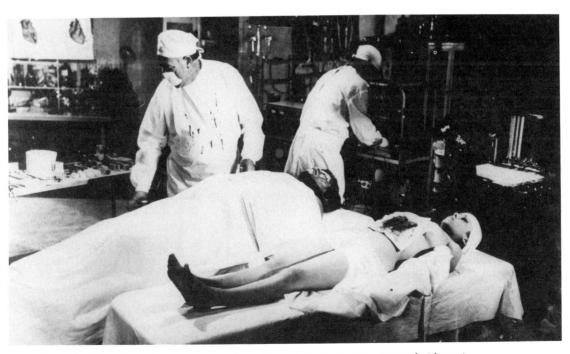

Dr. Krallman (José Elias Moreno) prepares to operate on his son Julio the Ape Man (Armando Silvestre) to give him the heart of a lady wrestler. Well, it seemed like a good idea at the time, but it leads to the *Night of the Bloody Apes.*

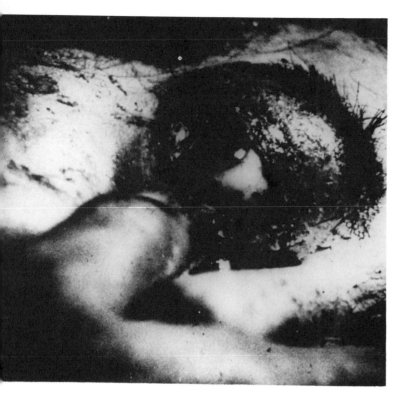

A tasteless eye-gouging scene from the relentlessly tasteless *Night of the Bloody Apes*.

**SCREENPLAY:** René Cardona and René Cardona, Jr.
**CAST:** José Elias Moreno, Carlos Lopez
Moctezuma, Norma Lazareno, Armando
Silvestre
**ORIGINAL RELEASE:** Jerand Productions
**VIDEO:** Gorgon Home Video

This painfully bad exploitation flick, made in Mexico and released in English in 1972, is brought to you by the director of the wrestling women movies, which admittedly are very weird but basically entertaining movies. *Night of the Bloody Apes* is weird, too, but definitely not entertaining, even though it is essentially a remake of Cardona's *Las Luchadoras Contra el Médico Resino (Doctor of Doom)* of 1962, the first of the wrestling women films. There are significant differences, of course, between the original and the remake. For one thing, *Doctor of Doom* has no nudity or gore, while *Night of the Bloody Apes* has virtually nothing else. The original is about brain transplants, but the remake is about heart transplants. And while *Doctor of Doom* features two female wrestlers who are the stars of the show, the later film has only one wrestling woman who really has no reason for being in this flick at all . . . except

hey, what's a Mexican sci-fi movie without a pro wrestler and some gratuitous mat action?

Lucy Ossorio (Lazareno) is a guilt-ridden masked wrestler who has fractured the skull of her opponent Elena by throwing her out of the ring. Dr. Krallman (Elias Moreno) is called in to do brain surgery on the injured woman.

Meanwhile, Krallman has some other things going on the side. His son Julio (Silvestre) is terminally ill, and so the good doctor and his weird assistant Goyo steal a gorilla from the city zoo, and Krallman transplants the gorilla's heart into Julio to give him strength. It probably seemed like a good idea at the time, but the operation transforms the handsome Julio into an ugly apelike creature that escapes and slaughters a woman in a nearby apartment house. Krallman and Goyo capture Julio using a tranquilizer gun, but it's obvious that things aren't going well.

Detective Arthur Martinez (Lopez Moctezuma), Lucy's boyfriend, is assigned to the case, and the murder is blamed on the gorilla missing from the zoo. But Julio escapes again—Krallman and Goyo are remarkably careless—and attacks a couple in the park, ripping out the guy's throat and assaulting the girl, who manages to escape. Then he gouges another guy's eyes out before

The half human, half ape claims another victim for no particular reason in *Night of the Bloody Apes*.

his father recaptures him and takes him back to the lab. When Goyo asks the doctor, "What plans do you have now, master?" Krallman explains that Julio needs a human heart, so he's going to take Elena's and transplant it into his son.

The operation seems to work, and Julio returns to normal. By this time, though, Arthur has figured out something of what's going on. He tells his chief: "Whatever committed these atrocities is a beast, yes, but a terrible half beast, half human." Of course the chief laughs and says that Arthur has been watching too many horror films on TV.

For no particular reason, Julio reverts to his apelike state and escapes yet again after pulling Goyo's head off. In the end, after chasing Lucy through the park, the monster is shot down by the cops, and Dr. Krallman sees the error of his ways: "Please, Julio, forgive me. I acted against the dictates of God in trying to save you."

My guess is that, between the making of *Doctor of Doom* in 1962 and *Night of the Bloody Apes* in 1968, Cardona saw H. G. Lewis's *Blood Feast*, because he uses the same tight close-up gore shots that Lewis's film made famous. Unfortunately, Cardona doesn't have Lewis's zany sense of humor, and so the gory stuff in *Night of the Bloody Apes* is simply relentlessly grim. Even the effort to add sex to the film fails. It seems that, once the gorilla man has gotten hold of a naked woman—he always tears her clothes off first thing—he wants to rape her, but he can't figure out what to do.

Apparently Cardona changed his mind about a few things in doing the remake of *Doctor of Doom*. The doctor of the original seems like a nice guy, but in fact we soon learn that he is a typically evil mad scientist who wants to transplant gorilla brains into human beings just to see what will happen. Dr. Krallman, however, really *is* a nice guy who does what he does to save the life of his son, and the use of a more complicated character in the scientist role is really the only aspect of the remake that is more interesting than the original.

What made *Doctor of Doom* interesting, though, was the fact that Cardona went against all the rules of science fiction and horror films by making the women the characters who not only figure everything out and continually rescue their bumbling cop boyfriends but who even do the physical work of duking it out with the bad guys and the monsters. There is none of that in *Night of the Bloody Apes*, where women exist only to be stripped and slaughtered. That's too bad, because while *Doctor of Doom* and the other wrestling women films are interesting and fun in their own bizarre way, *Night of the Bloody Apes* is just another stupid, violent flick.

# PHANTASM

1979

**DIRECTOR/PRODUCER/SCREENPLAY:** Don Coscarelli

**CAST:** Angus Scrimm, Michael Baldwin, Bill Thornbury, Reggie Bannister, Ken Jones, Kathy Lester

**ORIGINAL RELEASE:** New Breed Productions, Inc.

**VIDEO:** Embassy Home Entertainment

This is an alien invasion movie that through almost its entire length doesn't seem to be an alien invasion movie at all.

When their friend Tommy is found dead, apparently a suicide, Jody (Thornbury) and Reggie (Bannister) are crushed. We know, of course, that Tommy did not kill himself—he had a lot of help from a nameless young woman (Lester) who stabbed him in the opening segment. Jody and Reggie are at Tommy's funeral. Jody's thirteen-year-old brother Mike (Baldwin) is there, too, spying on the ritual because Jody wouldn't allow him to attend.

After the funeral, Mike sees something that really scares him. The funeral director, known throughout the movie only as the Tall Man (Scrimm), lifts Tommy's casket out of the grave as if it weighed nothing at all, loads it back into the hearse, and takes it away.

Later, again near the mortuary, Mike sees some creepy dwarf-like creatures dressed in brown robes and hoods. They chase him and try to kill him, but when he tells his brother and others about the dwarves, no one will believe him.

Mike is a gutsy kid who decides to go to the mortuary to investigate the weird things he's seen. He breaks in, gets caught by the caretaker (Jones), and is almost killed by a strange silver ball bristling with jagged blades that flies through the mausoleum all by itself. Mike ducks in time, and the ball strikes the caretaker in the head, bores a hole through his skull, and pumps out most of his blood.

Next the Tall Man chases Mike, but the kid manages to slam a door on the big guy's hand, lop off some of his fingers with a hunting knife, and take one of the fingers away as proof of what he's been saying. When Jody and Reggie see the wriggling digit resting in a box in a pool of yellow blood, they are convinced.

From here on in, things happen pretty quickly. Reggie, Jody, and Mike kill one of the weird dwarves and find out that it is their friend Tommy, apparently brought back to life and crushed down to half of his original size. The guys suspect that this might have happened to others in the graveyard and the mausoleum. As Mike says, "What about Mom and Dad? They're up there, too."

Eventually Mike, Jody, and Reggie get into the mortuary again, where Jody destroys the deadly silver ball with a shotgun blast. Then they discover a room full of packaged dwarves with a portal that opens onto another world. It seems that the Tall Man is an alien who is on Earth to reanimate the dead and compress them to suit the pressures of his own planet. He then ships them to his home world via the portal; there they are used as slaves for eternity.

The guys destroy the portal, and the mortuary vanishes. Then the girl who killed Tommy shows up again to stab Reggie; in fact, she is not a girl at all but the Tall Man in another incarnation. Now furious at having lost another friend and aware of the fact that their parents are probably dwarf slaves on some distant planet, Jody and Mike lure the Tall Man to a mine shaft, where they bury him alive.

When I first saw *Phantasm,* it was playing on a double bill with *Dawn of the Dead,* and it didn't seem to hold its own against the amazing second installment of George Romero's zombie trilogy. Since then, though, I've seen *Phantasm* a couple more times, and it really is a fine movie in its own right. The pacing and the camera work are excellent, and the story really clips along. Unfortunately, the movie has one of those "it was all a dream—or was it?" endings tacked on to allow for a sequel, and that's too bad, because the closing sequence weakens the film as a whole, and *Phantasm II*—done with a bigger budget and more special effects—is no great shakes.

*Phantasm* owes a lot to the original *Invaders From*

In *Phantasm,* Mike Pearson (Michael Baldwin) is stalked by the Tall Man (Angus Scrimm) in the mausoleum.

188

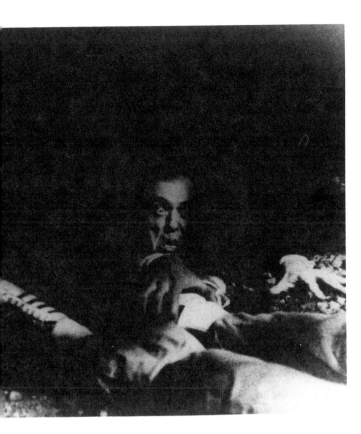

The Tall Man emerges from a freshly dug grave to claim his next victim in *Phantasm*.

Mike finds an unexpected visitor nesting in his hair in a particularly bizarre scene from *Phantasm*.

*Mars* of 1953. There, too, a kid becomes aware of an alien invasion but can't get anybody to believe him. Of course, throughout the fifties and beyond, this idea would get a lot of play, from *The Blob* to *Invasion of the Saucer Men* to *Night of the Creeps*. The reason for the popularity of this notion is obvious. Kids became the heroes of sci-fi and horror films primarily because kids were the audience for these movies.

But *Phantasm* and other movies like it remind us of something important. The kid hero becomes a hero because he sees what other people—usually older people—do not see, and he sees what the others don't

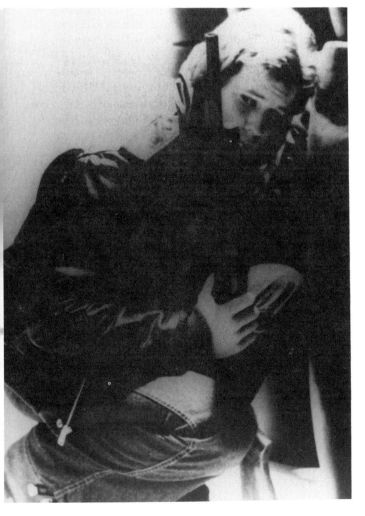

Mike's brother Jody (Bill Thornbury) discovers the containers used to ship compressed living corpses to another planet in the closing moments of *Phantasm*.

because he has fewer preconceptions about the world. In other words, because he is young, he hasn't decided ahead of time about what is possible and what is not. The kid-hero film suggests that, young or old, we must keep our options and our minds open, and that's good advice.

# THE PHANTOM PLANET

1961

**DIRECTOR:** William Marshall
**PRODUCER:** Fred Gebhardt
**SCREENPLAY:** Fred Gebhardt, William Telaak, and Fred de Gorter
**CAST:** Dean Fredericks, Coleen Gray, Anthony Dexter, Dolores Faith, Francis X. Bushman, Richard Kiel

**ORIGINAL RELEASE:** Four Crown Productions
**VIDEO:** Nostalgia Family Video and Sinister Cinema

This film doesn't have a lot going for it, though it does feature veteran actor Bushman as leader of the planet Rayton and an early appearance by Kiel—Jaws from the James Bond flicks—as the Solarite monster. But in many ways, *The Phantom Planet* is typical of fifties and early sixties sci- fi films, so it's worth a look, if only to see what was going on then.

Two spaceships sent out from our lunar base have disappeared, and now Captain Frank Chapman (Fredericks) and his copilot are sent out to investigate. When their ship is damaged in a meteor storm, Chapman is injured and his copilot is killed, but mysteriously the ship is drawn to a large asteroid and brought in for a landing. There Frank is found by a bunch of miniature people, and before he knows what's going on, he shrinks, too. He is taken prisoner and informed that he is now a subject of the planet Rayton, and for security reasons, he will not be allowed to leave.

Frank meets Seson (Bushman), the leader of the little

Astronaut Frank Chapman (Dean Fredericks) is shrunken down to a height of six inches when he arrives on *The Phantom Planet*.

190

planet, along with his daughter Liana (Gray), who immediately starts flirting with the Earthling. This angers Herron (Dexter), a high-ranking official who wants Liana for himself. Frank, however, is more interested in Zetha (Faith), a beautiful young Raytonian who is mute. Our captain isn't exactly a brilliant conversationalist, so maybe this is why they hit it off.

Herron challenges Frank to a duel, which involves trying to push your opponent onto a gravity plate and disintegrating him. Chapman wins, of course, and spares his enemy's life, so Herron decides to be a pal and help Frank get back home.

While this is going on, the Solarites attack. Solarites are the traditional enemies of Rayton, and as Seson explains: "If we don't stop them, they'll eventually attack your Earth." Frank meets a big, ugly Solarite prisoner (Kiel) who is so monstrous that when Zetha saw him some years before, she was stricken dumb.

Rayton wins the battle against the Solarites and wipes them out in a few seconds—if it was that easy, you have to wonder why they never did this before. During the battle, however, the prisoner escapes and grabs Zetha, who is so shocked that she gets her voice back. Frank and Herron manage to defeat the Solarite, and Herron keeps his promise by helping the captain return to normal size so he can go home again, though unfortunately Chapman must leave Zetha, his one true love, behind.

Like so many sci-fi movies of the fifties and sixties, *The Phantom Planet* suffers from what I like to call the Tarzan syndrome. The novels of Edgar Rice Burroughs and the movies featuring his classic character are based on a significant assumption: If a white guy is accidentally dropped into the African jungle, he will not only survive but prove himself superior to the natives there and eventually become ruler of the whole place.

*The Phantom Planet* makes the same assumption. If a white Earthling finds himself on a strange planet, he too will prove himself superior to the natives and eventually take over. Frank Chapman isn't built like Tarzan—though he does manage to keep his shirt unbuttoned throughout the entire flick—but the analogy still holds. The women of Rayton fall all over him, and though he doesn't seem to be particularly bright, Seson seeks his advice again and again. After the battle with the Solarites, during which Frank does absolutely nothing but stand around, Seson tells him: "You are wise, Chapman. One day you and Herron will lead our world." Here's a guy who's been on the planet for about a day and a half, and he is promised supreme executive authority by the planetary leader. Why? Because he's an Earthling and therefore deserves to rule over the inferior Raytonians.

The Tarzan syndrome doesn't make sense, of course, but it crops up in American popular culture all the time—and in real life, too. This is the kind of thinking that has gotten the United States into trouble all over our own planet since the end of World War II. Maybe it's time for us to think again before we really do take off for other worlds.

# PIRANHA

1978

**DIRECTOR:** Joe Dante
**PRODUCERS:** Jon Davison and Chako Van Leeuwen
**SCREENPLAY:** John Sayles
**CAST:** Bradford Dillman, Heather Menzies, Kevin McCarthy, Keenan Wynn, Dick Miller, Barbara Steele, Bruce Gordon, Paul Bartel, Richard Deacon
**ORIGINAL RELEASE:** New World Pictures
**VIDEO:** Warner Home Video

When *Jaws* hit the big screen in 1975, it was followed by a tidal wave of aquatic monster movies looking to cash in on the big bucks—*Tentacles, Orca, Alligator, Blood Beach, Island Claw, Barracuda,* and *Killer Fish,* not to mention *Jaws 2, Jaws 3,* and *Jaws: The Revenge.* You can add *Piranha* to that list, too, though this is a lot more than just another *Jaws* rip-off.

*Piranha* is an early effort by Joe Dante, who went on to direct *The Howling, Gremlins, Gremlins 2, Innerspace,* and *The 'Burbs.* Dante is a master of the postmodern serio-comic film, the kind of movie you can watch straight or as a parody of its genre, and *Piranha* is certainly one of these. The screenplay by John Sayles (*Return of the Secaucus 7, Brother From Another Planet, Matewan*) gives Dante everything he needs to make *Piranha* a very funny, very scary sci-fi/aquatic monster flick.

And take a look at this cast, which is a who's who of the science fiction and horror genres: Bradford (*Moon of the Wolf, Bug*) Dillman, Heather (*Sssss*) Menzies, Kevin (*Invasion of the Body Snatchers, The Howling*) McCarthy, Dick (*Little Shop of Horrors, Bucket of Blood*) Miller, the legendary Barbara (*Black Sunday, She-Beast*) Steele, Paul (*Frankenweenie, Eating Raoul*) Bartel, Keenan (*The Clonus Horror, Orca*) Wynn, and Richard Deacon, whom most will recognize as Mel from the original *Dick Van Dyke Show* but who also appeared in *Invasion of the Body Snatchers* with McCarthy back in '55. Just the chance to see all these good people in the same movie is worth the price of admission.

Maggie McKeown (Menzies) is a private detective

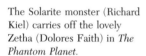

The Solarite monster (Richard Kiel) carries off the lovely Zetha (Dolores Faith) in *The Phantom Planet.*

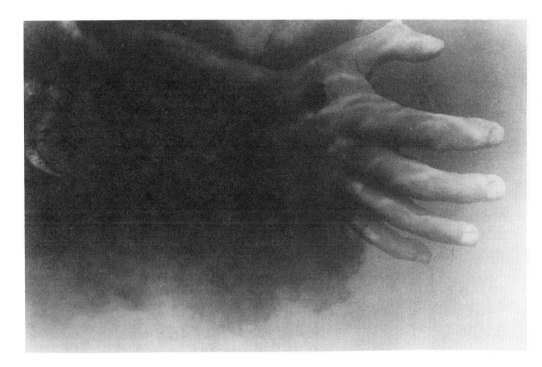

The *Piranha* attack in Joe Dante's excellent re-working of *Jaws*.

looking for two teenagers who disappeared while hiking on the mountain where Paul Grogan (Dillman) lives as a drunken, burned-out hermit. Working together, they discover an abandoned military research base where mad Dr. Robert Hoak (McCarthy), the scientist in residence, is continuing experiments with piranha that the army gave up on at the end of the Vietnam War. The idea was to develop a strain of super killer fish that could reproduce rapidly, could live in fresh or salt water in any climate, and would be hungry as hell—the ultimate weapon to destroy the enemy's river system. In fact Hoak's piranha were responsible for the disappearance of the teens. Unfortunately and accidentally Maggie and Paul release the fish from their holding tank and into the river, and as Hoak points out: "There'll be no way to stop them."

Maggie and Paul can try, though, and they race against time and fish to save the new resort and the summer camp that are located on the river downstream. On the way, the piranha kill Hoak and Paul's best friend, Jack (Wynn), so we know the little critters mean business.

The military enters the conflict, but General Waxman (Gordon) and Dr. Mengers (Steele), the evil scientist of the movie, want only to cover everything up, so they do whatever they can to stop Paul and Maggie. In fact Waxman is a large investor in the new resort, owned by cowboy star Buck Gardner (Miller), and he doesn't want rumors of killer fish ruining the opening day celebrations.

The little monsters do invade the summer camp, much to the dismay of Mr. Dumont (Bartel), the dictato-

Jack (Keenan Wynn) has a pretty good life on the river until the *Piranha* come along and chew off his feet.

Maggie McKeown (Heather Menzies), Dr. Mengers (Barbara Steele), and Colonel Waxman (Bruce Gordon) look on as a soldier uses some meat as bait to see if there are any mutant *Piranha* in the river.

As it turns out, there really are *Piranha* in the river.

The *Piranha* attack a summer camp. (Courtesy Hollywood Book and Poster)

Little Betsy (Belinda Balaski) tries to save a couple of her camp counselors from the *Piranha*.

195

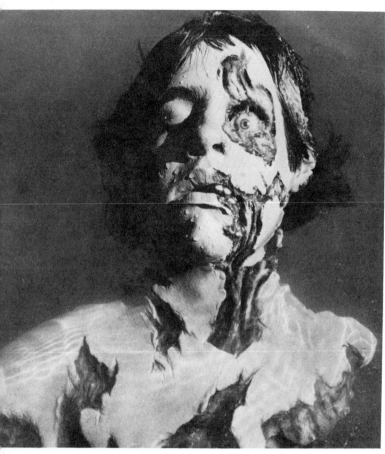

An example of Rob Bottin's fine makeup in Joe Dante's *Piranha*.

shark video game, fish cartoons, a clip from *The Monster That Challenged the World* (a 1950s aquatic monster flick), a girl on the beach reading *Moby-Dick*, etc. Even the cast of sci-fi and horror regulars shows the filmmakers' awareness of the genre they are sending up. But, of course, like so many Steven Spielberg films, *Jaws* was also a parody of earlier watery monster movies like *Creature From the Black Lagoon, It Came From Beneath the Sea, The Monster That Challenged the World*, and Roger Corman's *Creature From the Haunted Sea*—which was also a parody.

So that would make *Piranha* a parody of a parody of a parody, right?

We really do live in confusing times.

# PLANET OF THE VAMPIRES

1965

**ALTERNATE TITLE:** *Terro nello spazio*
**DIRECTOR:** Mario Bava
**PRODUCER:** Fulvio Lucisano
**SCREENPLAY:** Callisto Cosulich, Antonio Roman, Alberto Bevilacqua, Mario Bava, Rafael J. Salvia
**CAST:** Barry Sullivan, Norma Bengell, Angel Aranda, Evi Marandi, Fernando Villena
**ORIGINAL RELEASE:** Italian International Film/ Castilla Cinematografica
**VIDEO:** HBO Home Video

rial director, then make their way on to the resort, where Gardner's assistant informs him: "The piranha . . . they're eating the guests, sir."

Paul manages to release the waste from an abandoned smelting plant into the river, hoping to poison the water and the piranha as well, but in the end, despite Dr. Mengers's assurance that "There's nothing left to fear," we can't help suspecting that some of the fish made it to the ocean after all. If so, the river systems of the world are doomed.

Sci-fi movies are almost always anti-science, and since the late sixties, a lot of them have been anti-military, too. *Piranha* goes them one better by suggesting that evil science, the military, and big business are in cahoots for their own good and that they certainly aren't concerned with our welfare, despite constant claims of "national security." As General Waxman says, "Some things are more important than a few people's lives."

This is serious stuff, but as I suggested above, *Piranha* is also a parody of the *Jaws*-inspired movies, and a very funny one. The movie is full of self-reflexive gags—a

Director Mario Bava (*Bay of Blood, Black Sabbath, Baron Blood, Twitch of the Death Nerve*) has a solid cult following, and this Italian-Spanish coproduction is one of the reasons why. Despite the English title, there are no vampires in this flick, but there are walking dead people, lots of fog, and plenty of atmosphere.

Spacecraft Argos and its sister ship Galliant land on a fog-shrouded planet to investigate strange signals indicating there might be life there. During the landing, the Argos loses contact with the Galliant, and everyone on board except Captain Mark (Sullivan) blacks out. When the crew members come to, they start attacking each other, then seem to come out of a trance, unable to remember what they have done.

The Argos is damaged, and when a landing party goes out to look for the Galliant, they find her crew dead. Mark and his people bury their comrades and return to the Argos. Then in the most striking visual moment of the film, we see the dead come out of their graves, tear their way through transparent body bags, and wander off into the fog.

Back at the Argos, crew members are disappearing, then turning up dead. Mark and Sanya (Bengell) go exploring again and discover an abandoned spacecraft manned by gigantic alien skeletons—earlier victims of the strange planet.

Wess (Aranda) is trying to repair the Argos, and Tiona (Morandi) claims to have seen some of their dead colleagues up and walking around. Then two survivors of the Galliant show up, looking and acting weird and asking for help. Eventually Mark and the others discover that the "survivors" are really dead, and one of them explains that they are being controlled by the natives of the planet who exist only as pulses of light but who can inhabit any creature.

The planet's sun is dying, and the natives have been sending out signals for centuries, trying to lure others to their world so they can escape. Now they want to inhabit the bodies of Mark and the others and use the Argos to leave their planet.

Needless to say, the living crew members object to this plan and fight back, but by the time the Argos is ready to take off, only Mark, Sanya, and Wess are left. Even worse, Wess soon discovers that Mark and Sanya

Visitors to the *Planet of the Vampires*—Sanya (Norma Bengell), Wess (Angel Aranda), Dr. Karen (Fernando Villena), and Mark Markary (Barry Sullivan).

are hosts to the alien life-forms, and he dies in a effort to destroy the ship and keep the aliens from invading his home world.

The Argos is damaged, and Mark knows it will not take them all the way home. They must land on the nearest planet, which in a painfully hokey ending turns out to be our Earth; the aliens will now conquer it and make their own world.

With this disappointing climax, *Planet of the Vampires* becomes another one of those end-of-the-world-as-we-know-it science fiction flicks that have become so com-mon since the end of World War II. Prior to 1945, of course, the end of the world was not a real possibility—it was pretty much unthinkable. With the advent of the atomic bomb, however, all that changed, and the fifties saw the first wave of doomsday films. By the late sixties, nuclear disaster movies became for the most part eco-logical disaster movies. Every now and then aliens from another planet did the job. Whatever the cause, how-ever, human life on planet Earth has bitten the dust hundreds of times.

It seems worth asking: Why has the end of the world

In a scene that would be repeated in *Alien,* Mark and Sanya discover a gigantic skeleton on board an alien spacecraft on the *Planet of the Vampires.* (Courtesy Hollywood Book and Poster)

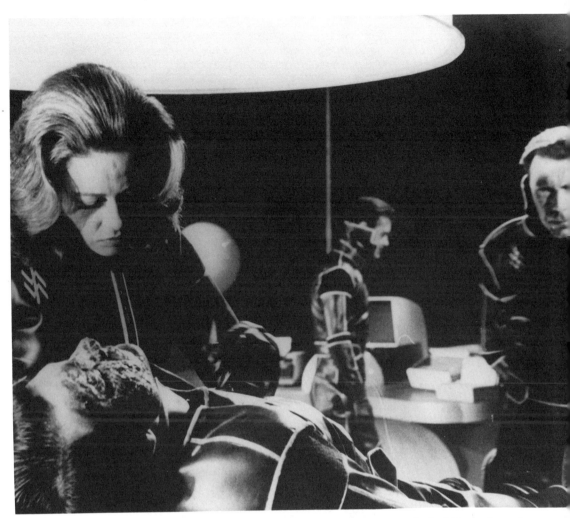

Sanya checks the body of one of
her dead comrades in Mario Bava's
*Planet of the Vampires*.

Tiona (Evi Morandi) freaks out
when one of her dead colleagues
returns to a semblance of life.
They don't call this place the
*Planet of the Vampires* for nothing.

199

The living battle the living dead on the *Planet of the Vampires.* (Courtesy Hollywood Book and Poster)

Mark doesn't look at all well. He's probably sorry he ever came to the *Planet of the Vampires.*

to take a sledgehammer to my car when it won't do what I want it to do. It is at such moments that I realize my car owns me, not the other way around. Of course I don't destroy my car—that would be stupid—but I kind of get a kick out of those crash-em-up *Smokey and the Bandit* flicks, maybe because at some level I'm pretending the car going over that cliff in the movie is my old clunker.

Maybe that's what end-of-the-world movies are good for, too. We don't really want to see human life on Earth obliterated, but it's fun now and then to imagine what it would be like not to have to get up in the morning and go to work. And if it *was* the end of the world, that would sure get me off the hook for those credit card payments.

# QUEEN OF OUTER SPACE

1958

**DIRECTOR:** Edward L. Bernds
**PRODUCER:** Ben Schwalb
**SCREENPLAY:** Charles Beaumont

become such a popular theme? Is it possible that we are so sick of our civilization that we enjoy the idea of its complete destruction?

Probably not, but all of us get the urge now and then to destroy what we value. I, for one, have often wanted

Guided by Talleah (Zsa Zsa Gabor), the guys from Earth—Professor Konrad (Paul Birch), Mike Cruze (Dave Willock), and Neil Patterson (Eric Fleming)—run into trouble on Venus in *Queen of Outer Space.*

**CAST:** Zsa Zsa Gabor, Eric Fleming, Laurie Mitchell, Paul Birch, Barbara Darrow, David Willock, Lisa Davis, Patrick Waltz, Marilyn Buford

**ORIGINAL RELEASE:** Allied Artists

**VIDEO:** Fox Video

If there is some mysterious force that draws you irresistibly to really bad movies—and believe me, I know exactly how you feel—then you can't afford to miss this one. Of course, any movie that stars Zsa Zsa Gabor has a couple of strikes against it right from the start, but *Queen of Outer Space* has some of the lowest production values I've ever seen, the acting is incompetent, the story is downright stupid, the pacing is painfully slow—*and* it has Zsa Zsa Gabor! If you are really a student of bad cinema, you really couldn't ask for much more in a sci-fi film.

The year is 1995, and Captain Neil Patterson (Fleming of TV's *Rawhide*), Mike Cruze (Willock), Larry Turner (Waltz), and Professor Konrad (Birch) are on their way to Space Station 8 some ten thousand miles from Earth to check on reports of hostile alien activity. En route they see the station destroyed by a mysterious ray. Then their ship is hit, and the blast accelerates them all the way to a crash landing on Venus.

The men are soon captured by a band of beautiful women in miniskirts and spiked heels and taken to meet the masked Queen Yllana. Now the ads and trailer for *Queen of Outer Space* suggest that Zsa Zsa is the regent

Talleah pretends to capture Earthlings Neil Patterson and Larry Turner (Patrick Waltz) to maintain her cover as a loyal subject of the *Queen of Outer Space*.

of the title, but she isn't. Laurie Mitchell plays the evil Yllana, and Zsa Zsa is Talleah, the planet's leading scientific genius—typecasting.

The Amazon society of Venus has been monitoring Earth broadcasts for some time, so all the women there speak perfect American English—except for Talleah, who must have been listening to Hungarian broadcasts. Yllana accuses the Earthlings of coming to Venus to spy on their civilzation and plan an invasion. The guys deny this, but she orders them imprisoned.

Talleah, who is secretly part of a disgruntled group that opposes the queen, visits the Earthlings in their cell and explains what's been going on. Ten years ago, there was a devastating war between Venus and the planet Morto. Venus won, but after the war, Yllana seized control of the government and executed or banished all the men. It was Yllana who destroyed Space Station 8, using the beta disintegrator ray. Now she plans to destroy the Earth as well, because there are men there and she hates all men.

The queen sends for Neil, and the other guys tell him to sweet-talk her and win her over, which he agrees to do. But Talleah likes Neil, and she immediately becomes jealous. As Larry explains, "Twenty million miles from Earth, and the little dolls are just the same."

Neil tries romancing Yllana, and for a minute or two he does okay. "Even a queen can be lonely, Captain," she says. But she refuses to remove her mask, and when Neil takes it off for her, we see that her face is horribly scarred by radiation burns received in the war. "Men did this," she snarls.

Captain Patterson ends up back in the cell with his men, but Talleah and a couple of her followers set them free. The group sets off to disable the disintegrator ray before Yllana can use it on Earth, and after they escape from the palace, they make their way through the Venusian forest and into a cave, where they run into that same giant spider that seems to attack all Earthlings who visit other planets in 1950s science fiction movies.

Yllana's guards track them down, and eventually Talleah and her friends have to turn the men over again, pretending that they captured the Earthlings to keep themselves from being imprisoned, too. Back at the palace, Talleah pulls a gun on Yllana and takes her mask, hoping to pass herself off as the queen. This doesn't work, and soon all the good people are prisoners, men and women alike.

Yllana powers up the disintegrator ray, but when she fires it at the Earth, it doesn't work—Talleah's forces have sabotaged the weapon. In fact the ray blows up, burning Yllana to a crisp, and Talleah takes over as the new leader.

Well, all the problems on Venus are solved, but Captain Patterson and his men are informed that it could be a year or more before a rescue ship from Earth can come to take them home—a whole year as the only four men on a planet full of women. Hoo-hah!

In many ways, *Queen of Outer Space* is yet another remake of *Cat-Women of the Moon*—just what the world needs. It's hardly worth mentioning how incredibly sexist this movie is. The basic assumption here is that the only thing women really want is to cook and clean for men—even women who manage to run their own civilization and create high-tech devices like the beta disintegrator ray. Oh, well, some women say they don't want to devote their whole lives to men, but they're only the ugly ones like Yllana, who couldn't get guys anyway and who have to pretend not to want men even though they really do. Again, according to Lieutenant Turner, no matter where you are in the universe or how advanced a civilization you encounter, "the little dolls are just the same."

Did you ever wonder where movies like *Queen of Outer Space* come from? Making a film involves a lot of people—not just actors and directors and producers and screenwriters but crew members and investors and

Konrad, Cruze, and Patterson seize Yllana (Laurie Mitchell), the *Queen of Outer Space,* while Talleah looks on.

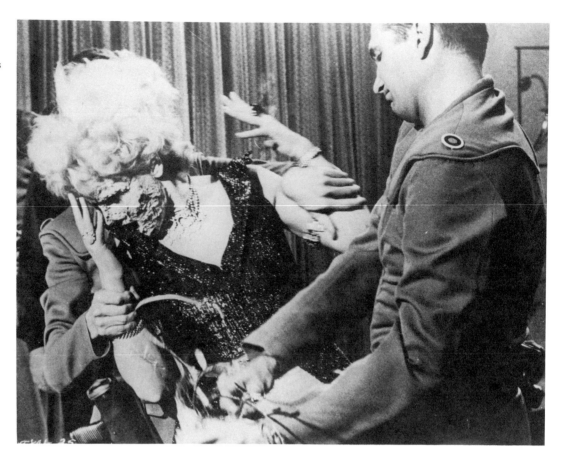

Captain Patterson unmasks the horribly disfigured *Queen of Outer Space*.

publicity people and drivers and caterers and others. With all those individuals taking part in this production, it's amazing that during the whole process of bringing *Queen of Outer Space* to the screen, nobody ever stood up and said, "This is really stupid. Let's just stop everything and go home."

In any case, *Queen of Outer Space* demands a lot from the viewer—a high tolerance for boredom and silliness, among other things—but if you can take it, I recommend it highly. The fact is, there's nothing else quite like it.

# RABID

1977

**DIRECTOR/SCREENPLAY:** David Cronenberg
**PRODUCER:** John Dunning
**CAST:** Marilyn Chambers, Frank Moore, Joe Silver, Howard Ryshpan

**ORIGINAL RELEASE:** Cinepix/Dibar Syndicates/ Canadian Film Development Corporation/Famous Players
**VIDEO:** Warner Home Video

For a good part of his career, David Cronenberg has been showing us the frightening things that can happen to the human body and the human mind, and more often than not in Cronenberg's films, these horrors are brought about by the very scientists who are supposed to be preventing them—physicians.

*Rabid* is a virtual remake of Cronenberg's movie of 1975, known variously as *Shivers, They Came From Within,* or *The Parasite Murders.* Both films are responses to the sexual revolution of the sixties and seventies, and both are terrifying prophecies of the AIDS epidemic to come. Hard-core porno star Marilyn Chambers might seem like a strange choice for the lead in *Rabid*—Cronenberg wanted the then-unknown Sissy Spacek for the part—but in fact Chambers's presence adds an additional dimension to the movie. In a sense, she is symbolic of the sexual revolution the film addresses.

Hart Read (Moore) and his girlfriend, Rose (Chambers), are involved in a terrible motorcycle accident not far from Dr. Dan Keloid's (Ryshpan) clinic for plastic surgery. Hart is injured, but Rose needs an operation immediately to save her life. Keloid has been experimenting with what he calls neutral field grafts, in which skin taken from one part of the body is treated so that it will actually become one with the area where it is applied—thigh skin will become cheek skin and so on.

He uses this new grafting technique to restore some of Rose's damaged internal organs.

Rose is in a coma at the Keloid Clinic for a month, and when she comes to, something is wrong. She has developed a weird phallic-looking thing that emerges from a hole in her armpit, and she uses it to puncture the skin of her victims and drink their blood. No one at the clinic knows of this, of course, and she manages to attack several people there, including Dr. Keloid

Rose (Marilyn Chambers) and Hart (Frank Moore), just before the motorcycle accident that causes all the problems in David Cronenberg's *Rabid*.

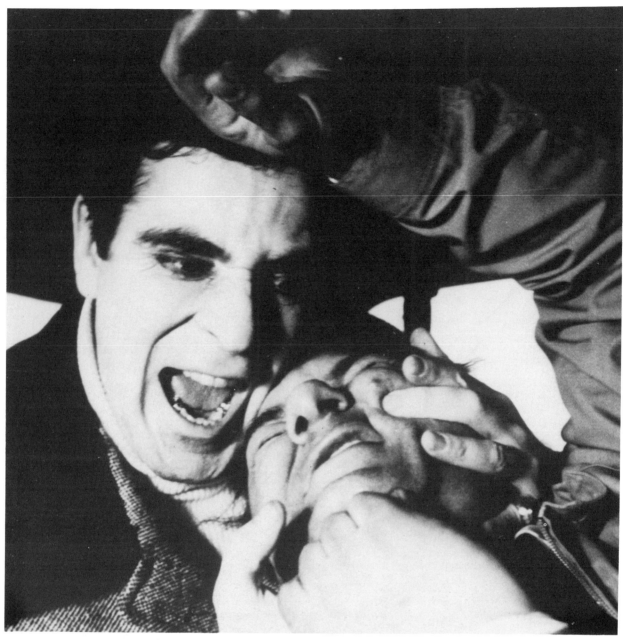

A passenger attacks and kills a helpful cabdriver. What's this guy's problem? He is *Rabid*.

himself, before she runs away and hitchhikes back home to Montreal.

Most of her victims don't die, and they don't remember the attacks—even Rose doesn't seem to be very clear about what she is doing. But the people she has contact with develop a virulent form of rabies that drives them murderously insane before it kills them. One of her victims from the clinic bites a cabdriver in the neck. A local farmer bites a waitress on the arm. In surgery, Keloid cuts off the finger of another doctor and drinks the flowing blood. Anyone who is attacked by one of

the rabies victims becomes rabid himself, and soon there is a full-scale epidemic under way.

The Department of Health comes up with a preventive vaccine, but there is no hope for those already infected, so the provincial government declares a state of martial law in Montreal. Anyone who has the disease is to be shot on sight.

Rose goes to stay with her best friend in the city and continues to find new victims, usually by pretending to offer them sex, then giving them the needle. Meanwhile, Hart and Keloid's business partner Murray Cypher (Silver) know that she has left the clinic and are trying to find her. The streets of Montreal are full of soldiers and garbage trucks for collecting the dead, and people are attacking each other on street corners, in shopping malls, and in the sanctity of their own homes.

The health officials manage to trace the epidemic back to Keloid's clinic, and they suspect that there is a carrier, a modern Typhoid Mary. When Hart finally does track Rose down, he arrives in time to see her attacking her girlfriend and realizes that she is the carrier the authorities are looking for. Rose denies it and runs away to try a little test. She picks up a man, pretends to seduce him, ingests his blood, then stays around to see if he gets the disease. He does, of course, and he kills her. In the closing scene, an army patrol finds Rose's body in a vacant lot and dumps her into the back

Dr. Dan Keloid (Howard Ryshpan) foams at the mouth as his partner Murray Cypher (Joe Silver) looks on in *Rabid*.

of a pickup truck with the rest of the bodies, never realizing that she is the source of the infection, and potentially the source of a cure.

This is a very disturbing film because there are no villains. Rose is not at fault for what happens. Nor is Dr. Keloid, though it is his technique that causes the disease. Keloid seems like a good guy. Admittedly he makes his living doing nose jobs and face-lifts for rich people, but he isn't satisfied with that. When Murray presents the idea of using his clinic to start a franchise chain, Dan replies, "I just sure as hell don't want to become the Colonel Sanders of plastic surgery." Maybe if Keloid *had* been satisfied with simply doing cosmetic surgery, none of this would have happened, but he uses his neutral field grafts on Rose because without them, she would have died. Keloid is simply doing what, as a physician, he's supposed to do.

But if there are no bad guys here—no mad scientists, no evil vampires, no heartless seductresses—then disas-

ter comes about simply because sometimes, through nobody's fault, science goes wrong. In a society that is as dependent on science and its discoveries as ours is, this is not a comforting thought.

# ROBOT MONSTER

1953

**ALTERNATE TITLE:** *Monster From the Moon*
**DIRECTOR/PRODUCER:** Phil Tucker
**SCREENPLAY:** Wyott Ordung
**CAST:** George Nader, Claudia Barrett, Selena Royle, Gregory Moffett, Pamela Paulson, George Barrows, John Mylong

Ro-Man (George Barrows) stands before his cave with his bubble machine in *Robot Monster*.

Johnny (Gregory Moffett) confronts Ro-Man in a supremely dramatic moment from *Robot Monster*.

**ORIGINAL RELEASE:** 3-Dimensional Pictures
**VIDEO:** Rhino Home Video, Sinister Cinema, and Scorched Earth Productions.

If you are writing a book about cult science fiction films, this movie is pretty hard to avoid. *Robot Monster* has the reputation of being one of the worst flicks ever made, a reputation it certainly deserves, but you ought to take a look at it anyway, if only to see what one of the worst movies ever made is like.

Here's what passes for the plot. Little Johnny (Moffett) is playing spaceman with his sister Carla (Paulson) during a family picnic when he meets two archeologists, the professor (Mylong) and Roy (Nader), working in a nearby cave. Mother (Royle) and big sister Alice (Barrett) arrive and take the kids back to clean up after the picnic. Then the four of them lie down in the middle of nowhere to take a nap.

Johnny wakes up and sneaks back to the cave. Suddenly lightning strikes nearby and Johnny falls down. When he gets up again, he discovers strange equipment in the mouth of the cave, including a bubble machine like the one they used to use on the old *Lawrence Welk Show*. He also discovers Ro-Man (Barrows), an alien in a gorilla suit and diving helmet. From his hiding place,

the kid listens as Ro-Man contacts his boss, the Great Guidance (Barrows again in the same costume, and for some reason waving a violin bow). Ro-Man reports that he has wiped out all humans—he calls them Hu-Mans—with his calcinator death ray. GG points out, however, that Ro-Man has made a mistake. There are still eight humans left. "Eliminate error," GG warns him. "Is this not the law?" Ro-Man must take care of the survivors or be put to death himself as punishment for failure.

Johnny returns home, where now the professor from the cave is his father, a brilliant scientist who with Alice's help has developed electronic equipment to cloak their house from Ro-Man. As long as they remain inside the compound, Mother, Father, Alice, Carla, and Johnny are safe. Soon Roy returns to the house, too—now he is the professor's assistant, and together they have developed a serum to prevent all diseases. This might not seem to be particularly useful now that virtually all of humanity is dead, but it has the side effect of neutralizing the calcinator ray.

Roy reports that Jason and McCloud—whoever they are—are still alive and that they are going to try to reach the garrison stationed on the space platform in orbit around the Earth to get help. But Great Guidance destroys their rocket ship and the platform, and Ro-Man contacts the professor on his view screen to tell him: "There must be an end to your race."

Now this is the turning point of the film, so pay close attention. When Ro-Man sees Alice on the view screen, he is captivated. As we all know, there isn't an alien in the universe who can resist an Earth woman, and the emotionless, calculating Ro-Man is no exception, so he arranges to meet with her: "I do not understand, but it is only the girl called Alice that I want to see." She agrees to meet him—in fact she plans to give herself to the monster in order to save what's left of humanity, but Roy and her dad won't let her go and tie her up.

Johnny sneaks out again and meets Ro-Man, who tries the calcinator ray on him and finds out about the serum that makes it ineffective. Reluctantly Roy unties Alice so they can go look for Johnny, but they too run into Ro-Man and hide in a thicket.

Johnny returns home while Roy and Alice stay out for a while to get in some heavy petting, and by the time they come back to the compound, they are ready to announce their engagement. The professor marries them—Alice digs up a veil someplace, but Roy is willing to be married with no shirt on. Then the happy couple leaves the compound to go on a honeymoon (!?) in their favorite thicket.

Sweet little Carla leaves home to pick some flowers, and Ro-Man catches and strangles her. Then he stumbles upon Roy and Alice kissing in their thicket. Ro-Man pushes Roy off a cliff and carries Alice back to the cave. Mom, Dad, and Johnny are in the middle of Carla's funeral when Roy staggers back to the compound, informs them that Ro-Man has Alice, and drops dead.

Meanwhile, Ro-Man is tying Alice up at his headquarters when the Great Guidance calls up to complain: "You have captured the girl and not destroyed her." But Ro-Man has his own complaints; he wants to act on his emotions like the Hu-Mans. GG tells him to kill the girl or be killed himself.

Johnny comes to the cave and lures Ro-Man out so Mom and Dad can sneak in and free Alice. Just as Ro-Man is about the strangle the smart-mouthed little brat—something we've been waiting for throughout the whole picture—the Great Guidance zaps his underling, and Ro-Man falls, the victim of his own lust.

Now Johnny comes to for real, and he's back at the cave with his archeologist friends. Apparently he bumped his head and was out cold for a while. "Boy," he says, "was that a dream or was it?" Alice, Carla, and Mom are all glad to find the kid again, and they invite the professor and Roy back home for dinner. But after they leave, we see Ro-Man coming out of the cave. Oh, no! Was Johnny's dream really a premonition of things to come?

There are elements of a pretty good sci-fi flick here, one of those last-survivors-of-the-human-race-battle-aliens movies. And there are some surprises, too, like the strangling of cute little Carla—kids never met gruesome deaths in fifties movies—or the death of Roy, the male lead. But *Robot Monster* fails to take advantage of what little it has going for it. Certainly the *Wizard of Oz* bit about Johnny's dream doesn't help, and neither does the fact that a lot of the action is not shown but presented in tedious dialogue.

Still, there's something disturbing about this movie. Maybe it's the bondage scenes: Alice gets tied up by everybody, even her own father, and that's pretty weird. Or maybe it's the idea that an alien gorilla with a fishbowl on his head would want to make love to a pretty Earth woman. That's pretty weird, too.

Or maybe it's only that we never really find out what the damned bubble machine is for or why the Great Guidance keeps waving that violin bow around.

Well, check out *Robot Monster* and perhaps you can answer these questions for yourself. By the way, the Rhino Home Video version of the film is in 3-D, as was the original, and comes complete with green-and-red glasses. Have fun!

# SANTA CLAUS CONQUERS THE MARTIANS

1964

**DIRECTOR:** Nicholas Webster
**PRODUCER:** Paul Jacobson

Young lovers Roy (George Nader) and Alice (Claudia Barrett) may be the world's only hope after the invasion of the *Robot Monster*.

The evil Voldar (Vincent Beck) and his henchman are captured by Kimar (Leonard Hicks), the leader of Mars, in the appalling *Santa Claus Conquers the Martians*.

Droppo (Bill McCutcheon), destined to become the Martian Santa Claus, helps the Earth Santa (John Call) entertain Billy (Victor Stiles) and Betty (Donna Conforti) on board the Martian spaceship in *Santa Claus Conquers the Martians*.

**SCREENPLAY:** Glenville Mareth
**CAST:** John Call, Leonard Hicks, Vincent Beck, Pia Zadora
**ORIGINAL RELEASE:** Jalor Productions
**VIDEO:** Goodtimes Home Video

Frankly, I'm embarrassed to be a member of the same species as the people who made this movie. Sure, *Santa Claus Conquers the Martians* is intended for children, but no self-respecting kid could find this film anything but stupid.

It seems that the children of Mars are depressed and listless. Kimar (Hicks), the Martian leader, attributes this state to the fact that the kids spend too much time watching Earth video programs. That makes sense—after all, watching TV is what makes us Earthlings depressed and listless, too.

As it turns out, though, the Martian kids feel deprived. They've learned about Santa from Earth TV. But Martians don't celebrate Christmas, and Mars has no Santa Claus. So, for the good of his own kids, Bomar and Grimar (Zadora in her first movie role), Kimar leads an expedition to Earth to kidnap Santa (Call) and bring him to Mars. As he says, "Earth has had Santa Claus long enough."

The Martians raid the workshop at the North Pole

Everything ends happily for Betty, Santa, Grimar (Pia Zadora), Droppo, Bomar (Christopher Month), Kimar, and Billy in *Santa Claus Conquers the Martians.*

and take Santa back to Mars, along with Billy and Betty, two Earth kids. One member of the Martian expedition, however, opposes this whole plan. Voldar (Beck) is of the old school, and he believes that children should not be allowed to play or have fun. Bringing Santa and Christmas to Mars will only make Martians soft. As Voldar explains, "That old man's a menace."

Voldar tries to kill Santa, Billy, and Betty on the way back to Mars, but his plans fail. Then he tries to kidnap the jolly old fellow, but again Santa makes a fool of him. Eventually Kimar has Voldar imprisoned. Santa sets up a workshop and brings Christmas to Mars at last. Now the Martian kids are happy: "They've never laughed before," observes Kimar's wife, Momar. In fact everyone is happy, now that the evil Voldar and his henchmen are out of the way. Kimar would like to keep Santa on Mars, but instead, St. Nick nominates Dropo, the village idiot, to be the Martian Santa Claus, and Kimar agrees to take Santa, Billy, and Betty back to Earth.

Probably nothing could have saved this movie, but the cheap sets and costumes, bad acting, and clumsy direction don't help. But this is more than just a bad film. It's an insulting film.

According to *Santa Claus Conquers the Martians,* what other cultures really want is to be just like us Americans, and this is what they should want. In this flick, of course, the other culture is Mars, a highly advanced and technological civilization, but from our point of view, not perfect—after all, they aren't Christians and they don't approve of television. Fortunately for them, their children show them the error of their ways, and, at the end of the movie, Mars is just like Earth— actually, just like the United States.

Voldar is the bad guy in this film because he wants to retain Martian culture. Kimar is the good guy because he is willing to trash his own culture in order to make Mars a cultural colony of Earth, and the movie tells us that this is the way things should be.

212

In the real world, we of the West too often believe that other cultures and nations would be okay if they'd only embrace our values and live like we do. It never occurs to us that other peoples might not want to be like us and that what seems to be right for us might not even work for them. The only good thing about *Santa Claus Conquers the Martians* is that it can show us how shortsighted, foolish, and insulting these notions are.

And as long as we're talking about insulting notions, get this. Throughout most of this film, the Martians are a kind of metallic green color, but by the end the makeup has pretty much disappeared. Given the lousy production values of this flick, the makeup people probably just ran out of supplies or forgot. But the effect is rather striking. As it turns out, Santa—our cultural representative—has not only converted the Martians to our way of life. He has even managed to turn them white!

# SCANNERS

1981

**DIRECTOR/SCREENPLAY:** David Cronenberg
**PRODUCER:** Claude Heroux

**CAST:** Jennifer O'Neill, Stephen Lack, Patrick McGoohan, Lawrence Dane, Michael Ironside
**ORIGINAL RELEASE:** Filmplan International
**VIDEO:** Columbia TriStar Home Video

In the late 1970s, in an effort to bolster its own film industry, Canada provided tax incentives for investors willing to put money into Canadian movie projects. As a result, there was plenty of money around, and Canadian director David Cronenberg had the opportunity for a time to do almost anything he wanted. As we all know, what he wanted to do was to direct some of the strangest, most powerful horror and science fiction movies ever made. *Scanners* was one such project. Thank you, Canadian Film Development Corporation!

Cameron Vale (Lack) is a derelict with a problem. He is telepathic, and the voices he hears in his head—the inner thoughts of those around him—are driving him crazy. Then one day he is kidnapped and taken to ConSec, an international security organization, to meet Dr. Paul Ruth (McGoohan) who tells him he is a scanner. And he is not the only one.

Meanwhile, at a seminar sponsored by ConSec for the international intelligence community to demonstrate the security uses of scanning, a renegade scanner

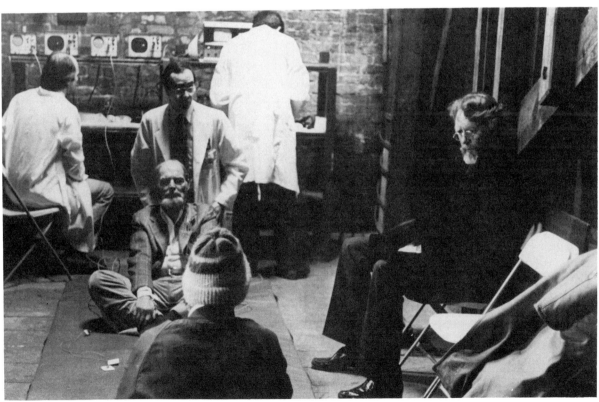

Dr. Paul Ruth (Patrick McGoohan), right, tests the psychic powers of Cameron Vale (Stephen Lack), foreground, in David Cronenberg's *Scanners.* (Courtesy Hollywood Book and Poster)

213

Cameron Vale visits fellow scanner and sculptor Benjamin Pierce (Robert Silverman), who has taken to living inside of his own head in *Scanners*. (Courtesy Hollywood Book and Poster)

named Darryl Revok (Ironside) offends the entire audience by telepathically blowing the head off the ConSec scanner. This is the famous exploding head scene that was widely advertised when the film was first released—"It'll blow your mind"—and it is every bit as effective now as it was in 1981.

Ruth believes that Revok heads an underground scanner organization, and he wants Vale to infiltrate that group for ConSec. In return, Ruth gives Cameron a drug called ephemoral, which can suppress his telepathic abilities and allow him to focus and control them. Ephemerol gets rid of the voices in his head.

ConSec has a list of 236 known scanners, and Cameron sets off to contact some of those who might know about Revok's operations. Unfortunately, almost everyone he contacts ends up dead, including the members of a scanner self-help group headed by Kim Obrist (O'Neill). Soon Vale and Kim are on the run from Revok's assassins.

As it turns out, Braedon Keller (Dane), head of ConSec's internal security, is secretly working for Revok and is using ConSec's computers to store information about Revok's plan for world conquest. Keller tries to kill Kim and succeeds in killing Paul Ruth, but Cameron

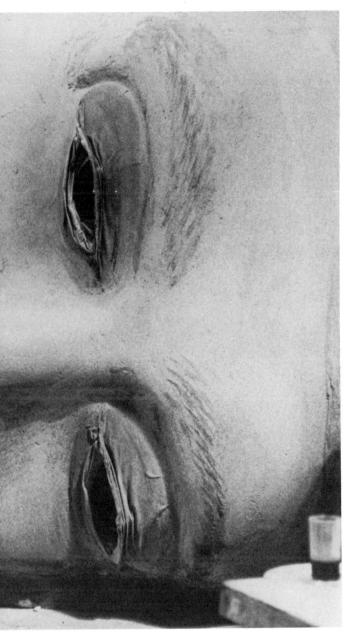

Cameron joins a scanner support group led by Kim Obrist (Jennifer O'Neill) in *Scanners*. Today these people would have their own TV talk show. (Courtesy Hollywood Book and Poster)

A couple of thugs from ConSec gun down several members of the scanner support group, but then the survivors turn their formidable powers on their assailants in David Cronenberg's *Scanners*. (Courtesy Hollywood Book and Poster)

manages to scan the ConSec computer system and comes up with a list of doctors who are giving ephemerol to their pregnant female patients—ephemerol that is being manufactured by a company run by Revok.

Revok finally captures Cameron and Kim and explains what's been going on; it's a good thing, too, because by now the plot has gotten a bit confusing. Back in the late 1940s, psychopharmacologist Paul Ruth developed ephemerol as a tranquilizer for use with pregnant women, but it had an unexpected side effect—it turned the babies into scanners. Most of them went crazy because they were unable to handle their powers, but

Ruth saw the military and intelligence potential of his drug and went to work for ConSec.

Ruth first tested the drug on his own wife during her two pregnancies, and his sons—Vale and Revok—are

215

the most powerful scanners around. Their father abandoned them to their own devices until Revok became a threat; then Ruth recruited Cameron to destroy his own brother. Revok's plan is to create more scanners for his own purposes—"There's a whole generation of scanner soldiers just a few months from being born"—and he wants Cameron to join him in ruling the world.

Vale refuses—he *is* the good guy, after all—and he and Revok engage in a scanning duel as Darryl tries to suck his brother's mind into his own. It's an amazing battle, full of bulging veins and popping eyeballs, and at the end, both brothers are in fact in Revok's body, though Cameron seems to be the one in control. Or is he?

This is a fine film, made even better by the casting of Patrick *(The Prisoner)* McGoohan in the role of Paul Ruth. In some ways, this is a classic mad scientist flick, and it owes a lot to the story of *Frankenstein.* As we all remember, through his experiments, Dr. Frankenstein "gives birth" to a son—the monster—then abandons him, only to have him return with a vengeance. Ruth does the same. He creates Darryl and Cameron, then cuts them loose. In the end, like Frankenstein, Ruth's own monster, Revok, is the cause of his destruction.

As played by McGoohan, however, Paul Ruth is not an evil man. Like other mad movie scientists since the late sixties, he is simply a guy doing his job. In fact, like far too many of us, he has sacrificed his family to his

This is the high-tech plant where ephemerol is being produced by renegade scanner Darryl Revok (Michael Ironside). Ephemerol is the drug that, when given to pregnant women, gives birth to *Scanners.* (Courtesy Hollywood Book and Poster)

work. And like many of us, he never stops to think about what the consequences of his work and that sacrifice might be—until it's too late.

# SUPERMAN AND THE MOLE MEN

1951

**ALTERNATE TITLES:** *Superman and the Strange People, Unknown People*

**DIRECTOR:** Lee Scholem
**PRODUCER:** Barney A. Sarecky
**SCREENPLAY:** Richard Fielding
**CAST:** George Reeves, Phyllis Coates, Jeff Corey, Walter Reed, J. Farrell MacDonald, Stanley Andrews, Ray Walker, Hal K. Dawson
**ORIGINAL RELEASE:** Lippert Productions
**VIDEO:** Warner Home Video

*Superman and the Mole Men* was a theatrical feature that served as a sort of pilot for the first Superman TV series starring George Reeves. *The Adventures of Superman* premiered in 1951 and ran until 1957, for a total of 104 episodes, and it is still playing in reruns. But by the time *Superman and the Mole Men* hit the theaters, audiences were already used to seeing the Man of Steel on the screen.

Superman first appeared in the pages of *Action Comics #1* in 1938, and only three years later, Fleischer Studios released the first Superman cartoon, *The Mad Scientist*. In all, the Fleischer Brothers and Famous Studios produced seventeen animated Superman stories between 1941 and 1943. Then in 1948 Columbia released *Superman*, a fifteen-chapter serial with Kirk Alyn in the title role. *Atom Man vs. Superman*, another cliff-hanger serial, followed two years later, again with Alyn, and it marked the screen debut of Lex Luthor, played by B-movie legend Lyle Talbot. Fortunately for fans of Superman, all of the cartoons and both serials are available on videocassette.

*Superman and the Mole Men* also appeared on television in a shortened form as two episodes of the regular Superman series, under the title *Unknown People*, but the Warner Home Video version restores all the material that was cut from the TV broadcasts, so it is definitely worth looking at if you take your Superman seriously.

The movie starts with a brief voice-over lecture on the origin of the Man of Steel and then gets on to the plot. Somewhere out west, in the town of Silsby, the National Oil Company has drilled the deepest oil well

Poster art from *Superman and the Mole Men*, starring George Reeves and Phyllis Coates.

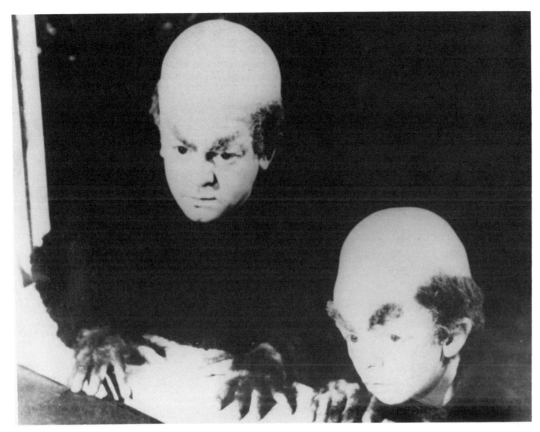

Two of the harmless creatures from the center of the Earth who cause all the commotion in *Superman and the Mole Men*.

Clark Kent (George Reeves) tries to stop Luke Benson (Jeff Corey) and his mob as Lois Lane (Phyllis Coates) and Bill Corrigan (Walter Reed) look on in *Superman and the Mole Men*.

in the world, but when reporters Clark Kent (Reeves) and Lois Lane (Coates) arrive from Metropolis to cover the story, they learn that manager Bill Corrigan (Reed) is closing down the project. Corrigan refuses to cooperate with the journalists or to explain why the effort is being shut down, though he does inform them that the well is 32,740 feet deep—nearly six miles. Clark thinks Corrigan is a very suspicious character, and so do we.

That night, when only watchman Pop Shannon (Mac-Donald) is around, the cap on the well opens, and two strange little men come out and look around. Later, when Clark and Lois return to the site to do some snooping, they find Pop dead of a heart attack. Lois sees something at the window of Pop's shed, and when Corrigan, the sheriff (Andrews), and Doc Saunders arrive in reply to Clark's phone call, she tells everyone what she saw: "They had the bodies of moles and great big human heads." Actually, what she saw was two midgets wearing fake bald wigs and fur suits with obvious zippers in the back, but hey, this is a low-budget flick, remember?

Everybody except Clark and Corrigan returns to town, and at this point the oil well manager spills the beans by showing Kent some soil samples that glow in the dark. Are they radioactive or simply phosphorescent? Corrigan isn't sure—he hasn't had time to test them—but he does know that at about 32,000 feet, his drill bit broke through an inner crust, proving that the center of the Earth is hollow! The bit also brought up some microscopic living organisms, suggesting that life could exist in the center of the world. In fact Corrigan suspects that Pop was frightened to death by something that came out of the well—possibly something radioactive!

Corrigan's suspicions are soon confirmed when some townsfolk see the little creatures, and Luke Benson (Corey), the local mean guy, organizes a hunting party to track them down and kill them. The crowd soon learns that the visitors from the center of the Earth might be radioactive and that they leave an eerie glow behind on any object they touch, and this doesn't make them any friendlier. Clark tries to talk the mob out of their plan to murder the mole guys: "They look strange to us, it's true, but we must look just as strange to them." Nobody listens, however, so Clark ducks into an alley and emerges as Superman, who sets out to stop the hunt.

Unfortunately he cannot prevent the mob from shooting one of the little guys, though he does manage to save the wounded mole man from a deadly fall and gets him to the hospital. The other creature escapes and goes back down the well.

The mob heads for the hospital to lynch the injured mole man, who has been saved by an operation performed by handsome young Dr. Reed. Once again Superman intervenes, and in a wonderful scene single-handedly disarms the entire crowd.

The mole guy who escaped earlier returns with two of his buddies and a huge weapon that looks a lot like a vacuum cleaner attachment, and they also head for the hospital, where Superman meets them and tries to explain that no one means them any harm. This isn't exactly true, though, because Benson tries to get the creatures with a shotgun, but they blast him with their ray. Superman saves Benson's life—he really is a great guy!—then returns the wounded mole man to his friends and escorts them all back to the well.

As it turns out, Corrigan proves that the glow left behind by the mole men is only a harmless phosphorescence, so no one was ever really in danger from the little visitors. It's too late to make friends, however. Once they are safely beneath the surface of the Earth, they blow up the well, sealing themselves off from the hostile surface dwellers forever.

At a time when we were quite intolerant of anything and anybody that wasn't 100 percent American, *Superman and the Mole Men* rises above most sci-fi films of the decade and argues that we have to try to understand and accept those who are not like us—a pretty impressive message for the early 1950s, even if in this film it is delivered with a very heavy hand. When Superman says to Benson, "It's men like you that make it difficult for people to understand one another," we know he is talking about bigots everywhere. He might even be talking about our political and military leaders—or about us.

# THE SWARM

1978

**DIRECTOR/PRODUCER:** Irwin Allen
**SCREENPLAY:** Stirling Silliphant
**CAST:** Michael Caine, Katharine Ross, Richard Widmark, Richard Chamberlain, Olivia de Havilland, Ben Johnson, Lee Grant, José Ferrer, Patty Duke Astin, Slim Pickens, Bradford Dillman, Fred MacMurray, Henry Fonda, Cameron Mitchell, Christian Juttner, Alejandro Rey
**ORIGINAL RELEASE:** Warner Brothers
**VIDEO:** Warner Home Video

This is another one of those Irwin Allen disaster movies with a cast of millions—if you count the bees. Reports of killer bees in South America led to a whole new subgenre of ecological disaster flick in the 1970s—*The Deadly Bees, The Savage Bees, Killer Bees,* and of course, *The Swarm,* which certainly features the biggest budget and the best cast of them all. I will now attempt to discuss this film without resorting to any stupid bee-movie jokes, but believe me, it isn't going to be easy.

In Texas, Major Baker (Dillman) and his men enter an ICBM installation where almost the entire crew has been wiped out by some mysterious force—the big brass suspects it was a chemical weapon attack. There Baker meets Dr. Brad Crane (Caine), a snotty entomologist who informs everyone, including General Slater (Widmark), that the soldiers were killed by bees. Crane has

Major Baker (Bradford Dillman) discovers an unauthorized civilian in the missile complex—Dr. Brad Crane (Michael Caine)—who tries to warn him about *The Swarm*.

School superintendent Maureen Schuster (Olivia de Havilland) looks out the window while dozens of her students are wiped out on the playground by *The Swarm*.

been predicting and planning for this bee invasion for years, but no one believes him, of course, until a gigantic swarm of African bees, arrived in Texas by way of Brazil, manages to down two air force helicopters. Much to General Slater's disappointment, the president of the United States puts civilian Brad in charge of operations, and the battle against the killer bees is on.

Dr. Helena Anderson (Ross) is an air force captain who is treating the survivors, but she isn't doing very well, because there is no known antidote for the killer bee sting. Brad sends for Dr. Walter Krim (Fonda), a close friend and the best immunologist in the country, in hopes that he will be able to come up with a mass antidote.

Meanwhile, outside of nearby Marysville, the Durant family is attacked by bees during a picnic, and Mom and Pop are killed, while young Paul (Juttner) manages to escape in the family car after receiving a couple of stings. He crashes into Marysville and informs Mayor Clarence Tuttle (MacMurray), school superindendent Maureen Schuster (de Havilland), and retired engineer Felix Austin (Johnson) about the bee attack. Brad and Helena visit Paul in the hospital, where he is hallucinating about giant bees—apparently, for some reason, this happens to everybody who gets stung and doesn't die right away.

Dr. Krim arrives in Texas and soon determines that three or four stings are fatal for most people, so he sets

Felix Austin (Ben Johnson) meets his end in a train crash caused by the killer bees of *The Swarm.*

to work on an antidote. More scientists arrive, including bee expert and ecological activist Dr. Hubbard (Chamberlain), and Crane calls a meeting to deliver a lecture on this mutant strain of African bees. General Slater wants to blast the swarm with insecticide, but Crane and other scientists veto this idea, because chemicals would kill all other insects in the area, including the good old American bee, who is a harmless and gentle creature and the friend of farmers everywhere.

Soon after, the swarm invades Marysville, killing 232 locals, and the event makes the network news, causing a nationwide panic. During the attack on Marysville, Helena is stung once and begins hallucinating about giant bees. At the same time, Krim discovers that some of those victims who seem to be getting better suddenly get worse and die for no apparent reason. Even those like Helena who have been stung only once are at risk, so Krim redoubles his efforts while Hubbard works on an effective poison that will kill only the African bees.

Marysville is evacuated, but the swarm attacks the train carrying the townsfolk and it crashes, killing almost everyone, including Clarence, Maureen, and Felix. By this time, the bees are only seventy miles from Houston.

Hubbard perfects his poison, and millions of pellets are dropped from helicopters, but the bees refuse to eat them—these are, it seems, very smart little insects. From this point on, cast members start dropping left and right. Little Paul has a relapse and dies. Krim tests

Dr. Walter Krim (Henry Fonda) and his assistants gather killer bee venom so he can work on an antidote to the deadly strings of *The Swarm.*

a new antidote on himself after taking a dose of bee venom, and he dies, too. Dr. Hubbard goes to a nuclear plant that is in the path of the swarm and tries to convince Dr. Andrews (Ferrer), the head of operations, to shut down, but before that can happen, the bees attack and cause a nuclear explosion, killing 36,422 people in the area.

Houston has been evacuated except for General Slater's headquarters, and he and Brad have their insecticide vs. ecological responsibility argument again. This time, though, the president sides with Slater, and the Air Force dumps chemicals that will kill all insect and plant life in the area for the next ten years—except for the bees, of course, which are immune to everything. The African bees enter Houston, and the president orders guys with flamethrowers to burn the city to the ground.

Brad finally figures out that a test signal from the ICBM site accidentally duplicated the frequency of the killer bees' mating call. This is what caused the initial attack on the missile base; the bees simply responded to a familiar sound. Brad manages to reproduce that signal, which he can use to lure the bees away from Houston. Of course, since he is an expert on these bees and has known all along that there was a sonic signal

Dr. Walter Krim, a noted immunologist, is one of many victims of killer bees in *The Swarm*.

that could control them, he could have saved tens of thousands of lives if he'd come up with this idea a little earlier in the flick, but better late than never. Unfortunately, before he can put his plan into operation, bees attack the headquarters, killing Slater and Baker and a whole bunch of other people, though Brad and Helena manage to escape.

Brad has the military spread an enormous oil slick in the Gulf of Mexico—so much for ecological responsibility—then lures the bees there with the mating call. Once they arrive, the oil slick is set on fire, and the problem is solved. Or is it?

You'd think that, given the kind of money and talent that went into making this flick, it would be a much

223

Noted bee expert and ecological activist Dr. Hubbard (Richard Chamberlain) is killed when *The Swarm* attacks a nuclear power plant, setting off a deadly explosion that wipes out a sizable chunk of Texas.

Major Baker and General Slater make a last stand against the killer bees in the final moments of *The Swarm*.

The soldiers who are burning Houston get a bit careless with their flamethrowers when they are attacked by *The Swarm*.

Another victim of *The Swarm*.

better film than it is. It definitely has its moments, but there are far too many unnecessary characters and subplots—the senior citizen love triangle involving Clarence, Felix, and Maureen is a good example of a minor point that takes up a lot of screen time and then is neatly resolved by killing off all three characters. As a result, the movie is much too long—more than two and a half hours in the expanded video version.

Even with all that screen time available, however, there are a surprising number of narrative gaps in this movie—apparently a lot of important footage was left on the cutting-room floor. For instance, during the bee attack on Marysville, Brad and Helena are accidentally locked in a walk-in freezer at the local restaurant. In the next scene, however, they are back at the ICBM base with no explanation as to how they managed to get out.

Ecological disaster movies like *The Swarm* are part of an American heritage of nature vs. civilization stories that have informed our literature and cinema for a long time, and generally these stories warn us that, in the face of the natural world, our civilization is a very fragile thing indeed. *The Swarm* says that, too—after all, a sizable chunk of the Southwest is wiped out because of the killer bees—but in the end, the movie says that with a little human ingenuity, we can still defeat nature.

Today, when the ecological disaster movies of the seventies could very well come true, this seems like a very irresponsible and dangerous message.

# TEENAGERS FROM OUTER SPACE

1959

**ALTERNATE TITLE:** *The Gargon Terror*
**DIRECTOR/PRODUCER/SCREENPLAY:** Tom Graeff
**CAST:** David Love, Dawn Anderson, Harvey B. Dunn, Bryant Grant, Tom Lockyear, Robert King Moody
**ORIGINAL RELEASE:** Topar Corporation
**VIDEO:** Al Taylor/Waltersheid, Sinister Cinema, and Scorched Earth Productions

*Teenagers From Outer Space* was made in the days when a guy like Tom Graeff could get a bunch of his

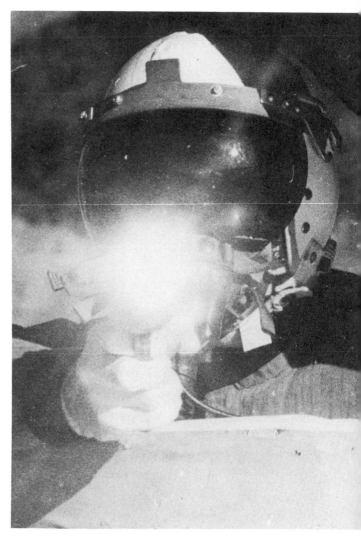

The evil Thor (Bryant Grant) uses the deadly disintegrator beam on a little dog in the opening moments of *Teenagers From Outer Space*.

friends together, make a movie for next to nothing, and get it distributed by Warner Bros. The film is terrible, of course—the title alone is enough to give *that* away. Everybody involved is pretty inept. When at the end of the flick, star David Love says, "I'm sorry I acted the way I did," you can't help but agree with him. And the shoestring budget shows. For instance, a physician in the film carries his instruments in a hatbox because apparently they couldn't afford a real-looking doctor's bag. And the horrible gargon monster is a lobster, pure and simple—I live in Maine, and I know what a lobster looks like.

On the other hand, all of the people who helped to make this movie really seem to be doing the best they can. Certainly everybody is very serious about the whole thing. A kind of dedication and affection comes through

Derek (David Love), the good alien, is one of the *Teenagers From Outer Space.*

Betty Morgan (Dawn Anderson) loves Derek, even after she learns that he is one of the *Teenagers From Outer Space.*

in the best moments—maybe because Graeff made the movie as a starring vehicle for his lover, David Love. Apparently, though, Graeff never made another film, and Love never acted professionally again, which is probably all for the best.

A spaceship lands on Earth with a crew of very human-looking aliens including young Derek (Love), Thor (Grant, whose real name is Bryant Geoffrey Pearson and who financed a big chunk of the movie), and the captain (played by Moody, who popped up occasionally on *Get Smart* and other TV shows of the sixties). Their mission is to find a planet where herds of gargon, the enormous and deadly creatures that provide their food, can be raised and harvested at a safe distance from their own population. Gargon start off very small—about the size of a lobster, as a matter of fact—but they grow to a million times their original size under the proper conditions. Earth looks like a good spot for a gargon ranch.

On landing, Thor, the bad guy, zaps a little dog with his focusing disintegrator ray, and Derek, the good guy, finds the mutt's tag among the bones, thus proving that there is civilized life on Earth. Derek objects to bringing the gargon to a populated planet, and when the others say they just don't care, he pulls a weapon and runs off to warn the Earthlings. Thor goes after him while the others take off for home, planning to lead hundreds of gargon-bearing ships back to Earth.

The rest of the movie is an extended chase scene,

Thor threatens a nurse (Helen Sage) in *Teenagers From Outer Space.* (Courtesy Hollywood Book and Poster)

with Derek running and Thor hot on his trail. Derek is befriended by Betty Morgan (Anderson) and her grandpa (Dunn, who has the distinction of appearing in a number of films by the legendary Edward D. Wood, Jr.), and he is also helped out by newsman Joe Rogers (Lockyear, actually producer-director-writer Graeff himself appearing under a stage name).

Meanwhile, Thor is disintegrating everybody in town—the guy at the gas station, Betty's sleazy friend Alice, and even a couple of cops—but eventually he is wounded and captured by the police. This doesn't solve the basic problem, though. The gargon ships are on the way, and a sample gargon that was left behind at the beginning of the movie has now grown to gigantic proportions and is moving toward the town.

Not surprisingly, Derek and Betty fall in love, and she doesn't change her mind even after she finds out that he is not of this Earth. Eventually Derek manages to repair Thor's damaged disintegrator and use it to stop the gargon, thus providing Earth with a valuable defensive weapon. By this time, though, the alien fleet is hovering overhead, and the advance ship lands again, ready to guide the others to the surface of the planet.

Derek finds out that he is the son of his planet's leader; in his advanced but sterile civilization, children are not raised by their parents, so he never knew. But the leader himself has come to Earth to meet his son and let him know that someday he will be the leader and dictator of their world. Derek pretends to go along with the idea. He even breaks Thor out of jail and brings him back to the ship. But then the crafty little guy fouls up the signals to the fleet, which brings the hundreds of alien ships crashing to the Earth, killing Thor and

Thor demonstrates the effects of the dreaded disintegrator ray in a shootout with the police in *Teenagers From Outer Space.* (Courtesy Hollywood Book and Poster)

228

Some locals are attacked by the gargon in *Teenagers From Outer Space*.

the leader—thus paving the way for a revolution on the home planet—and unfortunately, Derek himself. Sorry, no happy ending this time.

This is another one of those marvelous teen rebel movies of the fifties that pointed toward the youth movement of the sixties. It's also, in its own way, an immigrant film. Derek comes to America from an obviously communist planet, is welcomed here—Betty says, "I don't care where you come from"—and pledges his allegiance to his new home by providing us with a weapon to defend ourselves from commie aliens, by making a revolution possible on his native planet—he kills his own father to do this, thus marking a complete break with his past—and by giving his life for his new country. As he says, "I shall make the Earth my home, and I shall never, never leave it."

Norman Rockwell would have loved it. Maybe you will, too.

# THE TERRORNAUTS

1967

**DIRECTOR:** Montgomery Tully
**PRODUCER:** Max J. Rosenberg and Milton Subotsky

**SCREENPLAY:** John Brunner
**CAST:** Simon Oates, Zena Marshall, Charles Hawtrey, Patricia Hayes, Stanley Meadows, Max Adrian
**ORIGINAL RELEASE:** Amicus Productions
**VIDEO:** Charter Home Entertainment

Amicus Productions of England is best known for its series of horror anthology films—*Tales From the Crypt, Vault of Horror, Torture Garden, From Beyond the Grave,* and so forth—which borrow their style and even some of their stories from American horror comics of the 1950s. *The Terrornauts,* however, is an unusual Amicus excursion into science fiction, scripted by John Brunner, author of *Stand on Zanzibar, The Sheep Look Up,* and many other novels and certainly one of the finest British sci-fi writers. Even with this kind of talent behind it, however, *The Terrornauts* certainly doesn't measure up to the company's horror productions, though it has its heart in the right place.

Dr. Joe Burke (Oates) is a radio astronomer who heads Project Startalk and spends his time scanning the heavens with a radio telescope in hopes of picking up signals from alien life-forms. Unfortunately for Joe and his colleagues Ben Keller (Meadows) and Sandy Lund (Marshall), they've been at it for four years with no results.

Dr. Shore (Adrian) is the mean guy who is in charge

Space travelers Sandy Lund (Zena Marshall), Joshua Yellowlees (Charles Hawtrey), Joe Burke (Simon Oates), and Mrs. Jones (Patricia Hayes) discover a room full of talking cubes in an alien installation in *The Terrornauts*.

of the telescope Joe uses on a time-sharing basis, and he doesn't approve of the project, so he advises the Holmes Foundation, which supports Startalk, to cut off its funding. Luckily it is at this very time that Joe finally picks up a signal from outer space. Curiously Joe claims: "I've heard these signals before," and he tells Ben and Sandy a story from his childhood. It seems that his archeologist uncle once discovered a strange metal cube on a dig in France and gave it to Joe. That night, perhaps under the influence of the cube, little Joe dreamed of an alien world with two moons and heard a signal he believed to be a call for help. In fact this experience is what led him to become an astronomer and to found Project Startalk. Now, this time in real life, the same signal can be heard again.

Joe decides to spend the rest of his grant money on the equipment he will need to answer the signal. On the day when this is to happen, however, the Holmes Foundation sends accountant Joshua Yellowlees (comedian Hawtrey, best known for his work in the *Carry On* film series) to audit the books. The signal goes out and is received by a robot somewhere in a high-tech installation. The robot immediately sends out a spacecraft, which heads toward Earth.

Yellowlees is mostly around for comic relief, but he delivers one of the best lines of the film when he says, "Don't you think it dangerous to call attention to our-

selves?" Moments later the spacecraft arrives and lifts the entire Project Spacetalk building into the air, carrying Joe, Ben, Sandy, Yellowlees, and Mrs. Jones (Hayes), the tea cart lady, into outer space.

The spaceship delivers them to a robot, who feeds them, then leads them to a strange-looking creature in a very cheap costume. It seems hostile, but Sandy offers it something to eat and it disappears—it was only an illusion, and Sandy suspects it might have been some kind of test. Next the robot gives Joe a weapon and a cube just like the one he got as a kid. The cube seems to be some kind of book. "They've brought us here to do a job for them," Joe says.

They explore the installation and find the body of a long-dead alien, so it seems that the people who built this place have died out. Then Sandy stumbles onto a kind of matter transmitter and is zapped to the very world Joe dreamed of as a kid, where she is captured by some green humanoid savages who want to sacrifice

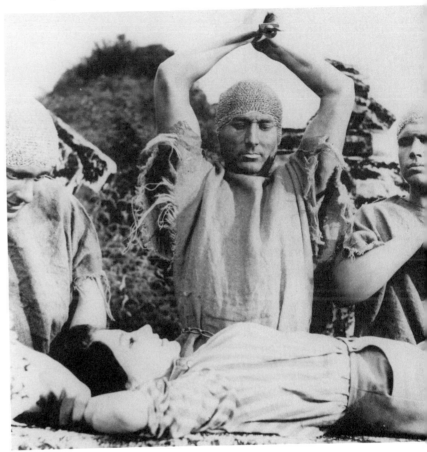

The savage green aliens prepare to sacrifice Sandy for no particular reason when she visits the planet of *The Terrornauts*.

Sandy meets up with a very low-budget alien in The *Terrornauts*.

her. Joe uses the transmitter to follow and saves her, and both return to the installation, where Joe finds a kind of shower cap full of wires that enables him to "read" the cubes.

Now we learn that the aliens were engaged in a centuries-long war with a civilization known only as the Enemy; this conflict reduced their original home planet to a state of savagery. The installation is a kind of fortress/outpost designed to monitor the Enemy, which is now approaching Earth.

The cubes also teach Joe how to use the weapons of the fortress against the Enemy, and by the time the very cheesy-looking Enemy ships arrive, the Earthlings are ready. It takes them only a few minutes to destroy the entire fleet, which makes you wonder why the original aliens didn't do that themselves if it was so easy. Then Joe readjusts the matter transmitter to take them

back to Earth, and they arrive in France at the site of his uncle's archeological dig, where they are promptly arrested for having no passports.

*The Day the Earth Stood Still, The 27th Day,* and other science fiction movies have suggested that we on Earth need the help of some alien intelligence if we are to solve our problems. *The Terrornauts* borrows a notion from *This Island Earth* by advancing the idea that one of those super-smart alien civilizations might actually need *us* to help solve its problems, and it's gratifying to see a movie that gives us lowly Earthlings a little bit of credit.

The problem with *The Terrornauts* is that it can't make up its mind whether it is intended for grown-ups or kids. The subject matter seems serious enough, but the juvenile comedy of Yellowlees and Mrs. Jones really hurts the movie after a while—and why in the world does this film need *two* comedians? On top of that, the special effects are so cheap, they remind me of those Saturday-morning kiddie-TV space operas of the 1950s.

The idea that Dr. Burke seems somehow destined from childhood to save the Earth from the Enemy is a strong one, but in the end, it's impossible to take *The Terrornauts* seriously.

# THX 1138

1971

**DIRECTOR:** George Lucas
**PRODUCER:** Lawrence Sturman
**SCREENPLAY:** George Lucas and Water Murch
**CAST:** Robert Duvall, Donald Pleasence, Don Pedro Colley, Maggie McOmie, Johnny Weissmuller, Jr.
**ORIGINAL RELEASE:** Warner Brothers
**VIDEO:** Warner Home Video

George Lucas's first feature-length film is based on an earlier version he made while still a student at the University of Southern California, which won a national award in 1965. Produced by American Zoetrope with Francis Ford Coppola as executive producer, *THX 1138* is a visual masterpiece. Lucas shoots in color but uses white costumes and backgrounds throughout, so it often seems that his characters are little more than disembodied, shaved heads drifting through a field of brilliant white. Unfortunately, the movie owes so much to George Orwell's *1984* and Aldous Huxley's *Brave New World* that the story line really has nothing new to offer, despite brilliant performances by Duvall and Pleasence.

THX 1138 (Duvall) lives in a futuristic underground society where all citizens look and dress the same and where robot policemen (one played by Weissmuller, Jr., the son of Tarzan) and video cameras keep everyone under almost constant surveillance. Drugs are used as a means of social control—one of the worst offenses in this society is criminal drug evasion—and confessionals are set up everywhere so troubled citizens can talk to a Christlike image called Om who comforts them with platitudes—"Buy more. Buy more now. And be happy."

Needless to say, nobody really is happy in this world. THX does very dangerous work with radioactive isotopes in a plant where death by radiation poisoning is

commonplace, so he is more than a bit tense. The real problem is that for some reason he cannot understand, he is losing his concentration, and that could be dangerous. "I feel as if something odd were happening to me," he tells Om.

THX's mate, LUH 3417 (McOmie), is also unhappy. Mates are assigned by computer, but THX and LUH seem to have something special between them and even engage in unauthorized sex. Still, both are dissatisfied with their lives, though they don't know why.

Things change for the couple when one of LUH's superiors at work, SEN 5241 (Pleasence), asks to see her. THX seeks out the brilliantly sleazy SEN, who informs him that he and THX are now going to be roomates. It seems that SEN's previous roommate has been destroyed for criminal activities—you get the idea that SEN had something to do with that—and now THX is to take his place. THX refuses, but SEN keeps pestering him and threatens to report LUH for drug evasion. SEN has some expertise with computers, and so he has the ability to make things happen in this computerized society.

Nervous and upset, THX makes a nearly fatal mistake on the job and is arrested for drug and sex offenses. A computer judge finds him incurable and sentences him to detention, where he is tortured by the police, studied by machines, and given drugs and cortex implants. LUH is apparently destroyed, and her number is reassigned to an unborn fetus in a jar, quite possibly the child of LUH and THX.

SEN is arrested and confined, too, and he spends his time in prison pestering THX and giving revolutionary speeches: "We're all in this together."

Finally THX has had enough and says he is leaving. He simply walks away—prisoners are not locked up because there is nowhere for them to go—and SEN follows him into a labyrinth of white hallways. On the way, they meet SRT (Colley), who is obviously insane and claims to be a hologram, but seems to know his way around the complex.

In a crowded hallway, SEN is separated from the others, and now on his own, he chooses to go back to detention. THX and SRT steal vehicles and are pursued through the tunnels by robot cops on motorcycles, and SRT crashes and is killed, as are a number of the police officers. Finally THX finds a ladder that leads to the surface, but the robots pursue him until they are informed that the project to capture THX has gone over budget and is therefore being called off. The film ends with THX arriving on the surface at sunrise with an uncertain future.

*THX 1138* is very heavy-handed in the way it presents its points, but there is no mistaking the elements of our

Visit the future where love
is the ultimate crime.

# THX 1138

Warner Bros. presents THX 1138 · An American Zoetrope Production · Starring
Robert Duvall and Donald Pleasence · with Don Pedro Colley, Maggie McOmie
and Ian Wolfe · Technicolor® · Techniscope® · Executive Producer, Francis Ford
Coppola · Screenplay by George Lucas and Walter Murch · Story by George Lucas
Produced by Lawrence Sturhahn · Directed by George Lucas · Music by Lalo Schifrin

Advertising art for George Lucas's first feature effort, *THX 1138*. (Courtesy Hollywood Book and Poster)

*THX 1138* (Robert Duvall) on the job in the dehumanized world of the future.

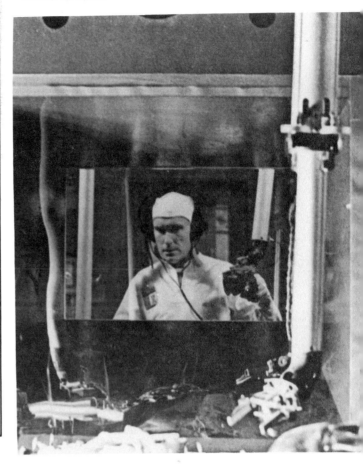

own consumer society in this futuristic culture. Lucas's film gets in its digs at pop psychotherapy, psychopharmacology, shopping malls, the Protestant work ethic, and lots more. In short, it's a pretty depressing film—but then ours is often a pretty depressing world.

What seems most depressing about the film is its suggestion that there is nothing citizens of an oppressive society can do to change things. Remember that this movie appeared in 1971, in the midst of tremendous social and political upheaval in this country—the protest movement against the war in Vietnam, the civil rights movement, the women's movement, and so on. It was a time when American society was being questioned and when many seemed eager to make changes in the way things were.

In *THX 1138*, those who claim to want to change society are all talk and are really cowards in the end; SEN is the example of this in the film, but the idea

NCH (Sid Haig) tortures a fellow inmate in the prison scene from *THX 1138*.

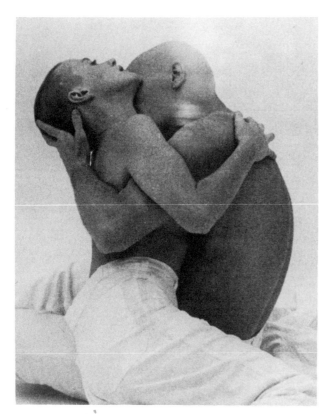

*THX 1138* and LUH 3417 (Maggie McOmie) engage in unauthorized sex, a forbidden act in the world of George Lucas's film.

clearly relates to sixties political activists. The only way to deal with an oppressive society is to do as THX 1138 does—run away. And it's impossible, of course, to fault THX for leaving a society that offers him nothing. The depressing thing about this message is that in many cases it might very well be true, though citizens of the former Soviet Union have done a lot in recent years to prove that people can change their societies and their lives for the better.

# THE TIME TRAVELERS

1 9 6 4

**DIRECTOR/SCREENPLAY:** Ib Melchior
**PRODUCER:** William Redlin
**CAST:** Preston Foster, Philip Carey, Merry Anders, John Hoyt, Dennis Patrick, Steve Franken, Forrest J. Ackerman

**ORIGINAL RELEASE:** American International Pictures
**VIDEO:** Thorn EMI HBO Home Video

Drs. Erik von Steiner (film and TV veteran Foster), Steve Connors (Carey, former cowboy actor and later soap opera star), and Carol White (Anders) are at work on a time portal designed to see into the past or the future, but when some circuits accidentally fuse, they discover that the portal is not a window but a door into the world to come. Along with technician Danny McKee (Franken, formerly Chatsworth Osborne, Jr., of TV's *Many Loves of Dobie Gillis*), they step 107 years into the future, only to find themselves trapped there when their time portal collapses.

Things in 2071 (1964 + 107) aren't very good. The Earth is a wasteland populated by subhuman mutants, but our heroes discover a cave leading to an advanced underground civilization and the last remaining humans on the planet. Varno (Hoyt), the council leader, explains that Earth was destroyed by a nuclear holocaust: "It was man's own folly," he says. "The destruction was total."

The Earth is hopelessly poisoned, and the mutants threaten to invade the underground sanctuary at any moment, so the humans are building a starship to take them to a planet in Alpha Centauri, where they will start over. Von Steiner and the others are invited to come along.

Unfortunately Councilman Willard, the bad guy in this movie, informs everyone that the starship will not hold four extra people. Varno offers to help rebuild the time portal, and von Steiner and Connors manage to complete it just as the starship is about to take off. But at the last moment the mutants break in, destroying the ship and killing almost everybody.

The four time travelers and a few survivors from the future go through the portal, back to 1964 and the lab where this whole thing started. But they soon discover that they have become unstuck in time. Everything around them is moving so slowly that it hardly seems to move at all, while they are living at an accelerated rate—more than one year per minute. If they stay there much longer, they will die.

The original time portal is still open, so the survivors go through again, this time more than 100,000 years into the future, where they discover a lush, green world. But the film isn't over yet. It seems the time travelers have gotten caught in a time loop, and in the closing moments of the movie, the entire story unfolds again and again in bits and pieces—immortality of a sort.

*The Time Travelers* owes a lot to the George Pal classics *When Worlds Collide* (1951) and *The Time Ma-*

*The Time Travelers*—Carol White (Merry Anders), Steve Connors (Philip Carey), Doctor Erik von Steiner (Preston Foster), and Danny McKee (Steve Franken).

A technician of the future (Margaret Selden) spends her day rolling her eyes in an android factory in *The Time Travelers*.

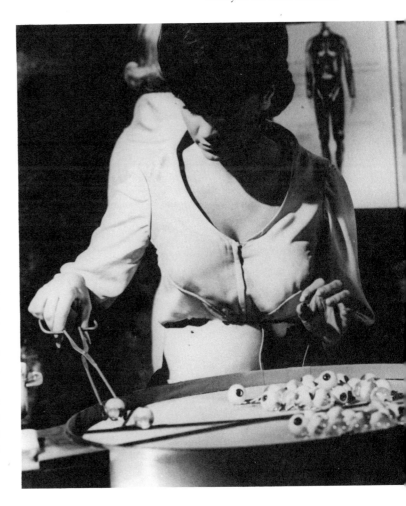

*chine* (1960), and the time portal might very well have been the inspiration for the late sixties TV series *The Time Tunnel*. There really isn't much of a plot to this film, but it's still fun, mostly because it is chock full of neat futuristic stuff—fast-growing orange trees, electronic musical instruments that also produce light shows in the comfort of your own cubicle, matter transmitters, and so forth. The tour through the android assembly plant is really the high point of the film—it's like a 1950s industrial documentary, complete with insipid, bouncy music on the soundtrack. Unfortunately there are also a lot of pretty boring lectures on photons, lasers, Alpha Centauri, and the like. But the final battle between the humans and the mutants is very effective, and it's a kick to see horror/sci-fi expert Forrest J. Ackerman in a bit part as a technician in the android factory.

In 1888, the American writer Edward Bellamy published *Looking Backward,* a novel that depicted Earth in the year 2000 as a socialist utopia. As it has turned out, Bellamy's optimism has proved to be the exception rather than the rule in the history of science fiction. Most futuristic novels and movies, including *The Time Travelers,* present us with a era to come that is much worse than the present.

But why? Given that for the most part, life for humankind has improved from the past to now, why do we seem to believe that this will not hold true in the future? Maybe we simply know too much about the

Radioactive mutants of the future war against the androids in the closing moments of *The Time Travelers*.

possibilities of nuclear weapons and ecological disasters to be optimistic. Also, whether it's true or not, many of us remember our childhood as being better than our present life as adults; perhaps when we think about the future of humankind, we're merely projecting our own feelings onto civilization as a whole. We could also be simply preparing ourselves for the worst, just in case.

Or perhaps we're so tired of civilization that some part of us would prefer to see the end of it in preference to more of the same. Maybe we're like kids who look forward to a blizzard to give them a break from the routine of school.

If this is the case, then we should start thinking about what we *really* want from the future.

# THE 27TH DAY

1 9 5 7

**DIRECTOR:** William Asher
**PRODUCER:** Helen Ainsworth
**SCREENPLAY:** John Mantley

**CAST:** Gene Barry, Valerie French, George Voskovec, Arnold Moss, Stefan Schnabel, Ralph Clanton, Frederick Ledebur
**ORIGINAL RELEASE:** Columbia Pictures
**VIDEO:** Goodtimes Home Video

Eve Wingate (French) is on a Cornwall beach in England when an alien arrives to spirit her away to a waiting spacecraft. At the same moment, the same thing happens to Los Angeles newspaper man Jonathan Clarke (Barry), Chinese peasant Su Tan, Soviet soldier Ivan Godovski, and German professor Klaus Bechner (Voskovec). On board the spaceship, the alien (Moss) explains: "We are here to help you save your beautiful planet." The Alien's planet is doomed, and they would like to make a new home on Earth, but their moral code will not allow them to invade and conquer another world. Therefore, they plan to make it possible for humankind to decide whether it wants to live or die.

Each of the Earthlings is given a small box containing three capsules. The capsules are weapons that will destroy nothing but human life, and though only the owner's thought waves can open the box, anyone can use the capsules themselves. One need only speak the longitude and latitude of any location on Earth into one of the

An alien voice speaks to the visitors from Earth (Valerie French, Gene Barry, Marie Tsien, George Voskovec, Azenath Janti) and explains why *The 27th Day* is so important. (Courtesy Hollywood Book and Poster)

The alien (Arnold Moss) gives Soviet soldier Ivan Godovski (Azenath Janti), American newspaper writer Jonathan Clarke (Gene Barry), British citizen Eve Wingate (Valerie French), Chinese peasant Su Tan (Marie Tsien), and German Professor Klaus Bechner (George Voskovec) capsules that have the ability to destroy all human life on Earth. These weapons will be effective until the end of *The 27th Day*.

capsules, and all human life will be destroyed within a diameter of 3,000 miles from that point. If one of the Earthlings dies, that person's capsules will disintegrate. The Earthlings are free to do whatever they want with the weapons, but if the capsules are not used in twenty-seven days, they will be neutralized—then humans will live and the aliens will be doomed.

The five Earthlings are sent back, and Eve immediately throws her capsules into the sea. Su Tan kills herself, thus neutralizing her capsules. Professor Bechner takes his capsules with him to a conference in the United States, and Jonathan and Ivan decide simply to keep their mouths shut until the twenty-seven days pass. Eve calls Jonathan and says she is coming to the States to meet with him, though he suggests that she too just lay low for a few weeks.

Then, however, the alien takes control of the world's communications media and explains what has happened, giving the names of those Earthlings who have received the special "gift." Immediately Ivan is taken prisoner, and Jonathan disappears. Professor Bechner is struck by a car and injured. When Eve arrives at the airport, Jonathan meets her and takes her to a safe hiding place.

A world panic follows as people speculate about the alien weapons and their power. Mr. Ingram (Clanton) and Dr. Neuhaus (Ledebur) of the U.S. government want to analyze the professor's capsules but of course cannot open the box. Meanwhile, the Soviet leader (Schnabel) interrogates Ivan, who claims to know nothing. Eventually Ivan is tortured but still won't talk, and the professor refuses to disclose any information to the American authorities.

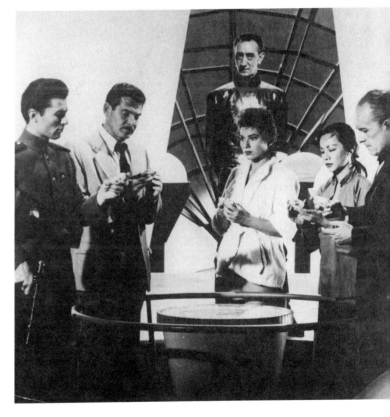

Jonathan and Eve give themselves up to the authorities to help stop the panic, and in the Soviet Union, Ivan is given truth serum and forced to disclose the secret of the capsules. The Soviet leader immediately claims world domination for his country and orders the U.S. military out of Europe and Asia; otherwise, he threatens to use the capsules to destroy North America.

237

Dr. Karl Neuhaus (Frederick Ledebur) studies the deadly alien capsules in *The 27th Day*. (Courtesy Hollywood Book and Poster)

Jonathan, Eve, and Bechner are brought together at the Pentagon, where military leaders decide to test one of the capsules at sea. Neuhaus volunteers to be the test subject—he has given himself a fatal dose of radiation to make it impossible for the authorities to refuse his request. The test is set up, and the capsule works.

The United States begins its military withdrawal in hopes of lasting out the twenty-seven days, but Bechner is convinced that the Soviets will use their capsules at the last minute. The professor also discovers a secret mathematical code on the capsules and tries to decipher it as midnight of the twenty-seventh day approaches.

The Soviet leader does indeed plan to wipe out North America with the capsules, but Ivan manages to delay the attack. At that moment Bechner launches both his and Jonathan's capsules, blanketing the entire world. Thanks to the coded message, however, Bechner has learned how to alter the capsules so that they kill only "confirmed enemies of human freedom"—including the Soviet leader. This, apparently, was the alien plan from the beginning, and now a world in harmony offers an invitation to the aliens to come share the Earth with us, an invitation they accept.

At a time when Hollywood was cranking out hundreds of evil alien invasion films, it's refreshing to see a movie in which the aliens are good guys. *The 27th Day* is a remarkably intelligent movie, though it is clearly a product of the cold war. When Bechner launches the capsules, communist leaders throughout the world all drop dead, but no authorities in the United States seem to die—apparently, according to this film, there were no "enemies of human freedom" in the American government in the 1950s. But *The 27th Day* makes a clear distinction between governments and ordinary citizens. Su Tan and Ivan may live under military dictatorships, but they themselves are good, decent human beings. As Bechner says of the Soviet ultimatum: "This is not their people speaking."

Though the movie is more than a bit naive, *The 27th Day* suggests that worldwide human harmony is a possibility for us, a message audiences of the fifties desparately needed to hear. Unfortunately, the film also suggests that our human problems are so vast that we will not be able to solve them without outside help from an intelligence greater than ours. Needless to say, that intelligence has not come forward yet.

# WAR OF THE COLOSSAL BEAST

## 1958

**DIRECTOR/PRODUCER:** Bert I. Gordon
**SCREENPLAY:** George Worthing Yates

**CAST:** Sally Fraser, Dean Parkin, Roger Pace, Russ Bender, Charles Stewart, George Becwar
**ORIGINAL RELEASE:** American International Pictures
**VIDEO:** Coumbia TriStar Home Video

*The Amazing Colossal Man* of 1957 was an amazing colossal success, so Bert I. Gordon followed it up with this sequel the following year.

In Guavos, Mexico, John Swanson (Becwar) sees the police about a missing truck full of groceries and supplies for the tourists at his gun club. A local cop says that they have found the driver, and he takes Swanson to the hospital to see Miguel, who is suffering from shock and cannot speak. Swanson also investigates the site where Miguel was found. There are tire tracks but no truck.

In Los Angeles, Joyce Manning (Fraser), sister of the gigantic Glenn Manning, hears this story on the TV news and goes to Mexico to talk to Miguel, who manages to say only one word to her: "giant."

Joyce believes that her brother is still alive, and though the army is convinced that he is not, Major Mark Baird (Pace) and Dr. Carmichael (Bender) arrive in Mexico to investigate. Mark and Joyce come upon the ruins of more trucks, which apparently her brother has been raiding for food. Then Glenn (Parkin) shows up—his face is now horribly disfigured because of his fall from Boulder Dam at the end of *The Amazing Colossal Man*, and he only grunts and roars like an animal. Baird and Carmichael use drugged bread to capture him and fly him back to the States.

After some difficulties, Mark gets permission to lodge Glenn in a hangar at the airport in Los Angeles until government officials can decide what to do with him. Glenn has to be kept tied down, and he doesn't seem to remember Joyce or even his own name, though he does have occasional flashbacks, which consist of footage recycled from the first film.

Eventually he breaks free and wanders around the

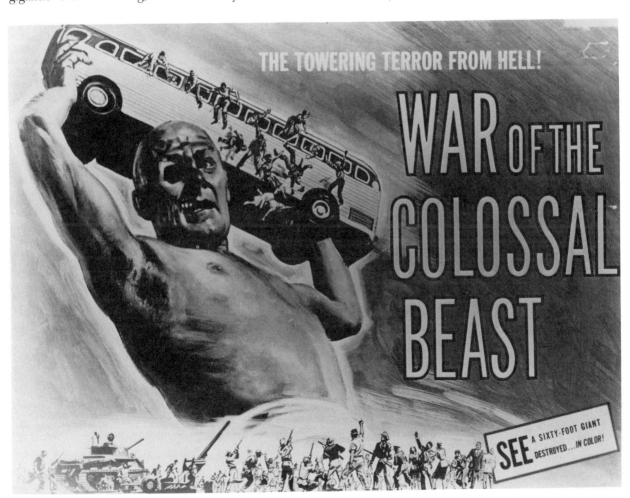

Ad art from *War of the Colossal Beast*, sequel to *The Amazing Colossal Man*.

Glenn Manning (Dean Parkin), the colossal man, hijacks trucks for food in the early moments of *War of the Colossal Beast*.

Glenn's sister, Joyce (Sally Fraser), Major Mark Baird (Roger Pace), and Dr. Carmichael (Russ Bender) wait to find out how the *War of the Colossal Beast* is going. It won't be long until they find out.

airport smashing stuff until the army subdues him with an anesthetic gas and puts him in chains. Dr. Carmichael doesn't know whether Glenn's problem is curable amnesia or hopeless brain damage, so he runs some tests to stimulate the giant's memory. Nothing seems to work, so the government decides to exile him to an island for life; presumably there he can cause no more harm.

Glenn escapes again, this time killing Carmichael in the process. Now he is on the loose in Los Angeles, and amazingly, the police can't find him, even though he is over sixty feet tall. Someone spots him in Griffith Park, and the army closes in. Glenn continues to make trouble, picking up a school bus full of kids on a field trip to the observatory, but Joyce manages to talk him into putting it down without harming anyone.

In the end, Glenn calls Joyce by name—he *does* remember, after all—then commits suicide by grabbing onto some high-tension electrical wires. For the climactic scene, the movie switches from black and white to color as Glenn electrocutes himself, and then for no conceivable reason disappears in a puff of smoke and sparks, thus neatly eliminating the problem of what to do with a sixty-foot-long dead body in Griffith Park.

As sequels go, this one isn't too bad, though screenwriter Yates—a veteran of 1940s serials—should have at least seen *The Amazing Colossal Man* before writing *War of the Colossal Beast*. In the first movie, much is made of the fact that Manning has no family, but in this sequel his sister shows up. Also in the original, scientists develop a serum that will reverse Glenn's growth problem, but in the sequel Mark simply tells Joyce that there is nothing medical science can do to help her brother. Since Bert I. Gordon produced and directed both films, you'd think he might have picked up on these contradictions, but if he did, they obviously didn't bother him.

The real problem with *War of the Colossal Beast*, however, is that Glenn Manning isn't the main character. The original movie works because we in the audience can identify with Glenn as a guy who has a terrible thing happen to him through no fault of his own, and we sympathize as we watch him fall apart mentally. In the sequel, Glenn is simply a mindless beast, as the title suggests, and the movie focuses on Joyce, though it's much harder to feel sorry for her. After all, she can still have a normal life, no matter what happens to Glenn, and it seems as if she is going to hook up with Mark and live happily ever after anyway. And if she is such a devoted sister, where the hell was she when her brother was going through all that misery in the first flick?

Well, sequels aren't supposed to be great movies. They're supposed to make money, and *War of the Colossal Beast* probably did, though apparently not enough to justify *The Amazing Colossal Man 3*.

# WARNING SIGN

1985

**DIRECTOR:** Hal Barwood
**PRODUCER:** Jim Bloom
**SCREENPLAY:** Hal Barwood and Matthew Robbins
**CAST:** Sam Waterston, Kathleen Quinlan, Richard Dysart, Yaphet Kotto, Jeffrey De Munn
**ORIGINAL RELEASE:** 20th Century-Fox
**VIDEO:** CBS/Fox Video

BioTek is a company working on improving agricultural yields in the pastoral farmlands of Utah—or at least

In *Warning Sign*, Major Connolly (Yaphet Kotto) tries to control the angry mob outside of BioTek, where a deadly biological weapon has accidentally been released. (Courtesy Hollywood Book and Poster)

that's the cover story. But when a test tube is broken in an accident and the BIOHAZARD sign starts flashing at five o'clock on a Friday afternoon, the locals begin to get some idea of what BioTek is really up to.

Joannie Morse (Quinlan), head of security for BioTek, follows established procedure and seals the building with everyone inside. Outside, her husband, Sheriff Cal Morse (Waterston), tries to keep friends and relatives from breaking into BioTek to rescue their loved ones. Then Major Connolly (Kotto) shows up with lots of technicians and equipment, trucks and armed soldiers.

Connolly works for some government agency, and though he tries to convince everyone that the accident is minor and that no one is in danger, the sheriff isn't convinced. Cal goes to see Dan Fairchild (De Munn), a scientist who was fired from BioTek but who has stayed on in the area, and what he finds out there does not cheer him up. Fairchild explains that though most employees don't know it, BioTek is involved in biological weapons research, kept secret because such weapons have been outlawed by international treaty. The bacteria that are now running rampant in BioTek cause victims to turn into crazed, murderous lunatics before they finally die. "This is not a disease," Dan explains. "It's a weapon of war. . . . It makes people crazy."

Back at BioTek, lots of people inside the building are getting sick, and some are trying to break out, despite Joannie's best efforts to keep the place sealed. Connolly's soldiers come inside in protective gear and kill a few employees, but they in turn are killed by some contaminated workers led by Dr. Nielson (Dysart), the

owner of BioTek and creator of the weapon that has now been set loose. Connolly decides to contain the problem by keeping the building sealed until everyone inside is dead.

Cal and Dan dress in protective clothes and sneak into the building to rescue Joannie, the only one there who isn't sick. Despite their efforts, however, Dan and Cal are both exposed to the bacteria, but Fairchild manages to figure out why Joannie is still okay. She is pregnant, and the hormones in her body are protecting her from the illness. Using her blood, Dan manages to make a working antitoxin. Cal still has to kill a few crazed employees, and Nielson shoots himself in a fit of insanity, but thanks to the antitoxin, most of the people at BioTek are saved. In the end, Cal and Joannie are together again, and Connolly slinks back to his secret agency until he is needed once more.

Sometimes the most effective science fiction films are the ones that are more science than fiction, and that's the case here. We know that everything that happens in *Warning Sign* is perfectly possible, and as in so many sci-fi movies since the late sixties, government agencies are not interested in protecting us. In fact they are willing to let innocent people die to cover up their mistakes.

It's a depressing message, but *Warning Sign* ends on an upbeat. The fact that Joannie's pregnancy proves to be the cure for the disease shows that new life triumphs

Sheriff Cal Morse (Sam Waterston) and Dan Fairchild (Jeffrey De Munn), a former BioTek employee, prepare to go inside the building to see what's going on in *Warning Sign*. (Courtesy Hollywood Book and Poster)

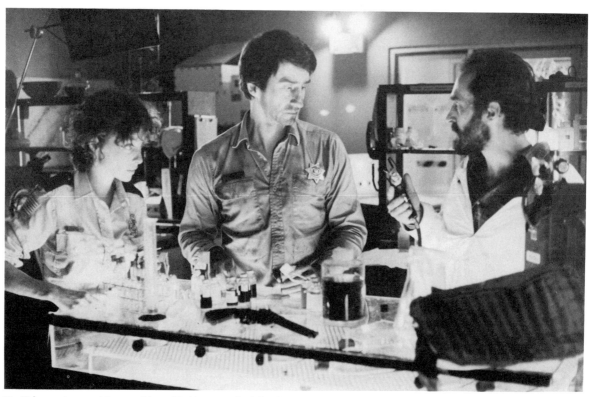

Bio-Tek security guard Joannie Morse (Kathleen Quinlan), her husband, Cal (Sam Waterston), and scientist Dan Fairchild find themselves trapped in a building with a crowd of homicidal maniacs in *Warning Sign*. (Courtesy Hollywood Book and Poster)

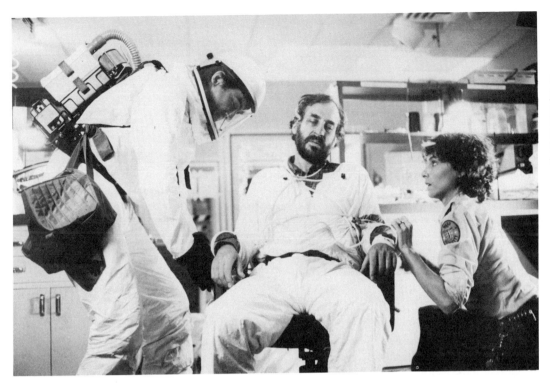

over death, that nature wins out over science and technology.

If only we could be sure that's true in the real world, too.

# THE WASP WOMAN

1960

**DIRECTOR/PRODUCER:** Roger Corman
**SCREENPLAY:** Leo Gordon
**CAST:** Susan Cabot, Fred Eisley, Barboura Morris, William Roerick, Michael Mark
**ORIGINAL RELEASE:** Allied Artists
**VIDEO:** Rhino Video

The plot is ludicrous, but this one gets a lot of points for originality. Business has fallen off at Janice Starlin Enterprises, a cosmetics company. Former model and company president Starlin (Cabot) has always appeared in advertising for their products, but now that she is forty, she refuses to do so. As she says, "Not even Janice Starlin can remain a glamour girl forever."

A Dr. Zinthrop (Mark) comes to her, claiming he has

Dr. Zinthrop (Michael Mark) has developed an enzyme from the jelly of the queen wasp which is supposed to reverse the aging process. Unfortunately, his invention can also turn an ordinary woman into *The Wasp Woman*, but hey, nobody's perfect.

Against Dr. Zinthrop's advice, Janice Starlin (Susan Cabot), head of Starlin Cosmetic, injects herself with the enzyme that will turn her into *The Wasp Woman*.

*The Wasp Woman* kills and prepares to eat Starlin Enterprises research and development man Arthur Cooper (William Roerick), even though R&D men are notoriously fattening.

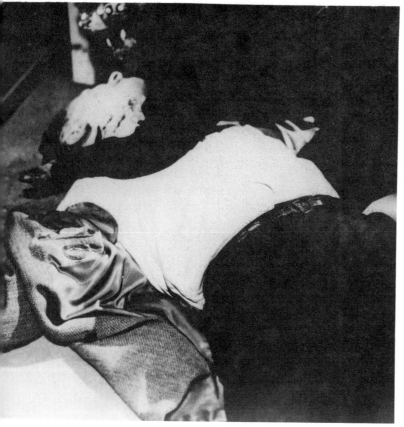

created a youth serum from the royal jelly of the queen wasp. Her research and development man, Arthur Cooper (Roerick), warns her against such extravagant claims: "Socially, the queen wasp is on a level with the black widow spider. . . . They kill their mates in the same way, too." But Janice plunges ahead and insists that Zinthrop test his serum on her.

The formula makes her young again, but now and then it also transforms her into a wasp woman—the makeup is absolutely ridiculous—and then she is driven to kill whoever happens by. Cooper is her first victim, then the night watchman, then a nurse. Apparently, she devours her prey completely, but she never seems to put on any weight. Eventually she tries to kill Mary, her secretary (Morris), and is pushed out of a window by ad man Bill Lane, played by Fred Eisley, who would later become Anthony Eisley on TV's *77 Sunset Strip*.

In our culture, most of us receive conflicting messages all the time concerning how we ought to behave, and this is particularly true for women. On the one hand, advertising insists that the ideal American woman is young and beautiful. On the other hand, when a woman who is not young and beautiful tries to live up to that ideal, she is seen as foolish, at best. This film even suggests that she is a danger to others and to herself and deserves whatever she gets. Janice Starlin is already wealthy, powerful, and successful, but she is shown to be a failure as a woman: first, because she isn't young, and second, because she tries unsuccessfully to become so. Apparently, no matter what she does, a woman can't win.

By the way, watch for producer/director Roger Corman in a cameo role as a doctor. Maybe his mom always wanted him to be one.

# WESTWORLD

**1973**

**DIRECTOR/SCREENPLAY:** Michael Crichton
**PRODUCER:** Paul N. Lazarus III
**CAST:** Yul Brynner, Richard Benjamin, James Brolin, Alan Oppenheimer, Dick Van Patten
**ORIGINAL RELEASE:** MGM
**VIDEO:** MGM/UA Home Video. ·

Delos is a theme park of the near future, where to the tune of $1,000 a day, visitors can live out their fantasies in Medieval World, Roman World, or Westworld—detailed re-creations of other times, populated by nearly perfect androids who fulfill every desire.

John Blane (Brolin) and Peter Martin (Benjamin) have chosen Westworld for their vacation. Blane has been there before, but Martin is a first-timer, trying to escape from the pain of a recent divorce. At first Peter has his doubts. As he picks out his cowboy clothes and gun, he tells John: "I feel silly. It's like a joke."

In Westworld itself, Peter is goaded into a fight by the Gunslinger (Brynner). After Peter draws his gun and kills the android, he decides: "This place is really fun."

Meanwhile, life goes on in Medieval and Roman Worlds, too, as well as behind the scenes, where technicians in white lab coats sit at computers and keep things running. At night, crews come out to fix the sets and repair "dead" robots. But there is some concern about a recent rash of mechanical breakdowns in the androids. As the chief technician (Oppenheimer) explains, something like an infectious disease seems to be spreading among the humanoid replicas, and those in charge don't know how to diagnose or fix the problem. "In some cases, they've been designed by other computers. We don't know exactly how they work."

Peter and John are still having fun shooting it out with the Gunslinger, breaking out of jail, playing cowboy. But minor things keep going wrong. Finally, in Medieval

*Westworld* visitors John Blane (James Brolin) and Peter Martin (Richard Benjamin) eye the man in black (Yul Brynner). No, he isn't Johnny Cash—he's a robot Gunslinger and part of the entertainment in the upscale theme park, Delos. (Courtesy Hollywood Book and Poster)

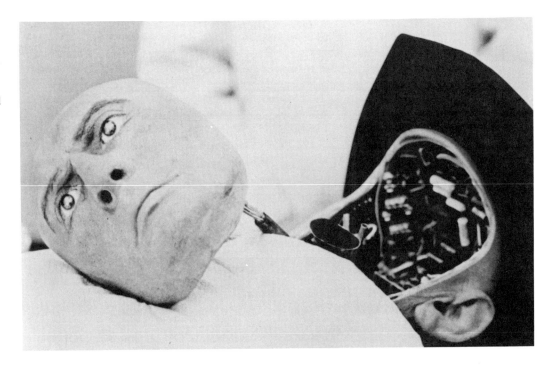

The robot gunfighter gets tired of losing face and rebels in the sci-fi/action thriller *Westworld*. (Courtesy Hollywood Book and Poster)

World, a robot knight challenges a guest to a duel and kills him.

In Westworld, the Gunslinger calls John out and shoots him dead. Peter runs for his life as the technicians realize that they have lost all control over the androids and that they have been locked in their computer rooms. Wholesale massacres take place in the various areas of the park, and the Gunslinger stays hot on Peter's trail.

Eventually Peter makes his way into the underground control areas, where he finds that the technicians have suffocated in their airtight booths. There is no one left there except Peter and the Gunslinger, who is still bent on killing him. Bullets don't stop the android; neither does acid. It is only when the Gunslinger is set on fire that he finally falls, leaving Peter a lone survivor in this dead fantasy world.

There are a lot of problems and unresolved contradictions in the story line, but this is still a well-made and effective film. Brolin, Benjamin, and the others are solid professionals, and casting Brynner as the robot gunfighter and dressing him in his black *Magnificent Seven* outfit was a stroke of genius—the man is almost unbelievably cold and menacing.

On the surface, this seems to be another one of those technology-runs-amok movies. Certainly, that is something people worried about in the seventies, though possibly not as much as we worry about it today. But *Westworld* also raises other important questions. For example, are we so lacking in imagination that we have to look to those who own and operate theme parks,

Most of the visitors to Delos are dead, but the robot Gunslinger still pursues Peter Martin in the closing moments of *Westworld*. (Courtesy Hollywood Book and Poster)

246

the TV networks, and the Hollywood studios to do our imagining for us?

*Westworld* also asks: What is real? That's a good question. In Delos, you can't tell the humans from the androids without a scorecard. In fact, in Delos, the distinction between real and unreal hardly makes sense.

In our world, too, that distinction is becoming harder and harder to make. Today we get most of our information about the world not from direct experience but from the mass media, notably from television. But what on TV is real and what is not? When an actor appears on a talk show, is he being himself, or is he acting? When I'm talking to the person I love, am I myself or am I playing a part, possibly even acting out a role I learned watching television? What's real and what isn't? What's the difference? These might well be the fundamental questions of our time.

If an android can go crazy, doesn't that make him human? If I behave in my life as I've been taught or programmed to behave, doesn't that make me an android?

At one point in the movie, Peter says, "I almost believe all this." John replies, "Why not? It's as real as anything else."

He might be right.

# YOG—MONSTER FROM SPACE

1970

**ALTERNATE TITLE:** *Nankai No Daikaiju*
**DIRECTOR:** Inoshiro Honda
**PRODUCERS:** Tomoyuki Tanaka and Fumio Tanaka
**SCREENPLAY:** El Ogawa
**CAST:** Akira Kubo, Atsuko Takahashi, Yoshio Tsuchiya, Kenji Sahara, Noritake Saito, Yukiko Kobayashi
**ORIGINAL RELEASE:** Toho Productions
**VIDEO:** Sinister Cinema

Okay, I'll admit it, I love Japanese sci-fi/monster flicks. They're weird and zany, but there's a kind of wacky sense to them, too. *Yog* certainly fits that description—and it doesn't even have Godzilla in it.

Helio 7 is an unmanned spacecraft on its way to Jupiter, but en route it is invaded by a strange flowing blue light that turns the ship around and takes it back to Earth, where it splashes down near a tiny Pacific island.

Meanwhile, Ayako Hoshino (Takahashi) works for a company that's planning to build a luxury resort on a tiny Pacific island—yep, the same one—and she hires photographer Taro Kudo (Kubo) to take publicity pictures of the place. They are accompanied by a scientist, Dr. Kyoichi Miya (Tsuchiya), who works for the company as an adviser. On the way, they are joined by a sleazy-looking, cynical guy named Makato Obata (Sahara), who claims to be an anthropologist hoping to study native customs.

When they arrive, they learn that their advance men have been attacked by a giant walking octopus. The islanders have long believed in the existence of such creatures, and when Obata tries to laugh the whole thing off, Rico (Saito), one of the natives, tells him: "The foreigners should not joke. Our god will be angry." In fact everybody is angry with Obata when they discover that he is not an anthropologist at all, but a spy

The visitors to the scenic Pacific atoll—Ayako Hoshino (Atsuko Takahashi), Makato Obata (Kenji Sahara), Dr. Kyoichi Miya (Yoshio Tsuchiya), and photographer Taro Kudo (Akira Kubo)—are about to meet *Yog—Monster From Space.*

from a rival company that also hopes to put a resort on the island.

Eventually the foreigners see the octopus for themselves when it destroys the village. Kudo and the others set fire to it with gasoline and destroy it, but we in the audience see the blue light leave its dying body and move on.

Soon the gang is attacked by a giant crab, which they manage to blow up with weapons left on the island after the war. But then the blue light enters Obata and takes control of him. It is at this point that the alien force admits that it has created the giant monsters and announces its purpose: "Our aim is to conquer the Earth."

Miya discovers that the giant monsters can't stand high frequency sounds like those produced by porpoises or bats, so they look around the island for bat caves where they can take shelter. In most of the caves, they find that someone or something has killed the bats, burned them out, but they soon find a cave where the bats are still alive, and they hide out there, hoping the sound of the winged rodents will keep the giant monsters away.

In *Yog—Monster From Space*, Dr. Miya examines the strange wounds on islander Rico (Noritake Saito)—wounds that seem to have been caused by a giant octopus.

The giant walking octopus is only one manifestation of the evil *Yog—Monster From Space*. (Courtesy Hollywood Book and Poster)

Rico goes to village wise man Ombo (Satoshi Naka-mura) to find out what the islanders should do about the recent invasion by *Yog—Monster From Space.*

Now there is a giant turtle running around, and it is soon joined by another giant crab. Worst of all, though, Obata shows up and tries to set fire to the cave and destroy the last remaining bats on the island. Miya quickly realizes that Obata is being controlled by the space beings, and Ayako pleads with him: "Try to fight off their hold on you. . . . You're still a human underneath."

Obata struggles with the alien that possesses him and sets the bats free. Their cries disturb the turtle and the crab, who begin to fight each other and who eventually fall into a volcano. Still tormented by his resident space being, Obata jumps into the volcano, too, taking the invader with him. According to Dr. Miya: "By killing the last alien, he saved mankind."

This is another one of those fear-of-space-travel films. Helio 7 is only an unmanned probe, and yet it's a kind of magic carpet for aliens who want to invade our planet. Obviously we should just stay at home and keep our probes to ourselves.

But there's more going on here. Ayako and Kudo start to think that maybe destroying the natural beauty and native life on the island with a resort isn't such a good idea. After all, the islanders were right when they said their god would be angry at the encroachment of civilization—it was civilization, in the form of a space probe, that brought the threat of extinction to them and to the whole planet. Dr. Miya learns a lesson, too.

Human beings can't be studied as objects of science, because if even a jerk like Obata can do the right thing under pressure, humans must have something very special going for them, whether they are islanders or products of civilization. And even Obata learns that some things are more important than sleaziness.

All in all, a fun movie!

This is the scene we've all been waiting for—the battle between the giant crab and the giant octopus in *Yog—Monster From Space.* (Courtesy Hollywood Book and Poster)

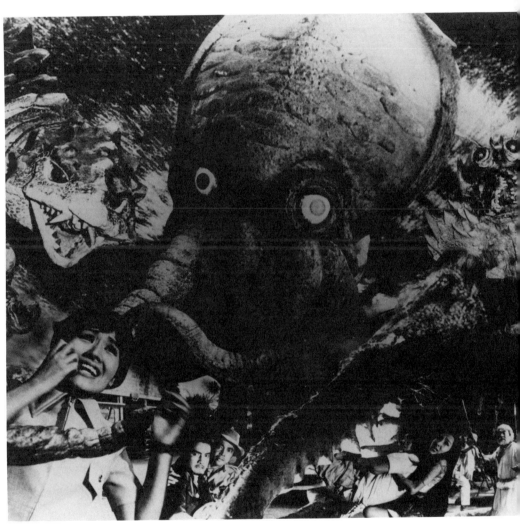

In fact, Ayako never really gets attacked by the giant octopus, the giant crab, and the giant turtle in *Yog—Monster From Space,* but it sure makes for a neat publicity shot.

# PHOTO CREDITS

Allied Artists; Ameran Productions; American General Pictures Corporation; American International Pictures; American Releasing Corporation; Amicus Productions; Anglo Amalgamated; Associated Producers and La Regina; AVCO Embassy; Banner-DCA; British Lion Films; Cine Artists Pictures; Cinepix/Dibar Syndicates/Canadian Film Development Corporation/Famous Players; Columbia Pictures; Dimensions Pictures; Embassy Pictures; Filmgroup; Filmplan International; Four Crown Productions; Goldstar Productions; Gorham Productions; Grosse-Krasne Productions; Hammer Productions; Howco International; Independent International; Italian International Film/Castilla Cinematografica; ITC Entertainment; Jalor Productions; Jerand Productions; Layton/Astor Pictures; Lippert Productions; M-G-M; Nike Cinematographica/Comptoir Français du Film; New Breed Productions, Inc.; New World Pictures; Planet Productions; RKO; Scotia International; Standard Club of California; 3-Dimensional Pictures; Toho Productions; Topar Corporation; TriStar Pictures; 20th Century-Fox; United Artists; United Artists of Japan/George Breakston Enterprises; Universal Pictures; Vogue Pictures; Warner Bros.

# INDEX

Ackerman, Forrest J., 234–36
Adams, Casey, 170–73
Adamson, Al, 95–99
Adler, Cynthia, 73–76
Adrian, Max, 229–32
Agar, John, 32–34
Ai, Kyoko, 59–61
Albertson, Jack, 52–54
Aldredge, Michael, 102–4
Alexander, Suzanne, 38–41
*Alien*, 122–23, 125
Allen, Irwin, 220–26
Allport, Christopher, 52–54
*Amazing Colossal Man, The*, 19–20
Anders, Merry, 234–36
Anderson, Dawn, 226–29
Anderson, Melody, 52–54
Andrews, Dana, 81–85
Andrews, Harry, 157–64
Andrews, Stanley, 218–20
*Angry Red Planet, The*, 20–22
Ankrum, Morris, 62–65
Aranda, Angel, 196–200
Asher, William, 236–38
Ashley, John, 78–81
Astin, Patty Duke, 220–26
*Atomic Submarine, The*, 23–25
*Attack of the Giant Leeches*, 25–27
Austin, Charlotte, 152–54
Axton, Hoyt, 70–73

Badel, Alan, 157–64
Baldwin, Michael, 187–90
Ball, Robert, 30–32
Bannister, Reggie, 187–90
Barnes, Raymond, 125–31
Barrault, Marie-Christine, 157–64
Barrett, Claudia, 208–10
Barrows, George, 165–67, 208–10
Barry, Gene, 15, 236–38
Bartel, Paul, 192–96
Bartok, Eva, 85–87
Barwood, Hal, 241–43
Barzell, Wolfe, 78–81
Basehart, Richard, 112–18
Bava, Mario, 196–200
Baxley, Gary, 113
Beaudine, William, 125–31
Beaumont, Hugh, 149
Beck, Vincent, 211–13
Beckley, Tony, 148–52
Becwar, George, 239–41
Bender, Russ, 239–41
Benedict, Richard, 123
Bengell, Norma, 196–200
Benjamin, Richard, 245–47
Bennet, Spencer G., 23–25
Benson, Joey, 95–99
Bent, Doris, 34–36
Bernds, Edward L., 200–204
Bestar, Barbara, 134–36
Bettoia, Franca, 139–43

Bice, Robert, 121
Birch, Paul, 49–52, 201–4
Bishop, Jennifer, 95–99
Bissell, Whit, 149
Black, Jeremy, 27–30
Blaisdell, Paul, 49–52
Blake, Larry, 62–65
Bloom, John, 104–8
Bolder, Cal, 125–31
Bolling, Tiffany, 136–39
Bostwick, Barry, 73–76
*Boys From Brazil, The*, 27–30
Brady, Scott, 131–33
*Brain Eaters, The*, 30–32
*Brain From Planet Arous, The*, 32–34
*Brain That Wouldn't Die, The*, 34–36
Breakston, George P., 154–57
Breck, Kathleen, 15, 81–85
Breck, Peter, 42–43
Brewster, Carol, 38–41
*Bride of the Monster*, 36–38
Brighton, Bruce, 34–36
Brolin, James, 245–47
Brynner, Yul, 245–47
Buford, Marilyn, 201–4
Burton, Richard, 13, 157–64
Bushman, Francis X., 190–92
Byrne, Eddie, 118–21
Byrne, Michael, 157–64

Cabot, Susan, 243–45

Cahn, Edward L., 108–12, 121–25
Caine, Michael, 220–26
Call, John, 211–13
Callan, Michael, 177–81
Cammell, Donald, 55–59
Carbone, Antony, 143–46
Cardona, René, Sr., 185–87
Cardos, John, 136–39
Carey, Harry, Jr., 70–73
Carey, Philip, 234–36
Carradine, John, 95–99
Carrel, Dany, 88–90
Carrera, Barbara, 66–68, 112–18
Carreras, Michael, 148–52
Carridia, Michael, 85–87
Carruthers, Benito, 148–52
Carson, John David, 68–70
Cass, David, 113
Castillo, Gloria, 108–12
*Cat-Women of the Moon*, 14, 38–41
Cavanagh, Paul, 152–54
Chamberlain, Richard, 220–26
Chambers, Marilyn, 204–8
Chaney, Lon, 20
Christie, Julie, 11, 55–59
Ciannelli, Eduardo, 168–70
Clair, Jany, 90–92
Clanton, Ralph, 236–38
Clark, Ken, 25–27
Coates, Phyllis, 218–20
Cole, Albert, 104–8
Colley, Don Pedro, 232–34
Collins, Joan, 68–70
Conforti, Donna, 211
Connors, Touch, 49–52
Conried, Hans, 170–73
Conway, Tom, 23–25
Coogan, Jackie, 165–67
Corey, Jeff, 218–20
Corman, Roger, 48–52, 143–46, 243–45
Corrigan, Ray, 8, 121–25
Coscarelli, Don, 187–90
Cossins, James, 148–52
Coyote, Peter, 70–73
Craig, Michael, 16, 177–81
Crane, Kenneth, 154–57, 167–70
Cravat, Nick, 112–18
*Crawling Hand, The*, 42–43
Crichton, Michael, 245–47
Cronenberg, David, 204–8, 213–17
Cunha, Richard E., 78–81
Curtis, Donald, 62–65
Cushing, Peter, 93–95, 118–21

D'Alberti, Delia, 90–92
Dalton, Audrey, 170–73
*Damnation Alley*, 43–48
Dane, Lawrence, 213–17
Daniel, Leslie, 34–36
Danieli, Emma, 139–43
Dante, Joe, 192–96
Darrow, Barbara, 201–4
Davenport, Nigel, 112–18
Davis, Jim, 125–31, 168–70
Davis, Lisa, 201–4
Dawson, Hal K., 218–20
*Day the World Ended, The*, 48–52
Day, Robert, 76–78
de Havilland, Olivia, 220–26
De Munn, Jeffrey, 241–43
Deacon, Richard, 192–96

*Dead and Buried*, 52–54
Dean, James, 43
DeBenning, Burr, 102–4
Dehner, John, 27–30
*Demon Seed*, 11, 55–59
Demura, Fumio, 113
Denning, Richard, 49–52
Dern, Bruce, 104–8
*Destroy All Monsters!*, 59–61
Dexter, Anthony, 190–92
Dillman, Bradford, 13, 192–96, 220–26
Dix, Robert, 95–99
Dooley, Paul, 70–73
Doran, Ann, 121–25, 152–54
Douglas, Paul, 85–87
Downs, Cathy, 19–20
Dressler, Lieux, 137
Dubov, Paul, 23–25, 49–52
Dunn, Harvey B., 36–38, 226–29
Duvall, Robert, 232–34
Dyneley, Peter, 155–57
Dysart, Richard, 241–43

*Earth vs. the Flying Saucers*, 12, 62–65
Edwards, Bill, 76–78
Eisley, Anthony, 131–33, 181–85
Eisley, Fred, 243–45
Elerick, John, 66–68
*Embryo*, 66–68
*Empire of the Ants*, 68–70
*Endangered Species*, 70–73
Endfield, Cy, 176–81
Englund, Robert, 52–54
Estelita, 125–31
Evers, Herb, 34–36

Fair, Jody, 30–32
Faith, Dolores, 190–92
*Fantastic Planet*, 73–76
Farentino, James, 52–54
Ferrer, José, 220–26
Ferrer, Mel, 88–90
Finlay, Frank, 147–48
*First Man Into Space*, 76–78, 103
Firth, Peter, 147–48
Fisher, Terence, 118–21
Fleming, Eric, 201–4
Fluellen, Joel, 168–70
Fonda, Henry, 220–26
Foran, Dick, 23–25
Foster, Preston, 234–36
Fowley, Douglas, 38–41
Fox, Edward, 83
Franken, Steve, 234–36
*Frankenstein*, 9, 103
*Frankenstein's Daughter*, 78–81
Franz, Arthur, 23–25
Fraser, Sally, 239–41
Fredericks, Dean, 190–92
French, Valerie, 15, 236–38
Frost, Alan, 30–32
*Frozen Dead, The*, 15, 81–85
Fujita, Susumu, 173–76
Fuller, Robert, 32–34

Gabor, Zsa Zsa, 14, 201–4
Gamin, Poupee, 131–33
*Gamma People, The*, 85–87
Gentilomo, Giacomo, 90–92
Geray, Steven, 125–31
Gerstle, Frank, 134–36

Gibson, Mimi, 170–73
Gilbert, Philip, 81–85
Gillespie, Dana, 148–52
Gillespie, John, 113
Gilling, John, 85–87
Gold, Jack, 157–64
Gordon, Bert I., 19–20, 68–70, 238–41
Gordon, Bruce, 192–96
Gorshin, Frank, 108–12
Gothard, Michael, 147–48
Gough, Michael, 27–30
Graeff, Tom, 226–29
Graham, Gerrit, 55–59
Grant, Bryant, 226–29
Grant, Lee, 220–26
Graves, Peter, 134–36
Gray, Bill, 181–85
Gray, Carole, 118–21
Gray, Coleen, 190–92
Green, Joseph, 34–36
Greenwood, Joan, 177–81
Greer, Dabbs, 121–25
Gréville, Edmond T., 88–90
Griffin, Robert E., 168–70
Gruner, Mark, 73–76
Guttenberg, Steve, 27–30

Hagen, Uta, 27–30
Hale, Alan, 42–43
Haley, Jackie Earle, 43–48
Halsey, Brett, 23–25
*Hands of Orlac, The*, 88–90
Hanley, Jimmy, 9, 148–52
Hatton, Raymond, 49–52, 108–12
Hawtrey, Charles, 229–32
Hayden, Nora, 20–22
Hayes, Allison, 42–43
Hayes, Patricia, 229–32
Haze, Jonathan, 49–52
Healey, Myron, 102–4
Heflin, Nora, 73–76
Henry, Tom Browne, 62–65
Henson, Basil, 15
*Hercules Against the Moon Men*, 90–92
Hertz, Nathan, 32–34
Hervey, Richard, 122
Hewitt, David L., 131–33
Hicks, Leonard, 211–13
Hill, Jack, 30–32
Hill, Mary, 165–67
Hilton, Arthur, 38–41
Hirata, Akihiko, 173–76
Hoey, Michael, 181–85
Holt, Tim, 170–73
Honda, Inoshiro, 59–61, 173–76, 247–51
Honoré, Jean-Pierre, 90–92
Hooper, Tobe, 146–48
*Horror Express*, 93–95
*Horror of the Blood Monsters*, 15, 95–99
Hoyt, John, 234–36
Hudson, Rock, 66–68
Hudson, William, 19–20, 152–54
Hughes, David, 30–32
*Humanoids From the Deep*, 99–102
Hylton, Jane, 155–57

*Incredible Melting Man, The*, 102–4
*Incredible Two-Headed Transplant, The*, 104–8
*Invasion of the Body Snatchers*, 30, 31–32

*Invasion of the Saucer Men*, 12, 108–12
Ironside, Michael, 213–17
*Island of Dr. Moreau, The*, 112–18
*Island of Lost Souls*, 112, 117
*Island of Terror*, 118–21
*It! the Terror From Beyond Space*, 8, 121–25

Jackson, Gordon, 157–64
Jaffe, Carl, 76–78
Janti, Azenath, 15, 237
Jergens, Adele, 49–52
*Jesse James Meets Frankenstein's Daughter*, 125–31
Johnson, Ben, 220–26
Johnson, Tor, 36–38
Jones, Gordon, 170–73
Jones, Ken, 187–90
Jones-Moreland, Betsy, 143–46
Jory, Victor, 38–41, 152–54
*Journey to the Center of Time*, 131–33
Judd, Edward, 118–21
Juttner, Christian, 220–26

Kanter, Marin, 70–73
Kardos, Leslie, 152–54
Kasem, Casey, 104–8
Kidd, Sam, 118–21
Kiel, Richard, 190–92
*Killers From Space*, 134–36
King, Loretta, 36–38
*Kingdom of the Spiders*, 136–39
Knapp, Robert, 165–67
Knef, Hildegard, 148–52
Knight, Sandra, 78–81
Kobayashi, Yukiko, 59–61, 247–51
Kochi, Momoko, 173–76
Kotto, Yaphet, 241–43
Kowalski, Bernard L., 25–27
Kroeger, Berry, 55–59, 104–8
Kruschen, Jack, 20–22
Kubo, Akira, 59–61, 247–51

Lack, Stephen, 213–17
Ladd, Diane, 66–68
Laloux, René, 73–76
Lamont, Adele, 34–36
Lancaster, Burt, 112–18
Landi, Marla, 76–78
Langan, Glenn, 19–20
Lansing, Joi, 23–25
Lansing, Robert, 68–70
Lanza, Anthony M., 104–8
*Last Man on Earth, The*, 139–43
*Last Woman on Earth, The*, 143–46
Lauren, Rod, 42–43
Laven, Arnold, 170–73
Lazareno, Norma, 185–87
*Le Voyage dans la Lune*, 10
Leaver, Philip, 85–87
Ledebur, Frederick, 152–54, 236–38
Leder, Herbert J., 81–85
Lee, Christopher, 88–90, 93–95
Lee, Joanna, 30–32
Leigh, Suzanna, 148–52
Leith, Virginia, 34–36
Lek, Niko, 165–67
Lester, Kathy, 187–90
*Lifeforce*, 146–48
Line, Helga, 94

Lloyd, Harold, Jr., 78–81
Locher, Felix, 78–81
Lockyear, Tom, 226–29
Lom, Herbert, 177–81
*Lost Continent, The*, 9, 148–52
*Lost World, The*, 95, 96
Love, David, 226–29
Lu, Lina, 55–59
Lucas, George, 232–34
Lugosi, Bela, 36–38
Lupton, John, 125–31

McCallum, Neil, 148–52
McCarthy, Kevin, 192–96
McClure, Doug, 99–102
McCoy, Tony, 36–38
McCutcheon, Bill, 211
MacDonald, J. Farrell, 218–20
McDowall, Roddy, 66–68
McGoohan, Patrick, 213–17
McLean, David, 136–39
MacMurray, Fred, 220–26
McOmie, Maggie, 232–34
*Man Who Turned to Stone, The*, 152–54
*Manster, The*, 154–57
Marandi, Evi, 196–200
Marco, Paul, 36–38
Mark, Michael, 243–45
Marlowe, Hugh, 62–65
Marshall, William, 190–92
Marshall, Zena, 229–32
Martin, Eugenio, 93–95
Mason, James, 27–30
Mason, Pamela, 181–85
Maurice, Paula, 34–36
May, Mathilda, 147–48
Meadows, Joyce, 32–34
Meadows, Stanley, 229–32
*Medusa Touch, The*, 13, 157–64
Melchior, Ib, 20–22, 234–36
Méliès, George, 10
Menzies, Heather, 192–96
Merrill, Gary, 177–81
*Mesa of Lost Women*, 165–67
Meyes, Fred, 95–99
Miller, Dick, 192–96
Miller, Martin, 85–87
Miller, Marvin, 73–76
Mitchell, Cameron, 220–26
Mitchell, Laurie, 201–4
Moctezuma, Carlos Lopez, 185–87
Moffett, Gregory, 208–10
Mohr, Gerald, 20–22
*Monster From Green Hell, The*, 167–70
*Monster That Challenged the World, The*, 170–73
Moody, Robert King, 226–29
Moore, Frank, 204–8
Moreno, José Elias, 185–87
Morris, Barboura, 243–45
Morrow, Susan, 38–41
Morrow, Vic, 99–102
Moss, Arnold, 236–38
Murphy, Donald, 78–81
Mylong, John, 208–10
*Mysterians, The*, 13, 173–76
*Mysterious Island*, 16, 176–81

Nader, George, 208–10
Nakamura, Satoshi, 155–57, 250

*Navy vs. the Night Monsters, The*, 181–85
Nelson, Edwin, 30–32
Nelson, Lori, 49–52
Nelson, Ralph, 66–68
*Night of the Bloody Apes*, 185–87
Niven, Kip, 43–48
Nixon, Allan, 165–67

O'Neill, Jennifer, 213–17
Oates, Simon, 229–32
Olivier, Laurence, 27–30
*One Million B.C.*, 95, 96
Onyx, Narda, 125–31
Oppenheimer, Alan, 245–47
Ormond, Ron, 165–67
Osborn, Lyn, 12, 108–12

Pace, Roger, 239–41
Paiva, Nestor, 126
Palance, Brooke, 68–70
Palk, Anna, 81–85
Palmer, Lilli, 27–30
Parkin, Dean, 239–41
Pataki, Michael, 52–54
Patrick, Dennis, 234–36
Paulson, Pamela, 208–10
Peck, Gregory, 27–30
Peeters, Barbara, 99–102
Penya, Anthony, 99–102
Peppard, George, 43–48
Perreau, Gigi, 131–33
*Phantasm*, 187–90
*Phantom Planet, The*, 190–92
Phillips, Greigh, 30–32
Phillips, Leslie, 85–87
Phipps, Bill, 38–41
Pickens, Slim, 220–26
Pine, Robert, 68–70
*Piranha*, 192–96
*Planet of the Vampires*, 196–200
Pleasence, Donald, 88–90, 232–34
Polani, Anna-Maria, 90–92
Porter, Eric, 148–52
Powell, Eddie, 149
Powers, Bruce, 95–99
Price, Vincent, 139–43
Priest, Pat, 104–8

*Queen of Outer Space*, 14, 200–204
Quinlan, Kathleen, 241–43
Quinn, Tandra, 165–67

*Rabid*, 204–8
Railsback, Steve, 147–48
Rebar, Alex, 102–4
*Rebel Without a Cause*, 43
Reed, Walter, 218–20
Reeves, George, 218–20
Remick, Lee, 157–64
Rey, Alejandro, 220–26
Rigaud, Jorge, 93–95
Rilla, Walter, 85–87
*Robot Monster*, 208–10
Roerick, William, 243–45
Rogan, Beth, 177–81
Romero, Cesar, 149
Ross, Katharine, 220–26
Rossi-Stuart, Giacomo, 139–43
Royle, Selena, 208–10

Rubinstein, John, 27–30
Rudolph, Alan, 70–73
Ryshpan, Howard, 204–8

Sachs, William, 102–4
Sage, Helen, 228
Sahara, Kenji, 173–76, 247–51
Saint-Simon, Lucille, 88–90
Saito, Noritake, 247–51
Salkow, Sidney, 139–43
Salmi, Albert, 68–70
Sanda, Dominique, 43–48
Sande, Walter, 181–85
*Santa Claus Conquers the Martians*, 210–13
Savalas, Telly, 93–95
*Scanners*, 213–17
Schaffner, Franklin J., 27–30
Schedeen, Ann, 66–68
Schnabel, Stefan, 236–38
Scholem, Lee, 218–20
Scott, Jacqueline, 68–70
Scrimm, Angus, 187–90
Sears, Fred F., 62–65
Seay, James, 19–20, 134–36
Selden, Margaret, 235
Semand, Britt, 95–99
Shatner, William, 136–39
Sheppard, Jan, 25–27
Sherman, Gary A., 52–54
Sherman, Orville, 30–32
Shimura, Takashi, 173–76
Shirakawa, Yumi, 173–76
Shoop, Pamela, 68–70
Silver, Joe, 204–8
Silverman, Robert, 214
Silvestre, Armando, 185–87
Smight, Jack, 43–48
Smith, Shawn, 121–25
Sofaer, Abraham, 131–33
Sokoloff, Vladimir, 168–70
Spalding, Kim, 121–25
Steel, Alan, 90–92
Steele, Barbara, 192–96
Steele, Bob, 23–25

Steffen, Sirry, 42–43
Stepanek, Karel, 15, 81–85
Stewart, Charles, 239–41
Stewart, Patrick, 147–48
Stiles, Victor, 211
Stock, Nigel, 148–52
Strock, Herbert L., 42–43
Strode, Woody, 136–39
Sullivan, Barry, 196–200
*Superman and the Mole Men*, 217–20
*Swarm, The*, 13, 220–26
Sweeny, Ann, 102–4

Takahashi, Atsuko, 247–51
Talbot, Lyle, 165–67
Taylor, Don, 112–18
Taylor, Joan, 62–65
Taylor, Kent, 42–43
Tazaki, Jun, 59–61
*Teenagers From Outer Space*, 226–29
Terrell, Steve, 108–12
*Terrornauts, The*, 229–32
Terry, Phillip, 181–85
Tevos, Herbert, 165–67
Thompson, Marshall, 76–78, 121–25
Thor, Larry, 19–20
Thornbury, Bill, 187–90
*THX 1138*, 9–10, 232–34
Tilvern, Alan, 81–85
*Time Travelers, The*, 234–36
Todd, Sally, 78–81
Tortosa, Silvia, 93–95
Travis, Richard, 165–67
Tremayne, Les, 20–22
Tsien, Marie, 15, 237
Tsuchiya, Yoshio, 59–61, 247–51
Tucker, Phil, 208–10
Tufts, Sonny, 14, 38–41
Tully, Montgomery, 229–32
Turkel, Ann, 99–102
Turner, Barbara, 168–70
*27th Day, The*, 15, 236–38

Urich, Robert, 70–73

Van, Bobby, 181–85

Van Doren, Mamie, 181–85
Van Hawley, Norman, 155
Van Patten, Dick, 245–47
Vaughn, Robert, 55–59
Ventura, Lino, 157–64
VeSota, Bruno, 25–27, 30
Vickers, Yvette, 25–27
Villena, Fernando, 196–200
Vincent, Jan-Michael, 43–48
Volante, Vicki, 95–99
Voskovec, George, 15, 236–38

Waggoner, Lyle, 131–33
Wain, Edward, 143–46
Walker, Ray, 218–20
Waltz, Patrick, 201–4
*War of the Colossal Beast*, 238–41
Warde, Harlan, 170–73
*Warning Sign*, 241–43
*Wasp Woman, The*, 243–45
Waterston, Sam, 241–43
Weaver, Fritz, 55–59
Webster, Nicholas, 210–13
Weintraub, Cindy, 99–102
Weissmuller, Johnny, Jr., 232–34
*Westworld*, 245–47
Widmark, Richard, 220–26
Wilder, W. Lee, 134–36
Willes, Jean, 152–54
Williams, JoBeth, 70–73
Willock, David, 201–4
Windsor, Marie, 38–41
Winfield, Paul, 43–48
*Wolf Man, The*, 20
Wolfit, Sir Donald, 88–90
Wood, Edward D., Jr., 36–38
Wu, Samuel, 165–67
Wynn, Keenan, 192–96

*Yog—Monster From Space*, 247–51
York, Michael, 112–18

Zadora, Pia, 211–13
Zaremba, John, 62–65
Zimmern, Terri, 155–57

# ORDER NOW! - Citadel Film & Television Books

If you like this book, you'll love Citadel Press's other television and movie books. A complete listing of these books appears below.

And if you know what books you want, why not order now? It's easy! **Just call 1-800-447-BOOK and have your MasterCard or Visa ready. (Tell the operator code #1602) Or use our toll-free sales fax 1-800-866-1966.**

## FILM:
### STARS
Al Pacino
Arnold Schwarzenegger
Audrey Hepburn
Barbra Streisand Films; Scrapbook
Bela Lugosi
Bette Davis
The Bowery Boys
Brigitte Bardot
Buster Keaton
Carole Lombard
Cary Grant
Charlie Chaplin
Clark Gable
Clint Eastwood
Curly
Dustin Hoffman
Edward G. Robinson
Elizabeth Taylor
Elvis Presley
The Elvis Scrapbook
Errol Flynn
Frank Sinatra
Gary Cooper
Gene Kelly
Gina Lollobrigida
Glenn Close
Gloria Swanson
Gregory Peck
Greta Garbo
Harrison Ford
Henry Fonda
Humphrey Bogart
Ingrid Bergman
Jack Lemmon
Jack Nicholson
James Cagney
James Dean: Behind the Scene
Jane Fonda
Jeanette MacDonald & Nelson Eddy
Joan Crawford
John Wayne Films; Reference Book; Scrapbook; Trivia Book
John Wayne's The Alamo
Judy Garland
Katharine Hepburn
Kirk Douglas
Laurel & Hardy

Lauren Bacall
Laurence Olivier
Mae West
Marilyn Monroe
Marlene Dietrich
Marlon Brando
Marx Brothers
Moe Howard & the Three Stooges
Olivia de Havilland
Orson Welles
Paul Newman
Peter Lorre
Rita Hayworth
Robert De Niro
Robert Redford
Sean Connery
Sexbomb: Jayne Mansfield
Shirley MacLaine
Shirley Temple
The Sinatra Scrapbook
Spencer Tracy
Steve McQueen
Three Stooges Scrapbook
Tom Hanks
Vincent Price
Warren Beatty
W.C. Fields
William Holden
William Powell
A Wonderful Life: James Stewart

### DIRECTORS
Alfred Hitchcock
Cecil B. DeMille
Federico Fellini
Frank Capra
John Huston
Steven Spielberg
Woody Allen

### GENRE
Black Hollywood, Vol. 1 & 2
Classic Foreign Films: From 1960 to Today
Classic Gangster Films
Classic Science Fiction Films
Classics of the Horror Film
Cult Horror Films
Cult Science Fiction Films
Divine Images: Jesus on Screen
Early Classics of Foreign Film
Great Baseball Films

Great French Films
Great German Films
Great Italian Films
The Great War Films
Harry Warren & the Hollywood Musical
Hispanic Hollywood
Hollywood Bedlam: Screwball Comedies
The Hollywood Western
The Incredible World of 007
Jewish Image in American Film
The Lavender Screen: The Gay and Lesbian Films
Martial Arts Movies
Merchant Ivory Films
The Modern Horror Film
Money, Women & Guns: Crime Movies
More Classics of the Horror Film
Movie Psychos & Madmen
Our Huckleberry Friend: Johnny Mercer
Second Feature: "B" Films
They Sang! They Danced! They Romanced!
Thrillers
Words and Shadows: Literature on the Screen

### DECADE
Classics of the Silent Screen
Films of the Twenties
Films of the Thirties
More Films of the '30s
Films of the Forties
Films of the Fifties
Lost Films of the '50s
Films of the Sixties
Films of the Seventies
Films of the Eighties

### SPECIAL INTEREST
Bugsy (Illustrated screenplay)
The Citadel Treasury of Famous Movie Lines
Comic Support
The Critics Were Wrong (Misguided Movie Reviews)
Cutting Room Floor
Did She or Didn't She: Behind Bedroom Doors
Film Flubs

Film Flubs: The Sequel
Filmmaking on the Fringe
Final Curtain
First Films
Hollywood Cheesecake
Howard Hughes in Hollywood
How to Meet & Hang Out w/Stars
Jim Carrey Scrapbook
Lost Films
More Character People
Most Influential Women in Film
The Nightmare Never Ends: A Nightmare on Elm Street
100 Best Films of the Century
701 Toughest Movie Trivia Questions
Sex in Films
Sex In the Movies
Sherlock Holmes
Shot on this Site
Son of Film Flubs
Total Exposure: Nude Scenes
Who Is That?: Familiar Faces and Forgotten Names
Women's Book of Movie Quotes
The Worst Movies of All Time
"You Ain't Heard Nothin' Yet!"

## TELEVISION:
America on the Rerun
The "Cheers" Trivia Book
Classic TV Westerns
Favorite Families of TV
Gilligan, Maynard & Me
Heather! (Locklear)
Mary, Mary, Mary! (Tyler Moore)
The Northern Exposure Book
The Official Andy Griffith Show Scrapbook
The 1001 Toughest TV Trivia Questions of All Time
The Quantum Leap Book
The "Seinfeld" Aptitude Test
Star Fleet Entrance Exam
The Star Trek Concordance
1201 Toughest TV Trivia Questions
What's Your "Frasier" IQ?
What's Your "Mad About You" IQ?

**For a free full-color Entertainment Books brochure** including the Citadel Film Series in depth and more, call 1-800-447-BOOK; or send your name and address to Citadel Film Books, Dept. 1602, 120 Enterprise Ave., Secaucus, NJ 07094.